WOODY HAYES

A Reflection

Paul Hornung

Foreword by Bo Schembechler

Sagamore Publishing Inc.
Champaign, IL 61824-0673

Production supervision and interior design: Susan M.Williams
Cover and photo insert design: Michelle R. Dressen
Cover photo: Chance Brockway
Production assistants: Brian J. Moore and Lisa S. Park
Developmental editor: Dan Heaton
Editor: Laurie McCarthy
Proofreader: Phyllis L. Bannon

10   9   8   7   6   5   4   3   2

Library of Congress Catalog Card Number: 90-64226
ISBN: 0-915611-42-2

Sagamore Publishing Co., Inc.
P.O. Box 673
Champaign, IL 61824-0673

Printed in the United States of America

To my long-suffering wife,
and to the unique man who made this book necessary

CONTENTS

ACKNOWLEDGMENTS

Special thanks go to Mrs. Anne Hayes and to Steve Hayes for their assistance and encouragement in preparing this book, including the loan of family pictures.

Thanks also go to Chance Brockway, who provided a number of photos from his extensive collection; to Joe Pastorek and other *Columbus Dispatch* photographers, and to Editor Robert B. Smith for permitting reprinting of *Dispatch* file photos; and to The Ohio State University Archives.

Grateful recognition is given the hundreds of *Dispatch* readers who contributed "Woody stories," although only a small portion could be included in the book.

Finally, most sincere thanks go to all of the Ohio State players, coaches, and others who shared the recollections and feelings reported in these pages.

PROLOGUE

My father was a complex man. He could charm the birds out of the trees in a humble, down-home manner. He could recite poetry or quote the ancient Greeks. Yet another day, he might shoot those same birds out of the trees or singe the ears of those nearby with quotes that were anything but classical prose.

Paul Hornung asked me to write this prologue on behalf of our family. A book about Woody Hayes is a vast undertaking. It is akin to night maneuvers in a minefield while wearing sunglasses. Yet no one is better equipped to capture the complete Woody Hayes than Paul Hornung. Paul and Dad were friends for many years. They had great respect for each other, both personally and professionally.

We have not yet read the book as we write this. But that is not important because we know the author. He's a winner! Paul possesses great journalistic integrity and commitment. These attributes will allow him to show all of Dad's many sides fairly and accurately.

Dad has been dead for more than four years, yet he is still fondly remembered. I am constantly reminded by people of the positive influence Dad had on their lives. I know that would please him because he always felt that people were important and material things were not. It also pleases our family.

Of all the good decisions Dad made, the best was to marry my mother, Anne Hayes. Mom is a strong woman who has cared about other people more than she has cared about herself. She has contributed to Dad's success behind the scenes. She gave Dad time to do his job, without any complaints and with enormous support. She is one in a billion.

After four years, I still remember my father as a man who was going to make you get the best out of yourself. He believed people were capable of accomplishing more than they felt they could. Dad could accept a grade of C if you were working as hard as you could, but if you were an A or B student who was getting Cs and Ds, you'd better duck. This was applicable to both his son and his football players.

I miss my father. He helped me bring out the best in myself. But he is not gone. He is still with us.

Steve Hayes
For the Hayes family
Columbus, Ohio 1991

FOREWORD

I loved Woody Hayes. That won't come as a surprise to many people because I've said it a couple zillion times. But dammit, it's a fact and I've never tried to hide it. After being associated with him for almost 40 years in one way or another, how could I feel any other way?

We had the greatest rivalry any two football coaches ever had, for ten glorious years. Man, did we compete! The sports writers called it a "war," and as far as the old man and I were concerned, it was.

You talk about tough ball games—Michigan vs. Ohio State games were. Every year but one, we battled for the Big Ten championship and the trip to the Rose Bowl, but the big thing was WINNING THE GAME!

Woody wanted to beat Michigan—and me—more than anything in the world, and you can believe that nothing got me as excited as beating Ohio State and the old man. What more could a couple football guys ever want?

But the more time goes by, the more I'm convinced that those ten years of intense rivalry and competition actually brought us closer together. I hate to do it or admit it, but I can get damned nostalgic and choked up when I think about Woody and those games and the wonderful relationship we had from the time I played for him at Miami University to the sad day he left us in 1987.

Woody Hayes was a unique individual, one that comes along only once. Believe me, I know, and I'm grateful for having shared so much of his life and for being in a position to appreciate his different perspectives and what a hell of a man he was.

I wondered for a long time why no one had written a comprehensive account of Woody's life and accomplishments. Now, happily, somebody has. *Woody Hayes: A Reflection* presents the many sides of this extraordinary man, not only as a famous football coach—the best of them all in my opinion—but as a teacher, a scholar, a molder of young men, a patriot, a community activist, and a humanitarian.

I'm pleased that Woody's story was written by Paul Hornung. He was the right man for the job. He was one of Woody's closest friends, from the day Woody came to Ohio State until the day he passed away. There's no doubt in my mind that Hornung really knew Woody Hayes, certainly better than any other sports writer.

That in itself qualified him to do the definitive Hayes book. But Hornung is also qualified by profession. He was a sports writer and sports editor for the *Columbus Dispatch* for more than 40 years, now retired, and was known nationally for his writings about Big Ten football and the Buckeyes.

I only had one complaint about him as a sports writer: he was too damned supportive of Ohio State. But at the same time I respected him for being loyal to his school and to Woody.

I believe you'll enjoy the history of my mentor and greatest friend, Wayne Woodrow Hayes, as Hornung has written it.

Glen E. "Bo" Schembechler
Ann Arbor, Michigan 1991

PREFACE

Maybe Marc Antony really did say it at Caesar's bier; or maybe Shakespeare just made it up; or maybe it was biting wisdom born of some long-forgotten seer, passed down through generations.

"The evil that men do lives after them,"quoth Antony, according to Shakespeare, "the good is oft interred with their bones."

It could have been a eulogy for Woody Hayes, but from only one narrow perspective. "Evil" is a term much too harsh. Woody never did a genuinely evil thing in his life.

As an intense, driven practitioner of a high-profile, heavy-pressure profession, he became involved in "incidents," although only one of truly serious consequences. In a fit of overwhelming frustration, he struck Clemson middle guard Charlie Bauman, whose pass interception during the closing minutes of the 1978 Gator Bowl had snuffed out Ohio State's late-game bid for victory.

The fateful swing was seen live by a national television audience. It was shown again and again, on networks and local stations. The press reported it copiously, complete with judgmental comment.

The University that Hayes had served with uncommon devotion for 28 years relieved him of his duties the next morning, ending one of college football's most distinguished and successful coaching careers.

Woody lived with it for almost 10 years. It wouldn't go away, even though he steadfastly refused to discuss it and usually terminated interviews when the question came up.

Bauman himself arrived at the point where he refused all interviews because, Clemson officials explained, he'd had enough and because of his admiration for Coach Hayes.

When Woody died in 1987, Bauman told a Columbus writer, "I was shocked. It brought tears to my eyes. There's a lot of feelings I still have inside about what happened (in the Gator Bowl).

"He was such a competitive man. I don't know, if I was in his shoes, maybe I would have done the same thing. It [Hayes' punch] didn't hurt. I didn't even feel it."

Prophetically and with resignation, he added, "Here we go again." And he was right. The Hayes/Bauman episode was re-run on television—including national networks—and rehashed in the press.

The "incident" confirmed in the minds of many, mainly outside of Ohio, an image of Woody Hayes that had been nurtured for some time by unfriendly segments of the media: that of an ill-tempered, tyrannical, self-centered dictator out of control; a not-so-lovable curmudgeon.

But it was a woefully false image, because it did not account for the whole man. It ignored Woody Hayes as the molder of young men, the teacher, the scholar, the benefactor to his fellow man, the patriot, and the winner, on the field and off.

This book seeks to present that total picture, the image held by those who knew him best and appreciated him most—the author included. Conceding his human foibles, sometimes disagreeing, but understanding, his football players remember the "old coach" with almost passionate loyalty. It's a fraternal distinction to have been one of "Woody's guys."

He was a stern taskmaster, but they remember how much he cared about them, as people more than as football talents and long after their college eligibility; how he drove them, because he believed "a man is always capable of achieving more than he thinks he can"; how he preached education and hounded them to "get that degree"; how he sold them on hard work—"nothing that comes easy is worth a dime"; how he prepared them for the "real world" with a philosophy of which he was an example; how he counseled them to practice respect for each other and humanity in general; how compassionate he could be inside a tough exterior.

His assistants remember him for his leadership, the incredible devotion to duty, his knack for anticipating problems, the thoroughness of detail, the integrity he represented, his always demanding more of himself than of them.

Ohio State followers remember him for winning, of course—205 times against 61 defeats and 10 ties; for the great teams—13 Big Ten championships, three national titles; for the great players—58 All-Americans and three Heisman Trophy winners; and for all the great games and great thrills.

They also remember him for his animated, into-the-game sideline gyrations and his demonstrated protectiveness of his team's best interests. Not forgotten either was his sportsmanship, the many times he raised his hands to the crowd, calling for quiet so that visiting teams could hear their signals—even at the OSU goal line.

His multitude of speeches and charity appearances were well known and widely appreciated, but his hospital visits and other good deeds usually went unreported. He wanted it that way. Publicity would have cast a false light on his motivation.

Woody Hayes is remembered fondly and with deep admiration by many, many people in Columbus, in Ohio, and around the country. They accept the reality of the Gator Bowl "incident," but they believe that his pluses so far outweigh the minuses that it's another resounding "win" for the old Buckeye coach.

Marc Antony was wrong after all!

Paul Hornung
Columbus, Ohio 1991

1

A COMPLEX
SUBJECT

An eager young television sportscaster, microphone in hand and camera crew trailing, interviewed selected subjects among Ohio Staters attending a reunion party.

He approached Esco Sarkkinen, a media favorite during his 32 years as a Buckeye assistant football coach because of his penchant for ear-catching phraseology.

"Tell me all about Woody Hayes," requested the TV type.

"How much time do we have?" Sarkkinen asked and the answer came: "30 seconds."

Sarkkinen may have laughed up the entire half minute. Recalling the incident later, he suggested, "it was like asking someone to do the life of Winston Churchill in 30 seconds. You don't describe Woody Hayes in one sentence or one paragraph—or 30 seconds, but chapter after chapter."

In accepting that challenge, I recalled one story that Woody repeated often enough to elevate—or demote—it to the status of borderline cliché.

A dignified gentleman of the old South would haughtily declare, according to Woody's version, that "what this country needs is an unbiased history of the Civil War—written from the Southern viewpoint, of course."

This book will make no such hypocritical pretense of total objectivity, because its perspective also would be suspect, considering the close personal friendship with the subject and an informed understanding of events and causes.

But I will also be guided by Woody's own counsel. When I approached him about new material for a (Columbus) *Dispatch Sunday Magazine*, Woody replied in historical reference, as he so often did.

"Like Oliver Cromwell, I'll give you permission," he stipulated, "provided you paint me warts and all."

To be entirely accurate, the distinguished British Prime Minister once agreed to sit for a personal portrait, but warned that he'd refuse to buy the finished product unless the artist promised to "faithfully paint me, warts and all."

But the message was clear.

Hence, albeit with some reluctance, Woody's "warts" will be duly recognized—including the most prominent of them all: the Gator Bowl incident of 1978 that abruptly ended his coaching career, though not, to his stature-magnifying credit, his service to Ohio State University and to mankind.

A background check will be helpful in evaluating this singular man who grew to truly legendary proportions during 28 colorful, controversial and eminently successful years as head coach of the football Buckeyes.

Woody had a way of turning criticism to humor that delighted banquet audiences. When his conservative, ground-game offense drew media barbs and some fan complaints, he reminded, "Three things can happen on a forward pass, two of them bad: incompletion and interception."

Sometime after a Clemson pass interception in the Gator Bowl prompted Hayes' career-ending swing, he informed an Agonis Club luncheon audience: "I used to say three things can happen on a forward pass, two of them bad. I don't say that anymore, because I found out four things can happen on a forward pass. The fourth thing is, you can get fired."

When "Columbus Roast" planners Moose Machinsky and Greg Lashutka discussed the dais for the 1987 "Night with Woody and Earle (Bruce)" a week before Woody's death, they wondered if Hugh Hindman should be one of the speakers.

Hindman was Hayes' offensive line coach who graduated to the position of OSU athletic director. He had dropped the ax on Woody after the 1978 Gator Bowl.

"Yeah, he should," Hayes answered. "We can have him discuss 'How I Fired Woody Hayes.'" He said it with a laugh and without rancor. When Hindman underwent major surgery, Woody visited him in the hospital, and Hindman insists that he said, "If you hadn't done what you did, I'd have no respect for you."

2

OPENING KICKOFF

Wayne Woodrow Hayes was an item in the birth announcements on Valentine's Day 1913 in a Clifton, Ohio, house that straddled a county line. With his proclivity for self-deprecating humor, that geographical accident provided Woody with a stock line years later: "Greene countians claimed I was born in Clark County, and Clark countians claimed I was born in Greene County."

In recruiting at Ohio State, he placed great store in "the youngster who comes from a good home." Obviously, it was in part a recognition of his own family background; his parents and their children—Woody had an older brother, Isaac, and an older sister, Mary—formed a close, nurturing unit.

Effie Hayes was "the balance wheel, driving, competitive, puritanical, and the businessperson of the family," according to Woody. "When she believed in something, all hell couldn't change her mind." That trait was transmitted unreservedly to her youngest son.

Wayne Benton Hayes was a dedicated teacher and inveterate seeker of knowledge, apparently a bit less practical than his wife. "Dad taught school before he even went to college," Woody recalled proudly. "After he finished the eighth grade, he took the Boxwood Exam, which allowed him to teach school in Ohio. A lady came up to me a few years ago in an airport and told me that my dad had taught her German in 1910. That really pleased me. Dad loved to teach, and he was a great teacher."

The elder Hayes did eventually earn a degree—at age 38 from Wittenberg University in Springfield, Ohio, the sixth college he'd attended. That belated certificate led to his appointment as superintendent of schools in Newcomerstown, Ohio.

On the train ride to their new home, the Hayes family stopped in Columbus. Seeing the State Capitol and other attractions of the "big city" impressed the visitors, but this also happened to be the day the circus arrived in Columbus with its traditional downtown parade.

"My first experience in Columbus was one of pleasure, awe and excitement," Woody recalled. Thirty-five years later he would experience a similar range of emotions on returning to Columbus on a permanent basis.

The move to Newcomerstown helped mold the character and destiny of young Woodrow. Small-town living complemented a home life that exemplified traditional American and religious values—with fringe benefits.

Woody remembered that his father always had half a dozen open books around the house. He would study from them and read to the family. It could be history, math, languages, philosophy, psychology, or science, but never romance or mystery.

Sunday dinner was an after-church dress-up occasion, sometimes of three hours' duration. Family matters were a common topic of discussion during that time, but so too were subjects as diverse as politics, world problems, music, theater, books, and sports. Whatever the topic in the Hayes family, intellectual curiosity was a virtue, and so was communication.

Though growing up in an educational environment would pay lasting dividends, young Woodrow saw drawbacks to his family situation at the time. "I believe there's nothing tougher than being the school superintendent's son," he maintained.

Woody idolized brother Ike, later calling him "the most colorful person I ever knew" and "the most intense and competitive football player I ever knew." After high school, Ike disdained college, but changed his mind several years later and enrolled at Iowa State. There he became an All-American guard in football and attained a degree in veterinary medicine.

Ike took enormous pride in Woody's coaching achievements. When Ohio State qualified for the Rose Bowl in 1954, Ike and his family headed for Pasadena. The brothers spent hours together, and as a grand climax to the week, Woody's Buckeyes whipped Southern Cal on New Year's Day. On January 25, Ike died of a heart attack, a shocking, soul-shaking tragedy for Woody in the days of his most glorious coaching.

Of all the thousands of clippings Woody received over the years, none touched him more than one that arrived after he had returned from Ike's memorial service. It glowingly recounted Ike's football career and praised him as a dedicated veterinarian and respected citizen of Waterloo, Iowa. Convinced that Ike had been a victim of excessive devotion to a profession he loved, Woody vowed, "This is a lesson to me. I'm going to slow down!" The conviction survived perhaps a week.

Young Woodrow found another role model during those early days in Newcomerstown. Manager of the town baseball team was Cy Young, who had pitched a record 511 major league victories and for whom baseball's annual pitching award was later named. He allowed Woody to do small chores around the park, fascinated him with baseball yarns, and kindled in him an interest in and appreciation of sports.

"It was great for a kid growing up to have a man like Cy Young to associate with and look up to," Woody said. With Young as a role model, his earliest aspiration was to a major league pitching career. Woody did play baseball in high school and at Denison University, but with no remaining illusions about reaching the "bigs."

A more lasting influence was his sixth- and seventh-grade history and English teacher, Clyde Bartholow. Wayne Benton Hayes had already instilled in his son a special interest in both subjects, and Bartholow so fanned the intellectual flame that Woody elected English and history as his academic majors at Denison.

In light of how Woody's career ended, it is noteworthy that the Hayes brothers developed a strong interest in boxing. They read about boxers and sparred in the family living room, much to the chagrin of Mary, particularly when practicing her piano.

Woody and Ike later staged bouts as special events, always under assumed names to avoid parental wrath. After one such exhibition at a stag picnic, a righteous spectator asked the boys if their father knew they were there, and Ike asked "Does your wife know you're here?" Indeed, when Hayes' father found out, Woody recalled, "He gave us hell!"

Bob Amos, one of Woody's roommates at the Sigma Chi

house at Denison, remembers that Woody had a habit of shadow-boxing. "Woody's reputation as a boxer soon came to the attention of the faculty," Amos says. "He was named student-instructor of boxing."

Wayne Woodrow Hayes and football, eventually synonymous, began their association at Newcomerstown High School, where he started at tackle for three years and captained the team as a senior. He also subbed on the basketball team. A three-year letterman at tackle for the Denison varsity, he was by his own testimony "a good player, but not great." That modest assessment has not been widely contradicted.

Teammates and others close to Big Red (Denison) football remember more his diligence, competitive intensity and utter intolerance of defeat. He waited tables at the fraternity, stoked furnaces, and did other chores to meet expenses.

Amos has other recollections that suggest several traits that would later distinguish Hayes: "Woody was a brilliant student in courses he liked and had a photographic memory. Particularly amazing was his ability to remember names, dates, and other particulars of past events." Hayes' gift for remembering players decades removed from his program—and not only the players themselves, but even their families—would become one of his most endearing trademarks.

"His personality blossomed as his college years rolled by," Amos adds. "He became more gregarious and a conversationalist extraordinaire. He had an amazing vocabulary for a student."

History buff Hayes would come to admire many generals, but one of the first was a fellow Ohioan, General William Tecumseh Sherman. A persistent theme in Hayes' coaching strategy echoed Sherman's plan of attack: "striking over a broad front with use of the alternate objective approach."

That strategy might also explain why, hours after receiving his diploma at Denison, economy-conscious Woody hitchhiked to Toledo to attend a football coaching clinic. Coaching was not a first career choice, but the alternate objective.

"I wanted to be a lawyer," he later recalled. "All my college work was in that direction." To accumulate funds for law school, however meager, he accepted an appointment as a seventh-grade teacher and assistant football coach at Mingo Junction, Ohio, the year following graduation.

"The next summer I applied for admission to the College of Law at Ohio State," he relates. "But they didn't take new students in the summer quarter." Instead, on the "broad front" theory, he began graduate work in education administration at Ohio State, "with law in the back of my mind."

That fall, he took a job at New Philadelphia High School as history teacher and assistant football coach. The move would have far-reaching significance: there he worked with influential John Brickels, and there he met Anne Gross.

Miss Gross, a pretty, popular, and independent graduate of Denison rival Ohio Wesleyan, became Mrs. Woody Hayes in 1942—six years after they were introduced by the Brickels.

They didn't know it until years later, but Woody and Anne Hayes shared a common football hobby. "I was supposed to go to the Super Bowl when it was in Detroit," Woody once related, "but I didn't go because I wanted to chart the game, and I felt I'd get more out of it that way. I learn a lot when I analyze game charts. I've been charting football games since 1928. I charted the Rose Bowl when I was a sophomore in high school and we got our first radio. I'd get a big cardboard and I'd chart every play." He was in Newcomerstown at that time.

"My brother and I used to chart football games all the time," reports Mrs. Hayes. "We used to chart the Rose Bowl games, chart every play." She was in New Philadelphia at that time.

The two Ohio towns are about 20 miles apart.

3

ESTABLISHING FIELD POSITION

During his legend-making days at Ohio State, Woody's standing as a practicing patriot received considerable attention and admiration. But it was not a new development.

While he wrestled with the problems of his first head coaching job—and his own temper and intensity—at New Philadelphia, he avidly monitored events in Europe. His study of history convinced him that "the war against Hitler couldn't be won without us [the United States]. We had to fight 'em." He also became convinced that his country would need its young men. He enlisted in the Navy five months before Pearl Harbor.

Because of his athletic background, Hayes was assigned to the Navy's training program, which was headed by former heavyweight boxing champion Gene Tunney. Later he was assigned to the training program of Admiral Tom Hamilton, a former football coach and star player at the Naval Academy.

But it wasn't the way Hayes wanted to contribute to the war effort. "I pulled a dirty trick on Commander Hamilton," he confessed. "I had been in the Navy over a year and wanted to get to sea so bad. I was at Pensacola [Florida] and I finally went to the yeoman and asked how I could get my orders [to sea] signed by Commander Clark.

"The yeoman said, 'I shouldn't tell you this, but the Commander usually reads the first three letters I give him every morning; he's got so many, he just signs everything after that. So if you write your letter, I'll put it down among the other letters and I think he'll sign it.' That's exactly what happened. In ten days, I had my orders. But just about that time, Commander Hamilton came down to Pensacola. I walked up to him and told him that I was leaving for sea duty the next day. He got mad as hell!"

All the people who were cowed by Woody Hayes might have difficulty accepting this, but he admitted that, "A couple of years later, Commander Hamilton came to Pearl Harbor and I saw him at the Officers' Club. He had his back to me, and I turned around and walked out. I was scared of him."

They finally got together after the war when Hamilton was athletic director at Pittsburgh. Woody recalled, "I took my Miami team to play Pittsburgh, and I was on a radio show with him that Friday night. I walked into the station and up to him and said, 'Admiral'—he had become an admiral by then—'I've never dreaded anything so much in my life.' He looked at me and laughed and said, 'You know what I was mad about, don't you? I was mad because you got to sea before I did.' We've been great, great friends ever since.

"Then in 1954, we [Ohio State] played Pittsburgh when Admiral Hamilton was the head football coach. He was athletic director and had taken over the team about midseason. Before the game, I told my players we weren't going to let an Admiral beat a chief boatswain's mate! We beat 'em by four touchdowns!"

Woody commanded a PC 1251 in the Palau Islands invasion and then the destroyer escort *Rinehart* in both the Pacific and the Atlantic. With each ship, he came aboard as executive officer, and approximately a year later he was given command.

During his sea duty, he received a pair of exciting messages. The first, in 1945, advised him that he'd become the father of a son, and that Anne and Steven Benton Hayes were both in excellent health back in the states.

The second, in 1946, was from his college coach, Tommy Rogers, who said he would not be returning to Denison and, reported Woody, "He asked me if I wanted the job. I was thinking of going back to high school teaching and coaching until I got Tommy's letter. I wired him back that I wanted the job, and they held it open for two months."

When the *Rinehart* steamed into drydock, Lieutenant-Commander W.W. Hayes headed immediately for Granville, Ohio, to confer with Denison University officials. He quickly agreed to a two-year contract for his first college-level head coaching opportunity.

The vision of "W.W. Hayes, Attorney at Law" receded to the most remote cranny of his mind. And once he espoused the "alternate" career, he pursued it with a fervor approaching passion. Nevertheless, through the years, he would become slightly rueful when he talked about his long-abandoned law aspirations, or even when he encouraged one of his players to seek the career he had bypassed, a counsel he often gave.

But regrets? He once answered that retrospectively: "I'd have to be greedy or stupid or both if I didn't appreciate the fact that I've had just about the best life a man could ever have. I don't think anybody ever was as fortunate as I was to be associated with so many good people, great coaches, great players, great friends. . . ."

Woody Hayes wasn't a fast starter in any of his three head coaching ventures, but he went 3-0 in righting the ship. In his debut year at Denison, the Big Red limped to a troubled 2-6 finish—his worst record and the first of only three sub-.500 seasons in Hayes' 33-year career. The recently mustered Navy lieutenant-commander admitted he didn't get along well with the ex-GIs who made up much of the squad. "They took a rather casual attitude toward football," he recalled later. And a casual attitude toward football was something Woody could never abide. Worsening the tension, he pushed them relentlessly on the practice field, conceding, "Maybe I was still striding the quarter-deck."

But he launched a new pattern when his second and third teams (1947-48) went undefeated. Their 18-game winning streak attracted the attention of officials at Miami University, which was then searching for a new head football coach. They found him at Denison.

Sid Gillman had left Miami for the head coaching job at the University of Cincinnati, and a number of Redskin football players had been seized by a sudden desire to pursue their studies at Cincinnati. Hampered by these defections, Hayes struggled through a 5-4 first season. "Sid took the best players out of my whole class," Bo Schembechler recalls, adding with a laugh, "but he left me at Miami."

Woody always insisted, "I don't hate anybody. Hating will destroy you." But if he didn't exactly hate Gillman, he managed to work up a strong case of dislike. Cincinnati's victory in their first field confrontation (1949) further aggravated the wound.

Woody's problems weren't all external. "That first year, the players disliked him considerably," confides Schembechler. "These were still mostly Sid's players and Sid's system, and Woody changed everything. [George Blackburn had served one year between Gillman and Hayes, but had continued Gillman's system]. Woody was wild, tough, and demanding. And we were losing. But the second year, the players all started liking him. We were winning, and they found out what kind of guy he was."

Woody's ability as a recruiter had been a key element in his comeback at Denison, and it was another reason for Miami's upswing in 1950. With talent replenished and morale revitalized, the Redskins dropped a strenuously contested 7-0 decision to Xavier early in the season. But they charged through the remainder of the schedule unbeaten, including the finale against Cincinnati, a game played in a swirling blizzard. "It was such a big game, and we whipped 'em 28-0," Schembechler remembers. "I mean that was B-I-G! Particularly in Woody's eyes."

Added to all the other incentives, Cincinnati had already received a bid to the Sun Bowl, but Hayes felt it belonged to Miami. He had understood that the Mid-American Conference champion would get the invitation, and Miami was the champ.

When it appeared that Miami also would be bypassed for a Salad Bowl invitation, Woody went after it with a vengeance— as he would react so many times in the future when he felt his team had been or might be shortchanged. He called the athletic director at Arizona State, the host school, and made a feverish pitch. But sensing rejection, he pitched a favorite ploy: he implied that Arizona State was afraid to play his team. It worked. Miami was invited.

"The reason we came so far is to win, and that's what we plan to do," Woody told a Salad Bowl luncheon in Phoenix several days before the game. His team backed him up. Though wilting in the second half in the Arizona heat, Miami prevailed 35-21.

One of Woody's favorite quotes, repeated often over the years, came from that sage of the Ozarks, Dizzy Dean: "Ol' Diz used to say that if you done it, it ain't braggin." In light of the final score, it didn't seem that Woody was braggin', either before or after the Salad Bowl.

He carried that philosophy with him to Ohio State. When the media asked for his outlook on an upcoming game, almost without exception, he replied, matter-of-factly, "We expect to win." It wasn't braggin'; he was right 205 out of the 276 times he marshalled his Buckeyes in major college battles.

Woody reconciled with Gillman years later when both were honored by the Ohio High School Football Coaches Association for their contributions to the game. Then after both had retired, he had Sid and his wife as his guests in the private booth atop the Ohio Stadium press box, from which he watched Ohio State home games. Explaining his decision to let bygones be bygones, Hayes recalled the words of President Buchanan: "He said that when he reached a certain age, he found that most of his friends were gone and his enemies didn't seem such bad people after all."

All branches of the military shared a niche in Woody Hayes' esteem, but the Navy remained his favorite. It was the Navy in which he served in World War II and it was during this Navy service that he developed and honed the leadership skills that, with intelligent application, came to full flower as a college football coach.

"He felt that the crew on a ship was no different than a crew on a football field," observes Esco Sarkkinen, who, in his 26 years as an assistant, heard most of Woody's sea references. "He tried to anticipate so many things he learned as a ship commander in order to get the most out of his crew."

Woody pressed his assistant coaches to establish close relationships with players at their particular positions, so close that any problems, however minor, would be known and solved—and if at all possible, anticipated and avoided.

"I first used this system of supervision aboard the Rinehart," Hayes said, explaining that he had designated officers for the various divisions aboard ship. "By close contact with his men, the officer could work on a problem before it got big."

When he confronted a disciplinary situation with a football player Hayes said, "I started the interview with an old Navy expression: 'Don't blow smoke.' The only possible way to start such a meeting is with the truth."

Once the young man reached the point of recognizing his mistake and appreciating how it adversely affected others, Woody noted, "I usually used the same technique I used at captain's mast in the Navy: I let the player set his own penalty and then I cut it in half."

4

THE HAY'S IN
THE BARN

E vents surrounding Woody Hayes' promotion from Miami
University to Ohio State University tipped a character trait
that would be primary in the longest—and most successful—
head football coaching tenure in the school's history: a dauntless
drive toward a desired objective.

In view of his eventual record-defying longevity, it seems
contradictory that Hayes was not the leading candidate in 1951
when OSU officials went searching for a new "pigskin professor," as one pundit phrased it at the time.

Paul Brown had produced the Buckeyes' first-ever national
championship in a brief but brilliant stint before serving in the
Navy and organizing the Cleveland Browns. With the resignation of Ohio State coach Wes Fesler in December of 1950, a clamor
for Brown's return immediately resounded throughout Ohio.
Brown had powerful backing in high places, including in the
business, political, and media areas. He appeared to be the
"people's choice."

The question was whether Brown would forego the high-
paying pros for Ohio State. But he gave a signal of availability by
accepting an invitation to be interviewed.

The evening he appeared before the six-member screening
committee, a petition in his behalf, signed by 1,800 students, was
delivered to the chairman. About 200 students rallied outside the
meeting place.

Chuck Mather, with an impressive record at Massillon (Ohio) High School, also had considerable support; so did Sid Gillman, a former Buckeye player and assistant coach, then head coach at Cincinnati; and Harry Strobel, a current OSU assistant who had previously been one of Ohio's top high school coaches.

The original "active and proposed" list of 30 also included a number of "name" coaches from other schools.

"I wasn't even in the top ten; I was a dark horse," Woody recalled. However, the screening committee, chaired by Athletic Director Dick Larkins, did include him among the eight selected for personal on-campus interviews.

Don Faurot, highly regarded head coach/athletic director at Missouri, had been second choice when Brown was hired in 1941. This time he was first choice. He reportedly agreed to take the job, but changed his mind two days later—even as OSU officials were in the process of setting up a welcoming press conference.

Hayes had been one of the first to openly declare his interest and one of the most industrious in campaigning. Meticulous preparation had always augmented his dogged determination, so he was, as expected, well-prepared when he faced the committee. He made it a point to know as much as possible about each member. He reasoned, "In a distance race, a dark horse can put on a sprint only once if he expects to win. It was time to sprint!"

As his lengthy session with the committee concluded, Woody's small-town background emerged in a parting shot. "Well, gentlemen," he said matter-of-factly, "I guess the hay's in the barn." University Vice President Bland Stradley, an influential member of the committee, lived on a farm near the hamlet of Canal Winchester, and the homey allusion brought an involuntary smile to his face.

That wasn't part of Woody's calculated strategy; simply one of his favorite throw-ins. During the early years of his Buckeye reign, he would finish Friday practice and greet sports writers with, "Well, the hay's in the barn."

Obviously, the search committee graded him on much more substantial observations, but Woody delighted in recalling that "Dick Larkins used to say that [hay reference] got me Bland's vote." One committee member suggested after the interview that "Mr. Hayes was frank, forthright, and full of *savoir-faire*. He rang the bell in all departments."

With Faurot's about-face—which did not become public knowledge until years later—the committee unanimously agreed on Hayes and submitted his name for approval by the 12-member Athletic Board.

At the outset the committee had established stringent qualifications for measuring the candidates. Six head football coaches had come and gone in the previous 12 years, and University officials grew sensitive to allusions in the press and among fans that their hallowed institution of higher education had become "the graveyard of coaches."

They sought a seventh coach with potential for greater job permanence. But 28 years must have been beyond their imagination!

The full membership of the Athletic Board—six faculty representatives, two alumni, two students, one trustee, and Stradley—quickly endorsed the committee's recommendation and approved Hayes' hiring, subject as always to approval by the University's Board of Trustees. Usually, the trustees' approval on personnel matters was a virtual formality, a rubber stamp. But as one amused bystander suggested, "This wasn't like hiring a dean; this was hiring a FOOTBALL COACH!"

It was one item, albeit the major item, on the agenda for the trustees' monthly meeting on February 12. After nearly three hours behind closed doors, a representative advised the assembled media: "Because three members of the Board of Trustees found it impossible to be present at today's meeting, and feeling that a matter of this importance should have a larger representation from the Board, a special meeting has been called for Sunday afternoon, February 18, 1951, at 4 p.m."

Those present February 12 declined comment, but the usual "unimpeachable sources" indicated that at least one and maybe two trustees did not support the screening committee's recommendation. So even though Woody "had" the job, he didn't.

The media, as might be expected, had a field day with this new development. The sports public buzzed. Brown's boosters renewed their campaign, although it became known that Larkins had declared Brown's return as coach would be "over my dead body." Feelings ran so hot that a move later developed to oust Larkins, and a state legislator introduced a resolution to investigate the Athletic Department's finances.

While he waited, Hayes received phone calls and letters suggesting he withdraw. One published report charged that a Columbus sports editor had threatened Woody with a "hard time" if he accepted the job, but Woody himself never confirmed it. Not that it would have made any difference. He wanted to be the Ohio State coach, and the University wanted him.

Those six long days of waiting showcased another attribute of Woody Hayes that would be manifested over and over: With jut-jawed defiance, he did not yield to pressure or disappointment or seeming slights.

In his 1969 book *Hot Line to Victory*, Woody would spend five pages telling high school coaches how to prepare for job interviews and how to give themselves the best chance of being hired. He was passing along wisdom gained in this struggle.

As the trustees checked in for the unprecedented special meeting, not all did so willingly. Upon arriving, Charles "Boss" Kettering, a distinguished OSU alumnus and General Motors bigwig, angrily brushed aside reporters and photographers with "You people are the cause of all this!"

As a further annoyance, Senator John Bricker's plane was temporarily grounded in St. Louis, and the start of the meeting had to be delayed for two hours. While the high-powered group waited, dinner was hastily imported from President Howard Bevis' University residence.

Did it seem like the fates were telling Woody something? Negative. Contrary to what his reaction might have been in later times, Hayes remained out of the spotlight—and silent. He went about his usual routine in Oxford and even continued recruiting for Miami.

Finally, once called to order, the trustees made it official: By unanimous vote, Woody Hayes and Ohio State had embarked on a journey, the scope of which neither could possibly have envisioned that Sunday afternoon in February 1951.

The skipper of this ship was not a dreamer with eyes on the far horizon, but a realist who recognized the shoals—the controversial hiring process, the divided alumni and Buckeye fandom, and finally, the "Columbus situation," as it was called.

Ohio State football generated boiling enthusiasm among its followers, the inevitable companion of which was a commensurate appetite for winning. Losing—particularly to archrival Michigan—had been a sin for which Woody's predecessors paid.

Nebulous groups called "Downtown Coaches" and "Disgruntled Alumni" supposedly wielded inordinate power.

The Athletic Board believed Hayes could handle it. One member confidently suggested, "No man who went up the ladder from chief petty officer to lieutenant-commander in the Navy in four years, and was skipper of a destroyer escort in several battles can be short of the courage to meet the 'Columbus situation.'"

As he would many times, Woody recognized the problem but refused to bow to it, figuratively rolled up his sleeves, and plunged into pursuit of his own priority. "I wanted this job very much," he said. "It's still the greatest coaching opportunity in the country."

Now that he had it, he was thinking positive—as always. He told a student group, "I didn't come to Ohio State to stay a short time," and said essentially the same at a Faculty Club dinner-dance that introduced Anne and Woody to academic society.

But fulfilling that intent proved a struggle for a while. Woody's early years at Ohio State paralleled those at Denison and Miami, except that it took him a few seasons longer to get the machine shifted into high gear.

Many thought that a coach jumping into the "big leagues" with only five years of college experience was taking a gamble in his first major decision, hiring a staff.

First of all, there were the holdovers.

It was standard practice in college football for the new head man to bring with him several trusted assistants from his previous situation and add others with whom he had coached, or at least knew well. Woody Hayes did not do the usual, a characteristic that would become more evident as his tenure progressed. He brought with him from the Miami staff only 24-year-old Bill Arnsparger, who had been a graduate assistant for one year.

After two of Wes Fesler's assistants followed him to Minnesota, Dick Larkins asked Hayes to consider retaining the four remaining members of Fesler's staff. The four included Harry Strobel, who had been a candidate for the head coaching job; Esco Sarkkinen, a former All-American end; Gene Fekete, a standout fullback on the 1942 OSU national championship team; and Ernie Godfrey, another former Buckeye player who had been an assistant for 22 years under seven previous head coaches. Hayes knew all of them, but had worked with none.

"I checked them out closely and kept all four," Woody said seasons later. "I never regretted it for a minute. They were good coaches and good people. Loyalty is a two-way street, not a blind alley, and I felt if I treated them right, they would treat me right. That's the way it worked out."

Besides, he admitted, "I couldn't have brought myself to get rid of them." He also needed their experience because he completed his staff by hiring two Columbus-area high school coaches, Doyt Perry and Bill Hess, neither of whom had coached on the major college level.

Then, in the fall of that first year, Woody hired one of his favorite Miami players as a graduate assistant. A fellow named Bo Schembechler, with no coaching experience at all on his resume.

If taking on those three seemed like a big part of the gamble, it paid off handsomely. Perry left after the unbeaten 1954 season to become the winningest head coach in Bowling Green State University history and a member of the National College Football Hall of Fame. The BeeGee stadium bears his name. Hess stayed three years longer before moving to Ohio University, where, like Perry, he became one of the most successful of his school's head coaches. Schembechler's career is too well-known to bear repetition here.

This was the first manifestation of Hayes' exceptional knack for hiring—and grooming—assistants of great promise. Of the 42 who served on his staff during the 28 years, 18 became head coaches in their own right and at one point, five, or half, of the head coaches in the Big Ten were Hayes proteges.

"Getting that [first OSU] staff in working order was no small job," Woody conceded afterward. As far as Anne Hayes is concerned, "I thought that was one of the best coaching jobs Woody ever did, to make all those coaches fit in and be successful."

"Successful" was not a word often applied to Ohio State, or Hayes, in the first few years. The transition from Fesler to Hayes was from calm to thunder and lightning, for both holdover players and the coaches.

Sarkkinen, who remained on Woody's staff until 1977, recalls, "You went through shock therapy as a coach or player when you went from Wes Fesler to Woody Hayes. They definitely had contrasting styles. Wes didn't have that fierce intensity of Woody, who wanted things done right now the way he wanted it, period. There were periods where there was nothing but a silent shock from the players and coaches."

"Woody really did have a rough time," agrees George Rosso, a starting safety in 1951. "Everybody was beefing. He came in and changed everything, and we weren't as good as they [the Buckeyes] were the year before. Because he came from that smaller league, we kind of thought he didn't know big-time football."

Rosso, switched to starting fullback in 1953, adds: "Woody proved everybody wrong. We hated him, but we adored him. He was a good guy."

The lightning and thunder didn't transmit into the stadiums in 1951; a 0-0 tie with Illinois ranked as the season's highlight. In cold figures, the record showed four wins, three losses, and a pair of ties, with a fifth-place finish in the Big Ten.

Vic Janowicz kicked field goals to win half of those four victories, but overall he fell far short of his Heisman Trophy/All American performance of 1950. Hayes' T-formation offense did not utilize Vic's all-around talent, which had flourished in Fesler's single-wing attack.

With customary self-deprecating humor, Woody confessed to banquet audiences, "I was the only coach who could stop Vic Janowicz." Signaling that all was not well between the new coach and his players, the players locked him out of the dressing room before one game.

Hayes, a handsome, black-haired man of 38, spoke with a slight lisp, but his message was always clear and straight-from-the-shoulder. Articulate, informed, thoughtful, and obviously sincere, he made a favorable personal impression with alumni, students, and press right from the start.

But they were less impressed with the results of his coaching. Mutterings of a segment of Buckeye disciples grew into an effort to have his contract terminated. Larkins quickly quashed that.

At that time, before athletic scholarships, football players earned tuition and maintenance money by working part-time for state departments and local businesses. Godfrey, who administered the job program, advised Hayes after the rocky 1951 season that the "downtown jobs" might be withdrawn.

"If I resign, will the players keep their jobs?" Woody asked.

Godfrey admitted that was the case. After an initial, x-rated response, Hayes set his jaw and thundered, with a defiance that would be a trademark in the future, "I'll mortgage my house and pay the players myself!"

Of course, neither the NCAA nor the Big Ten would have tolerated such an arrangement, however self-sacrificing. The situation was resolved in another—legal—manner.

At that early stage of their relationship, Hayes could have blamed Godfrey, dressed him down, or sent him packing. But he kept him, remained loyal, and repeatedly praised him. Ernie continued to tutor Buckeye place-kickers even after his retirement, and Woody often proclaimed him the "greatest place-kicking coach in the country."

The 1952 season represented an upswing, with a third place in the Big Ten, a 6-3 overall record, and, of monstrous importance, a 27-7 win over archrival Michigan—OSU's first since 1944. The Buckeyes had upset Illinois the previous week by the identical score, setting up one of Woody's favorite stories for the off-season banquets.

"This nice lady came up to me," he claimed, "and asked, 'What was the score of your Illinois game?' and I said '27-7.' Then she asked, 'What was the score of your Michigan game?' and I said, '27-7.' She commented, 'You aren't making much improvement, are you?'"

The Buckeyes did improve in 1952, but regressed in 1953. The rule-makers had wiped out the unlimited substitution rule, undermining the platoon system. The change affected all teams, but seemed especially costly to Ohio State. The record remained at 6-3. Not only did the team falter to fourth place in the Big Ten, but it lost to Michigan.

A particularly lackluster effort in the 1953 finale at Ann Arbor and what appeared a rugged start to the 1954 schedule led to a fairly general impression that Hayes might not survive the season. In fact, he heard it firsthand one warm July evening when he decided to sleep on the screened side porch of his Upper Arlington home. A neighbor was hosting a backyard party, and Hayes insists, "I heard someone say, 'This is the year we get rid of old Woody!'" His whispered reply to himself: Like hell you will! He set the alarm on his wrist watch permanently ahead by one hour.

The critics' timetable never materialized. The 1954 Buckeyes clicked off ten straight victories, beating Michigan for the Big Ten championship and Southern California in the Rose Bowl. They were voted the mythical national champion by the Associated Press.

In the next 24 years, Hayes' teams won 179, lost 52 and tied eight, all against major opposition; they won or shared 12 more Big Ten titles, including six in a row, and added two national championships.

In less than two decades, seven other head coaches had come and gone at Ohio State, six of them victims of the hot-seat job, with all its ramifications. Woody stayed within two years of three decades.

"They could break an ordinary man down," suggests Schembechler, a Hayes assistant for eight years, four as a grad assistant. "But they weren't dealing with an ordinary man. They couldn't break this son-of-a-gun down!"

Sadly, he self-destructed.

After the first and worst of his two losing seasons at Ohio State, Woody Hayes stuck out his jaw and went out on a limb. His 1959 Buckeyes had struggled to nothing more than a 3-5-1 record. But at the annual appreciation banquet, OSU President Novice Fawcett waxed poetic and attempted to deflect fan disillusionment over the sub-.500 season. Said he:

> *We don't criticize*
> *The vigorous guys*
> *Whose enterprise*
> *Helps them rise*
> *Above those who criticize.*

Later that evening Hayes himself promised the faithful:"We'll fight for the [Big Ten] championship next year, but I guarantee it in two years. If I don't bring you a championship then, this is no place for Woody Hayes."

Ohio State tied its 1961 opener (7-7 vs. Texas Christian), but finished the season 8-0-1. It gained the promised Big Ten Championship and the national championship, Football Writers of America version. But the Buckeyes were denied a Rose Bowl trip by the OSU Faculty Council.

5

THE WORK ETHIC

Steve Hayes debunks what he concedes to be a good story, though one obviously concocted by someone unfamiliar with his father's routine: "It was supposed to have happened after a Michigan game that Ohio State had lost," Steve relates. "According to the story, I met Dad at the door when he came home after the game and said, 'Dad, you ain't much of a coach,' to which he replied, 'Son, don't say "ain't!"'"

"That couldn't be true, because there's no way in the world that Dad came home after a Michigan game when I was little and still awake. He'd be at the office looking at films or getting ready for a bowl game."

Woody Hayes was not above using an occasional profanity, but his favorite four-letter word was spelled W-O-R-K. "Nothing in this world that comes easy is worth a dime," he said repeatedly, believed implicitly, and followed religiously. "I've never thought I was very smart," he also said sincerely, though anyone who ever shared a conversation with him knew better. "The only smarts I have," he insisted, "are that I'm smart enough to know that I can outwork 'em. If I can work a little harder, and we can be a little better prepared than the other guy, then we'll make luck come our way. [Longtime Texas coach] Darrell Royal says that luck is when preparation meets opportunity, and he's about right. If you get kids to believe that, you've really got something going."

Woody's capacity for work, his willingness to sacrifice almost everything for the job, and his ability to inspire others to a similar level of commitment made the foundation for an era in Ohio State football that was more memorably colorful and lavishly successful than any before or since.

For some coaches, the time immediately after a game is a chance to relax, an opportunity to catch your breath before starting to prepare for next week. Contrast that approach with Woody's postgame routine. First he would hold a closed-door, locker room session with his players, including a brief prayer. Then he met and talked with visiting recruits—typically 10 to 20 high school players whose talents qualified them as sought-after Buckeyes-to-be. He faced the media next, a session whose tone and duration corresponded to the success or disappointment of the afternoon's effort.

Then the real work recommenced. From the press conference, Woody went directly to his office. A student manager often had films of the first quarter in the projector already; if not, the films would arrive momentarily. Films of the remaining three quarters were delivered as they were developed. Woody ran them through, then again, with myriad stops, reverses, and starts. About midnight or 1 a.m., he'd snap off the projector and head for home. Too wound up to sleep, he'd read, then finally tumble into bed.

"But sometimes I'd get to thinking about something, something I might have overlooked," he admitted, "and I'd get up and go back to the office and look at the films again." The clock might say 3 or 4 a.m. "He did that many times," Anne Hayes attests, "even when it wasn't football season."

When the Buckeyes played on the road, the procedure depended on travel arrangements. If the team returned home after the game, Hayes went from the plane to his office for the same routine, pushed back a few hours. If the team stayed overnight, the films were processed at a local shop and delivered to Woody's room at the hotel.

"Out at Washington, when we played there in 1957, I was coming through the lobby and Woody spotted me," longtime assistant Gene Fekete relates. "He asked what I was doing, and I said I was planning to go out on the town with some of the other coaches. He said, 'Aw, let's go up and watch the films, they'll be delivering them pretty soon.' We went up to his room, and he paced back and forth, anticipating those films. They never did come. So he made us look at the films on the plane coming back."

On rare occasions, Woody would slip away from his film projector to have a quick dinner with Anne, or to see someone in the hospital, or drop in on a party. But the host had to be a very special friend or the guest list extraordinary. After the Iowa game of 1957, for example, which the Buckeyes won to qualify for another Rose Bowl trip, Woody and Anne accepted an invitation to the home of U.S. Senator John Bricker, who had as guests Richard Nixon, then the vice president, and wife Pat.

"I didn't go over the Iowa [game] films as much as I would have liked," Woody said later. He gloried in the evening, but he couldn't shake the fear that he'd given the "other guy" (his next opponent, Michigan coach Bump Elliot) a chance to outwork him.

In the early years of Woody's regime, assistant coaches personally scouted upcoming opponents, an expensive procedure all but abandoned in later years by virtue of exchanging films. Esco Sarkkinen acquired the nickname "Super Sleuth" because of his minutely detailed espionage reports.

The coaching staff heard the scouting report on Sunday morning, although Hayes usually had been briefed earlier. "Woody's trademark question, before the scout even presented his report, was, 'Can we beat 'em?'" recalls Fekete, who shared in the "gumshoe" detail. "If you said yes, before you could hardly get it out of your mouth, the old man would ask 'How?'

"One time, Sark was supposed to give his scouting report on Michigan. We were having a mediocre season, and Michigan was loaded. As usual Woody asked if we could beat 'em, and Sark replied, 'Well, Woody, if we do thus and so. . . .' Woody asked again, 'Can we beat 'em?' and again Sark says, 'If we do thus and so. . . .' Woody was getting mad and he told Sark, 'I want you to go out that door and come back in and I'm going to ask you once more!' Sark went out the door and came back in and Woody asked, 'Can we beat 'em?' and Sark said, 'If we do thus and so . . . .' Well, Sark went out that door and came back in two or three times that morning, and they kept on yelling at each other!" It finally went to a no-decision: time was being wasted, which Woody didn't like, and the other assistants could no longer suppress their amusement, which Woody also didn't like.

In those days, Woody met with the staff at 7 a.m. six days a week, and the assistant coaches usually headed home about midnight. "We were tickled to hit Saturday," Fekete admits. "The game, that was the fun."

There were some interruptions, though. On Sunday, those so inclined had leave to attend church. As an usher at First Community Church, I often saw Woody slip into a back pew and leave immediately after the service. On Mondays, he took time out for the media luncheon, and he accepted a limited number of other outside appearances. Anne Hayes often brought in sandwiches for the marathon coaching sessions. At other times, a graduate assistant or a manager would be dispatched to a nearby McDonald's for carry-in meals.

As the seasons passed, the regimen abated slightly; staff meetings started at 8 and lasted until 10 or 11 p.m. The offensive and defensive staffs generally held separate meetings, with Woody heading the offense, while the defensive coordinator— first Lou McCullough, later George Hill—headed the defense. "But Coach Hayes always knew what was going on [with the defense]," McCullough emphasizes. "He knew both sides of the ball, and he could coach both sides of the ball."

The assistant coaches worked Saturday nights, as did the head coach, dissecting and grading films of the day's game. When he succeeded McCullough, Hill made it a sort of social occasion, holding the Saturday night sessions at his home. "Getting all of that film work out of the way Saturday night was really a good system," Sarkkinen believes. "That way, you could start Sunday morning preparing for your next game."

McCullough remembers when Woody changed the system—for one season only: "We got Dr. Mel Olix, who had been Woody's quarterback at Miami and whom Woody liked, to tell him that it was psychologically unsound for us to come over Saturday night. If we could get off Saturday night, we'd be fresh on Sunday morning. So Woody told the staff one morning, 'Dr. Olix thinks you'd be fresher if you didn't have to come in Saturday nights, and it's probably a good idea. I'll be here, but you don't have to come in Saturday nights.' We had one whole season without Saturday nights. Then in the summer, we had a meeting in which he said, 'By the way, I don't want any of you SOBs to run to Dr. Olix, because you're going to be with me Saturday nights!'"

Still, Hayes came to realize that some time for recreation was important, that a break from work might actually improve the quality of the work done afterward.

In later years, Woody allowed the assistants "family nights," Wednesday and Thursday, although they were also supposed to use some of that time with the football players under their direct command.

And while Woody worked all year long, he insisted that the assistants get away for a month or more in the summer. He recognized that time off might be good for others, if not for himself. So the head coach worked on. "Woody pretty much ran the office by himself," Sarkkinen recalls.

Just as it took a visiting dignitary to break his postgame routine, only a special circumstance could induce him to take anything vaguely resembling a vacation. In the summer of 1952, his quarterback John Borton was serving on a ship as part of his Naval ROTC duties. With Anne and Steve, Woody set out by car for Toronto, where Borton's ship was to dock briefly. Hayes filled the car trunk with footballs, planning to work Borton out— "on the Plains of Abraham or something," Anne Hayes recalls.

The Hayes family planned to drive on through Canada on a sightseeing trip. But Borton's ship didn't arrive as scheduled; Steve became ill with what was first feared to be polio, but proved to be a one-day virus; and besides, Woody conceded, "I got to thinking of all the things I could be doing back at the office." They came home.

His first summer venture away ended just as abruptly. He flew to Europe, rented a car and toured. It was a rewarding adventure for a history buff—particularly an avid military buff. He avoided the usual tourist attractions and instead sought places where he might talk with the natives and enjoy each country's "grassroots."

Before leaving, he advised McCullough, "I will call you at 2:00 on June 5 for a report on eligibility. I want the entire staff there, because I'm going to question them about their players. I want them to know all the grade-point averages and how we did at the end of the term."

As June 5 drew near, McCullough recalls, "I knew we had a problem, because our star back made a flat 0.00." Woody called on cue at 2:00 from Belino, Italy. After a few amenities, he asked about the grades of the football players who had been in summer school. McCullough swallowed, then softly imparted the worst news. The other assistant coaches, seated around the conference table, heard Woody's reaction clear and very loudly—all the way from Italy: "I'm never going to take another vacation!" he promised, among other colorful declarations.

He reneged one summer years later. He went mountain climbing in Colorado with two OSU faculty colleagues. The group had planned to be away for all of one week, but after only a few days of training, Woody announced that he was going to climb Long's Peak—the biggie of the range. His colleagues protested that he wasn't ready, but he said, "I've got to get back to the office. I'm going to climb today.

"It took me a while to get up the mountain," he later reported. "I climbed at my own pace, but doggone, I got to the top!" The sense of accomplishment pleased him, and he found the mountains and the peaceful atmosphere a source of regeneration. But the job still sang its siren song.

Legend has it that Woody devoted 16 hours a day, seven days a week, 12 months a year to the Ohio State football program. That is a slight exaggeration, obviously, but anyone even casually associated with the Buckeyes during Woody's reign would agree that no man ever gave himself more completely to his calling. And no man ever had greater conviction in the principle of "working harder than the other guy."

"I heard Coach Hayes say it a thousand times: 'If you give me a big enough head start, I can beat Jesse Owens,'" recalled Bill Myles, once Hayes' offensive tackle/tight end coach, later OSU associate athletic director. "He figured if it could be done through hard work, he could get it done."

"I enjoyed working for Coach Hayes, because I like to work hard myself," McCullough declares. "He is by far the hardest working person with whom I have ever been associated. He was a tireless worker."

The 42 assistant coaches who served on his staff during his 28 years would agree with Fekete: "Woody was a very demanding person. But he was very fair. He never asked anything of his staff members that he wasn't going through himself." As the head coach, in fact, he did more. Time, like money, meant little.

Bill Wentz, a 1959-60 halfback, stayed on for two years as one of Woody's graduate assistants while working on his master's degree. If the assistant coaches ducked out of some film sessions, the GAs had no such seniority. "One Sunday night we were watching films of Saturday's game with Woody, and all of a sudden he exclaimed, 'He's not leveling off!'" Wentz relates. In Hayes football, it was a cardinal rule that ball carriers were to "level off to the goal posts" and plunge with maximum force as enemy tacklers closed in; no fancy didoes, just straight-ahead, smash-mouth power. "We watched a while longer and Woody said, 'Goddammit, he's not leveling off! Go get him!'"

"Him" was Bob Ferguson, who would eventually be an All-American fullback—twice. "This is 10:30 on a Sunday night," Wentz recalls. "I finally found Fergy's phone number, and he answered half-awake. I said, 'The old man wants to talk to you.' He said, 'Do you know what time it is? Tell him you couldn't find me.' I picked him up at his apartment, and we got back to St. John Arena about 11p.m. From then until 1 a.m., Woody, Fergy, and I went through the whole game film. When I finally took him home, Fergy said, 'I don't believe this!' But the following week, he had one of his best games."

"The guy was phenomenal at driving people to do work," says current Athletic Director Jim Jones, who served on Hayes' staff for four years. "I remember the first day on the job [freshman coach] Tiger Ellison told me, 'There's one thing you need to know: You will never outwork Woody so don't try.' I tried, I admit. I supposed that's what all of us did who worked for him. That was his goal. You tried to outwork him."

Sarkkinen, Fekete, Harry Strobel, and Ernie Godfrey found their routines radically changed in the switch from Wes Fesler to Woody Hayes. "In the four years Wes was here, I don't believe there were more than 10 to 12 night meetings," Sarkkinen observes. "There were player-coach meetings, but very few. It was almost like having a job from 9 in the morning to 6 at night. When Woody came in, the job was 7 in the morning to 10, 11, 12 at night. There were coach-player meetings during the day, at night, on weekends."

Tardiness for a staff meeting was a cardinal sin, and absence bordered on treason. In one oft-related episode, Woody himself had to use all of his determination and ingenuity to make the 8 a.m. starting time. Back then, the football offices were located in the old Men's Gym, now Larkins Hall. Immediately behind the building was a narrow lot with a handful of parking spaces. On this morning, Woody was running behind schedule. He cruised into the lot, finally spotting a single open space. He worked hard to back his car in, then discovered the space was so small he couldn't open his door to exit.

While the football staff watched from one window and Sports Information Director Marv Homan from another, Woody sat for a minute, studying his predicament. "Then, to our amazement, he pulled the car forward from the parking space," recalls Homan, "got out, went around to the front of the car, and pushed it back into the space!" The laughter had died down by the time Woody bustled into the staff meeting—on time.

Hayes understood when he accepted the Ohio State appointment that his assistants would be paid in part by the Athletic Department and in part by the Physical Education Department. They were to teach physical education classes for regular students in addition to their coaching duties. "He accepted that," Sarkkinen explains, "until the first season. We had staff meetings on Tuesdays and Thursdays, and it was getting close to 10:00. Several of us were stirring, looking at our watches. Finally we told Woody it was time for us to go teach a class. He said, 'Oh, goddammit, sonofabitch!' He was mad because he was losing some of his staff for two hours. Well, he changed that!" All assistant coaches hired from that point on were strictly full-time football staff. Coaching football at Ohio State was no longer a part-time occupation.

Much of the work for Woody and his staff took place in a myriad of meetings. Meetings, lots of meetings, were a Hayes trademark from the earliest years through the last. Some assistant coaches groused about it occasionally, but they made sure to keep their voices low. No detail was too insignificant for Woody's attention. He was a master of anticipation, and a relentless disciple of preparation.

As the Buckeye team boarded its buses for Michigan Stadium and its final game of Woody's first season, tackle Dick Logan whispered to a writer, "We may not be leading the league in won-lost, but we sure as hell are leading in meetings."

Staff meetings, according to Jones, ranged from raucous to philosophical to downright boring. Meetings in the latter category typically had to do with the Xs and Os of football; but even in those meetings, Hayes often tossed in enough of the other ingredients to help cut through the tedium.

Woody was a voracious reader of books, newspapers, and magazines. He clipped news stories, editorials, and columns he especially liked and had his secretary paste them in a scrapbook that bulged eight to ten inches thick. He often brought some of them to staff meetings, anything from clippings or a magazine article to a book he'd been reading, passages of which he had marked—anything he considered of sufficient interest to read aloud to his coaches. Sometimes he would quiz them or ask each for comment or interpretation.

"One night Woody read an article in *Reader's Digest* about a physical fitness program at a high school in California," McCullough relates. "He was all fired up for our 8 a.m. meeting the next day and promptly told us we were in lousy shape and should be running to the top of St. John Arena every morning. He started reading the article, then decided instead he would march us up to the top of the arena immediately. When we finally struggled up there, he lined us up and read the entire article. Then he marched us down to our offices and gave us a test. He got his point across. Everybody got 100 percent."

In another physical fitness effort at one spring practice, Woody decided that staff members—including the head coach— were carrying around too many extra pounds. He proposed a diet for all. When Buckeye players returned for fall practice, they were struck by how trim their coaches—including the head coach—had become over the summer.

But the coaches worked hard that fall, diet-diminished appetites revived, training table food was tasty and plentiful, and the pounds somehow crept back on. The head coach looked just about the same to fans attending the opening game in Ohio Stadium. He weighed in at a robust 220 pounds.

Woody didn't hire "yes men." Staff meetings were always exchanges of often contradictory ideas—though there was never any doubt whose ideas carried most weight. "He was a great listener," Myles says. "You could say something in a staff meeting and he'd shoot you down. Then three weeks later he might say, 'I've been thinking about what Bill said; maybe we ought to try it.' He'd remember what you said and give you credit. Of course, if it wasn't any good, you'd never hear about it."

"Woody listened to other ideas," Sarkkinen agrees. "In fact, he was a good listener as long as he felt you were making things worthwhile. Without telling them, he used the staff as a sounding board for some of his own ideas, a sort of trial balloon to see how you would react. It was a way of fortifying his own beliefs."

"He was brilliant and could read right through you," McCullough attests. "You had better be damned sure when you were talking with him that you knew what you were talking about."

Hayes wanted to hear his assistants' ideas on everything from strategy to game-day routine, but he particularly valued their insights on players. "He would challenge you about a player," Myles says. "He wanted to see how much you believed in the kid. If you were willing to stick your neck out for the kid, then you might know something about him that he didn't. He did that with Rudy Hubbard on Archie [Griffin]. Rudy pounded the table a lot. When Coach finally put him in and Archie did well, Coach said, 'I knew he was good.'"

But while Hayes encouraged debate, even heated debate, among his staff, he never relinquished the rights of his high office. "Woody loved votes, a tally of some sort to get a consensus," Sarkkinen says. "Many times, we assistant coaches would vote yes and Woody would vote no. Woody's no would wipe out our eight yeses."

Hayes' assistant coaches had a warning signal Bill Myles recalls. Whenever one spotted Woody coming, he would sound the alert by yelling "Geronimo!"

"He never said a thing about it or even acted like he heard it," Myles relates. "But not more than two weeks before he died, I was over at his office talking, and he asked with a little grin, 'Say Bill, have you heard from that Geronimo fella lately?'

"You didn't put anything over on him!"

6

IN A WORD: CARE

Big Ten teams participating in the Rose Bowl were, by custom, assigned a fleet of new automobiles—with chauffeurs—for use during their stay in Pasadena. Ohio State players were permitted use of the cars for sightseeing and after-dinner ventures around the Los Angeles area, in groups and under Woody Hayes' usual strict regulations.

After one Rose Bowl game, University officials staying at the team's Huntington Hotel headquarters lined up the cars for a caravan to a postgame party at another hotel in L.A. At least that was the plan until Woody heard about it. "To hell with that!" he bristled. "The players get those cars!"

Hayes took command. From the front of the hotel, he personally dispatched the cars that whisked the players in twos, threes, and fours off for their evening on the town—with his inevitable curfew requirements. The University "brass," including the president, trustees, and even Hayes' boss, Athletic Director Richard Larkins, scrambled for taxis and other emergency transportation.

Later, to a suggestion that he might have overstepped his bounds, he replied with conviction but without arrogance: "Who got us here? Who played the game? Our football players! They come first." This minor incident underscored a fundamental Hayes tenet that was one of his greatest strengths as a football coach and as a man: concern for the young men entrusted to his hands—during their playing days and long after. John Bozick, the sage of the OSU equipment room, is a man of many words, but he summarizes this trait of Woody Hayes in a cogent few: "The key word: C-A-R-E. He cared!"

"He was an outstanding coach, a great coach," attests Archie Griffin, the amazing little halfback who gilded four epic OSU campaigns with a pair of Heisman Trophies and a pocketful of Big Ten and NCAA records. "But the thing about Woody Hayes was the way he cared about his players. If any player came to Coach Hayes with a problem, you can bet he would do something to help."

The world saw Hayes as a sideline-stomping curmudgeon. His players knew that side of Woody too, but they also got a look at the human side.

"He might yell at you and scream at you and chew you out," admits Jan White, a 1970 All-American tight end, "but he cared about you as a person. He wanted you to succeed, on the field and off. He wanted good things for you, and he was going to do his best to see that you got them. He was some kind of person!"

And for Hayes, the coaching—and the caring—didn't end when a player's eligibility expired. "He cared before you went to Ohio State, while you were there, and after you were gone," says Larry Zelina, a talented wingback on the championship teams of 1968-69-70. "The guy was not just a football coach, he was a mentor!"

If you were one of "Woody's guys," anyone who played for him, from star to lowliest walk-on, you enjoyed the same assurance that you had a staunch ally in times of distress. "You knew there was one person who was always in your corner," declares John Hicks, an All-American tackle who won both the Outland and Lombardi Awards. "You could always go to the coach and talk with him, good or bad. He would come out with some pretty good solutions."

You didn't even have to seek him out. Vic Janowicz, the 1950 Heisman Trophy winner, had been involved in an auto accident in August 1956 that ended his pro football career. He was living in Chicago when Ohio State came to the Windy City to play at Northwestern. Woody invited him to have Friday night dinner with the Buckeye squad and was shocked when he saw Vic, as were Dick Larkins and others in the OSU party.

"I was in terrible shape," Janowicz confesses. "My left side was paralyzed, my speech was impaired, and my memory was shot." After dinner and after Vic had headed for his in-laws' home in south Chicago, where he was living with his wife and young daughter, Woody decided to take him back to Columbus on the team plane. He had team physician Bob Murphy contact University Hospital to arrange for Janowicz's admission upon his arrival Saturday night.

"They called me and told me to pack a bag, because I was going back to Columbus with the team," Vic recalls. Hayes called Skip Doyle, one of Vic's school buddies and teammates, advised him of developments, and secured his assistance. After his hospital check-up and early treatment, Janowicz stayed with the Doyles until he moved his family from Chicago and established his own home in Columbus.

"Woody Hayes was a great, great individual," Vic declares. "He brought me back to Columbus, he looked after me and got me back on my feet. I'm very, very grateful." While living at Doyle's house, he recalls, "The only place I went was to get treatment at Ohio State. Ernie Biggs [OSU trainer] worked with me every day and every night. When I came back with my family in January, I continued my treatments at University Hospital."

Janowicz was physically rehabilitated in a few months and went to work for the state of Ohio. He is now employed by the state auditor's office, not only serving in the department, but representing it in speaking engagements and personal appearances around Ohio, sometimes as often as five times a day.

Janowicz wasn't a charter member of the Woody Hayes fan club. He won his Heisman during Wes Fesler's last year as head coach. When Hayes replaced Fesler he brought with him an offensive system that failed to take full advantage of his star back's triple-threat skills.

"It was like I dropped out for a year," Janowicz says. "I was wasted. But I don't resent those things. This is life. Everybody has ups and downs. Mine came at the best time of my life, when I was 21 years old and my life was in front of me. But Woody did a lot for me. He knew I didn't like his football, but he was such a great, caring person. He brought me back and I'm very, very grateful."

Former halfback and graduate assistant coach Bill Wentz has especially poignant memories of Hayes' caring. One Sunday noon at their Dayton home, Bill's youngest, a toddler, somehow escaped the family and was crushed under the wheels of a backing automobile. Any parent can imagine the frightful impact of such a tragedy. A friend of Cindy and Bill Wentz put in a call for Woody. Anne Hayes took the message because Woody was at the team training facility watching films. She sped there and found the building locked. She banged on the doors until she could be heard over the whir of the film projector.

"Drive time from Columbus to Dayton is an hour and 30 minutes, and he was there in an hour and 20 minutes," recalls Wentz. "With what had happened, everything was kind of a blur. And of course, I didn't know he was coming," Bill continues. "When I opened the door and saw him standing there, I asked what he was doing here. And he said, 'I figured you needed to talk to somebody.'

"It just seemed as if everything was OK for that period of time. We talked about things in general, about the other two children, about my job. He engaged my mind on other things than what had happened. He stayed about an hour and a half, then he said he had to leave and asked me to walk with him to the car. He said, 'You understand this is going to be tough for you for a while. You can't blame yourself. One thing you've got to remember: You've got to be strong because you've got those other two kids and Cindy to worry about. It's important that you focus on them and their needs and nothing else. And if you need anything, give me a call.' More than anything that day, that was the thing that settled me down. It didn't make the tragedy any less a tragedy, but if I needed anything, Woody's being there was it."

Frank Kremblas quarterbacked the 1957 Ohio State team that won the Big Ten and the Rose Bowl, as well as UPI's version of the national championship. He was also one of those who followed Woody's urging to become an attorney. For some years after graduation, he would meet with a recruit now and then at Woody's request. But he hadn't really had much contact with Woody for several years.

Kremblas relates, "Then my daughter had a brain tumor and was in Children's Hospital for a long time. It was one of the more difficult operable tumors, and the day of the operation it was really touch and go. I hadn't talked with Woody, although [wife] Penny had talked with Anne a couple of times. But, lo and behold, about 8:30 in the morning, in walks Woody, and he stayed the whole day. Obviously, he was very supportive during a very difficult time. Also, this was during the time between the end of the football season and the Rose Bowl, when you knew how busy he was."

A few years later Woody caused a furor by refusing to speak to the media after Ohio State's bitter loss to UCLA in the 1976 Rose Bowl. He still wasn't available after returning from Pasadena two days later. "I knew where he was," recalls Dan Fronk, the gutty little center of the 1957-58 Buckeyes. "He grabbed a cab at the airport and came to the hospital where I was. I don't know how he got word I was in the hospital with cancer, but he came and spent five hours with me. I'll never forget it. I was down in the X-ray room and they came and told me that Woody was up in my room. I couldn't believe it. After all, I'd graduated in 1959, and this was 1976!

"Woody found out what was wrong and made sure I had the best doctors. His concern was my health, not what happened at the Rose Bowl. Everybody was ridiculing Woody for not talking to the press, and I wanted to tell them where he had been but he wouldn't let me. But that was typical Woody." Fronk, who had Hodgkins disease, a highly treatable cancer, is still doing well in 1991 and still remembers his debt of gratitude to an old coach.

But "caring" isn't only about coming to a friend's side in a crisis. Sometimes it's just treating a man like a man, when a large part of the world isn't willing to make that concession. Though his tenure at Ohio State spanned the turbulent years of the Civil Rights Movement, the only colors that ever mattered to Hayes were OSU's scarlet and gray; black and white were irrelevant.

John Hicks, later hailed by Hayes as the finest lineman he'd ever coached, heard hints of racism at OSU when he was being recruited back in Cleveland. But after meeting Buckeye players and having dinner with Woody, he found those slurs groundless. "Some people said I shouldn't go to Ohio State," he recalls, "because they said Woody was a racist and wouldn't play black players. I didn't find the coach to be that way at all. I found him to be a very loving person. He was tough, but he didn't show partiality to anybody."

Three OSU football seasons and 18 years later, the former Outland and Lombardi Trophy winner attests, "I loved the old man very much. I had a lot of one-on-one conversations with him. I'd call him up and we'd go to lunch, occasionally at the

Faculty Club at his suggestion. After you get done playing, you find out he's really a fun guy. I miss him so much."

Hayes recalled that his father, as a school superintendent, had worried about the plight of blacks and had done everything he could to encourage and assist them. His father doubtless influenced his attitude. But given his native intelligence and humanity, he surely would have arrived at the same conclusion anyway. In *You Win With People*, Woody noted without exaggeration, "We were involved with blacks long before it was either fashionable or politically expedient."

"Woody was a forerunner for integration and in giving the black athlete every opportunity," suggests Rev. Daryl Sanders, OSU offensive tackle in 1960-61-62, number-one draft choice of the Detroit Lions, and now a senior pastor of the Zion Christian Fellowship Church in Columbus. "He established a real special effort toward the black athlete, before anybody else I know of."

So it was not a big deal as far as Hayes was concerned to name Cornelius Greene as the first black quarterback at Ohio State in 1973, replacing the popular red-haired incumbent Greg Hare. Greene went on to direct the spectacular Archie Griffin-fueled Buckeye machines of 1973-74-75. "I started that first year as a sophomore against Minnesota," he recalls, "when Greg Hare was a co-captain of the team and going into his third year starting. I think it took a lot of guts for Coach Hayes to do that. But he took the pressure off me being the first black quarterback—and there could have been a lot of it. He never looked at me as color, he looked at me as one of his quarterbacks. He downplayed the color issue, and I never up-played it, so I think we established a good bond. I knew if I was good enough, I was going to play, and if I wasn't, I wasn't going to play, no matter what color I was. I respected him for that."

Always giving top priority to the physical well-being of his players, Hayes accepted the word of team physician Dr. Bob Murphy or his associates as law, particularly during games. If the medics recommended no further play for an injured warrior, that player remained on the sideline.

Greene, however, remembers a time when Woody conducted his own diagnostic test. "We were playing at Wisconsin in my sophomore year," he says. "It was my first away game. I remember running the ball and getting hit so hard that I almost lost my nerve and wanted to come out of the game. I had also hit my head pretty hard. I was shook up, and I went to Coach Hayes with the intent of coming out.

"Usually the doctors hold up two fingers, and if you want to come out of the game you say six. But Coach Hayes asked me what class I took at 1:00, and I proceeded to tell him. He asked me my teacher's name in my 10:00 class, and I told him. He said, 'Your head's OK, get back out there.' It was really something, because from that moment on, by going back out there, I really established a mental toughness!"

Hayes took great pride in the accomplishments of his players after they left OSU. But when the rare ex-Buckeye disappointed his former coach, Woody simply took that as a challenge to give that prodigal son further guidance.

A Texas high school star, Rod Gerald quarterbacked Hayes' 1976-77 teams to Big Ten championships with brilliant running and passing. As a senior, he was converted to wide receiver to make room for high-touted and enormously gifted QB recruit Art Schlichter.

Gerald left school after football season and returned to Texas without his degree, much to Woody's disappointment. What happened in the ensuing years disappointed Woody even more. Drugs and alcohol threw Gerald for a loss. With those burdens—and no degree—he was trapped in a dead-end, menial job. "He used to call me, just out of the blue," Rod reports. Hayes badgered his former player to come back to school and get his degree, but Rod was 600 miles away from Ohio State and Woody could pay only polite attention.

At Hayes' suggestion, OSU alumni in Texas staged a benefit for Gerald. Woody flew down, delivered the main banquet speech, and spent time with Rod, trying to affect a turnaround and arranging for a job as part of the reclamation. Eventually, Hayes' efforts took hold.

"He'd been on me since '84," Gerald recalls. "I thought he'd give up, but he never did. I really love the guy for that. I was at the end of the line, as far as you can go. But Coach Hayes opened the door for me to walk back up. He gave me a new lease on life. I credit Coach Hayes with my existence. Without him, I probably would have lost everything. Without him, I probably would have drifted off into oblivion. I probably would still be a bum."

As the cornerstone of all his encouragement, Hayes had preached to Gerald that getting his degree was a first big step back. "A week before he passed away, he called me in Dallas and said, 'Rod, we've been stretching this thing out for too long now. I want you to make a commitment to me. Either you can go to school down there or whatever you want to do, but you've got to get this done.'"

Woody's preference was that Gerald come back to Ohio State; Hayes had, in fact, taken preliminary steps toward that end. "But then he died," Rod continues. "A week after, Anne [Hayes] called me and said, 'Rod, I know what Coach wanted. I want to see this thing through.' Coach had already got me in touch with Greg Lashutka and Moose Machinsky [former OSU players]. That was March, and I came back to Columbus in June."

Gerald graduated from Ohio State in 1989 and is currently employed in the city of Columbus' Department of Regulations. "I've made a lot of strides," he acknowledges. " I have a wife and two kids, I have my degree, and I have a job. I've been completely free from drugs and alcohol since 1987. I'm here because of Coach Hayes and the impact of his tenacity."

Jim Parker, the only Hayes protege in both the College and Pro Football Halls of Fame, learned from a number of experiences about Woody's loyalty to his players, both while they were football-playing Buckeyes and long afterward. So convinced was the big fellow that he insisted, "If the old man said to move the stadium two yards or three inches, if he said it could be done, I believed it, and I would try!"

Parker had become an All-Pro tackle with the Baltimore Colts when Woody was inspired to look after what he considered Jim's best interests—and, coincidentally, that of another of his former players. "I didn't know anything about it, but Woody called [Colts head coach] Don Shula and told him, 'You've got the greatest guard in football playing tackle. If Vogel could be at tackle and Parker move to guard, you'd have a hell of a football team.'" Bob Vogel had been a standout tackle at Ohio State in 1960-61-62 and a number-one draft choice of the Colts.

"Shula asked me what I thought about it," Jim recalls, "and I said I'd mastered this [tackle] position, put a lot of man-hours into it, and knew most of my defensive opponents. Now I had to learn all over at guard?" Nonetheless, Parker was switched to guard, and Vogel was promoted to starting tackle in his place. Hayes' prediction proved true. "I sort of like guard anyway," Parker confesses. "That was my favorite position, pulling and trapping. All that stuff I learned at Ohio State came in handy, like Harry Strobel telling us how to pull in the direction you were going without losing a step. It all came back. I thought Harry was crazy doing all those things, and now I benefit from it."

It may be news to him, but Griffin also benefited from Hayes' intervention. After Archie's pro football career had ended and a business venture failed, Woody went to see University President Ed Jennings. "I felt Arch just HAD to be in our Athletic Department," Woody confided. (He continued to use "our," although his active connection with the department had been unceremoniously severed in 1978.) "He was just a natural for it. I knew we couldn't have a better representative of Ohio State and our athletics than Arch. So I asked the prexy if he would do something about giving Arch a job in the Athletic Department. When he finally said he'd take care of it, I jumped up and grabbed him and gave him a big hug. I shouldn't have done that, but I was so doggone happy, I couldn't help myself."

Archie joined the Athletic Department as special assistant to Director Rick Bay in 1985 and was promoted to assistant director when Jim Jones took over the department in 1987. As a fundraiser, a popular banquet speaker, and active community leader, he has been to the Athletic Department everything Woody envisioned.

You could add countless similar stories to these few—a benefit for ex-fullback Bob Ferguson, laid low by hypertension; moral support for Zelina when his mother was dying of cancer; a hundred phone calls to help ex-players find work or their way in life.

Multiply the examples here by the 28 years he coached at OSU, by the countless players and assistant coaches whose lives he touched, and you begin to get a notion of what "caring" meant for Woody Hayes.

Jim Stillwagon, Ohio State's greatest middle guard/linebacker (1968-69-70), recalls a time that Woody's caring "touched my life. When my mom suddenly passed away, it was the worst thing in my whole life," he remembers. "We held the Mass at the Catholic church in Mount Vernon, and my brothers and I were pallbearers. When we took the casket out, there was Coach Hayes in the church.

"I was just floored. I don't know how he even found out, but he was there! He was looking at me like he might cry. When we got in the car, he came over and said, 'She was a great lady. I'll be in touch with you. If you want to talk with somebody, call me.'" Mrs. Stillwagon died in 1980, ten years after Jim's last Ohio State football season under Hayes.

"When we got back home from the funeral that day," Jim adds, "my dad mentioned that Mom would have a special place in heaven today with sports fans. They would all come up to her when she gets into heaven and say, 'Woody Hayes was at your funeral today. That's unbelievable!'"

Woody Hayes always thought of his players' welfare, to the seemingly most insignificant detail. He suddenly decided late one Sunday afternoon to call a squad meeting. Assistants scrambled to round up the players.

"You know what?" Woody suggested, "They're going to be hungry. You guys [pointing to grad assistant Bill Wentz] go down to the drive-in and get some hamburgers and milk shakes."

Bill recalls, "I called a drive-in up on Olentangy River Road and said I was calling for Coach Hayes. We wanted 65 hamburgers and 65 milk shakes. One of the managers and I walked into the drive-in, and I said we were here for our 65 hamburgers and shakes. They said they thought it was a prank. I told them, 'I've got a guy sitting back there at St. John Arena, and if you call him you'll find out real quick if this is a prank.' We got the burgers and shakes."

7

THE "OTHER" FAMILY

Steve Hayes, at age 45 a lawyer and municipal judge, enjoys telling this story: "Dad was coming out of a hospital once, and somebody asked him how Steve was doing in law school. He said 'Steve who?' and they said 'Your son!' So he said, 'Oooooh, yeah.' He was trying to think of a football player named Steve who was in law school."

"Woody's family was the football team and Ohio State University," suggests Rex Kern, and Hayes' "other" family—wife Anne and son Steve—know better than anyone else the truth of Kern's assessment.

"I admitted it," says Anne Hayes, Woody's helpmate for nearly 45 of his 74 years. "Football and 90 boys—the football squad—came ahead of me, but I didn't mind that. I said it was better than having one thin blonde in an apartment someplace."

Anne met with natural humor and inordinate understanding the coach's "marriage" to a job that severely curtailed his time at home and left him unavailable for many things normally expected of a husband and father. "It was always that way," she conceded. "Woody loved the game and the guys who played it. It didn't bother me. I got used to being on my own. That was good, I was doing what I wanted to do."

As for ever persuading Woody to change, she once admitted in a speech: "I thought Woody Hayes should be the kind of man I wanted him to be, but I learned I had to let him be the kind of husband he wanted to be. But I get equal rights: I get to be the kind of wife I want to be!"

Which is not to say that Anne, a woman of quick and independent wit, was averse to the occasional joke about her status as a "football widow." During a question-and-answer session after another speech, someone asked if she ever thought of divorcing Woody. "Divorce no" she replied, "murder yes."

But on a more serious note, she says, "I felt he should live his life the way he wanted. I tried very hard to give him time to do his job. It was sometimes difficult, but he was a man of the world. You do what you have to do. I was part of his life."

She wasn't jealous or resentful of football, sensing that "Woody would have been as dedicated to any kind of job. I think most men are dedicated to a job. What's a woman going to do? Besides, I love the game of football. When we lost, I was a hard, hard loser."

Anne Gross Hayes' roots in athletics are deep and long-standing. "I was going to football games with my mother and dad when I was three, four years old," she pointed out. "Baseball, too. I saw Babe Ruth pitch for the Boston Red Sox when I was three years old. I saw Bobby Feller pitch his first home game. He was 18 years old. I knew everything about the Cleveland Indians.

"But football was my game. I just loved it. When I was in college [Ohio Wesleyan], I wouldn't miss a football or basketball game for love nor money. When Woody was an assistant football coach at New Philadelphia, we'd go somewhere and scout. That was my date. No sir, I didn't learn all of my football from Woody!"

Mrs. Hayes confessed to some spirited "differences of opinion" in their marriage, not uncommon between two positive, assertive people. But Woody's frequent absences kept conflict to a minimum. "You can't argue with silence," she suggested, adding, "People used to get a kick out of it when I said we didn't argue, we fought. But what the heck, he wouldn't have liked me if I'd been a milquetoast woman. He wanted a challenge. That was part of his nature, and I made up my mind he was going to get it from me."

She once amused a banquet audience by noting that she and Woody were married on June 19, "which is supposed to be Emancipation Day, but it didn't work out that way. I was sold into slavery. " But the independent Anne also took seriously her role as wife and helpmate; not only did she unstintingly grant

Woody the time he needed for his coaching, she helped his career in more concrete ways as well.

Hayes wrote three books, and wanting complete control of the contents, published each himself. Mrs. Hayes handled the business side of the projects, distribution, collections, and accounting—plus the tax headache. "I said I was going to write my own book," she said, "and it was going to be on sex and marriage. But being a football coach's wife, I wasn't an authority on either one."

Anne was also a first-rate public relations agent for the coach. The Hayes phone number was in the book for anyone who wanted to express an opinion, and Anne served as a buffer between Woody and fans who called at all hours of the day and night. She adroitly disarmed them, one way or another.

An angry Buckeye alumnus once phoned the Hayes home after a losing game and, along with several choice observations, termed Woody a "fathead." "I've called him a fathead a few times myself," she agreed. "What wife hasn't?"

So diplomatic and so agreeable was she that some fans became "phone pals." They'd call from Michigan or Texas or somewhere in Ohio just to talk, maybe to argue a little and be deftly ribbed. One late night, a caller bellowed into the phone: "I'm looking for your husband. I'm mad at him!" To which Mrs. Hayes responded, "If you find him, tell him I'm mad at him, too."

An irate fan called one Sunday morning, and after listening patiently Anne suggested: "I'm frying eggs and bacon; why don't you and your wife come over and we'll talk about this at the breakfast table?" They accepted the invitation—and left as Woody Hayes converts.

Anne's original ideas for holiday greeting cards were a source of pride and amusement for Woody. After the OSU Faculty Council denied Woody's 1961 Big Ten championship team a trip to the Rose Bowl, Mrs. Hayes worked up a card that showed a bouquet of wilted roses in a toilet, with the inscription, "Well, Happy New Year anyhow."

During one of Woody's early, mediocre seasons, an airplane flew over Ohio Stadium towing a banner reading, "Goodbye Woody." That Christmas, Mrs. Hayes' card showed an airplane over the stadium trailing the message "Happy Holidays."

"I have to keep my sense of humor," she once said. "If I can't laugh and laugh at myself, then I don't see any sense in living. I have serious thoughts, lots of them. I have serious interests. But laughter is such a wonderful thing. Everybody likes to laugh."

Anne made hundreds of speeches all over Ohio donating all the fees she received to the Ohio State University Development Fund or to charity. Her talks at banquets, luncheons, and sundry occasions often included tales about Woody and his foibles. "I didn't have to make up those stories, " she contended. "They were true."

One such speech followed Woody's highly publicized attack on the sideline equipment in a 1971 game at Michigan, after he had charged onto the field to protest an official's call. She began her talk, "I would have brought Woody along, but he's home repairing a set of yard markers." She said of the incident, "I knew Woody wasn't too old to coach football. It took four younger men to get him off the field. If Woody hadn't rushed onto the field to complain about the bad call," she said, "he would not have been Woody Hayes. Whatever he does, he isn't a phony. And let's face it, he did it within the rules. He knew he was going to get 15 yards."

The coach's displays of sideline temper during games triggered an increase in phone calls and unkind comments. "Sometimes," Mrs. Hayes notes, "when people ask how I can put up with it, I say 'It isn't easy, but I try.' Women ask how I can live with somebody like that, and I say, 'I don't know your husband, but I bet I could ask you the same question.'

"By the same token, somebody could ask Woody how he could manage to live with me. You can't like everything about the person to whom you're married. It's a two-way street. I don't see any sense getting upset about it."

Readily conceding Woody's temper, she observed, "When those things happened, he was mostly mad at himself, at his inability to handle the situation. He always took it out more on himself than on anybody else."

Recruiting was another area in which Anne Hayes played a significant role in Woody's success at Ohio State. In fact, son Steve suggests, "Mom was as great a recruiter as he was. How she supported him!" She convinced parents she would keep an eye on their football-playing son if he came to Ohio State, and she fulfilled that promise, becoming to Buckeye players a sort of "foster mom."

In the days when the NCAA didn't object, she entertained parents of potential Buckeye players, hosting a number of them overnight. "Since most recruiting visits came on the weekend, we went to a lot of different churches," notes Anne, who had minored in Bible study at Ohio Wesleyan.

Substantial recruiting gains were also made in the Hayes kitchen and breakfast nook. "Parents would come down in the morning and ask if there was anything they could do," Mrs. Hayes relates, "and I would have them do the toast or something like that. I learned more about the family that half-hour than if I spent half a day with them."

When Woody became Ohio State head coach, the family bought a modest two-story frame house, white with green trim, in Upper Arlington. Woody died there, and Mrs. Hayes still lives there. Their unpretentious home and lifestyle surprised many.

Anne recalls one Halloween night: "A youngster showed up at the front door and asked if Woody Hayes lived here. I said yes, and he looked in. Then he looked up at the house and said, 'Woody Hayes can't live here. Woody Hayes is rich!'"

Woody liked to tell this story: the Hayes sofa had seen better days, but every time they planned to replace it, some other need for the money intervened. When the society editor of a local newspaper did an in-home interview, she asked, "What is the decor of your drawing room?" Anne replied, with a glance at the well-worn sofa, "Modern split-T."

For many years, Mrs. Hayes has worn her hair pulled up severely and tied atop her head with a scarf-band. She wears casual clothes, usually slacks, for all but the most dressy occasions. Like her late husband, she is outgoing, loves people, and is an easy conversationalist. And she shares Woody's concerns for humanity. "It wasn't parties and big fancy things, because we just didn't do those things," Anne says. "Glamorous life? I suppose it could have been. But heck, I wouldn't know how to be glamorous."

The most difficult times for Anne Hayes—and Woody— came after his departure from coaching. From May of 1981, he battled a series of physical ailments that taxed them both. With little regard for her own well-being and interest, Mrs. Hayes became nurse, valet, chauffeur, errand-runner, and personal secretary. Those close to the family marveled at how she took care of every need without compromising his independence or his dignity.

Once asked what the best thing was about being Mrs. Woody Hayes, she answered, "Steve Hayes, that's the best!" She has always had a very special relationship with her son. "She had the ability to be a father and still be a mother, a woman," Steve recalls. "She was a good athlete. She's the one who taught me how to throw a football and a baseball, took me bowling and all that. She'd try to arrange times when we could be together, just the two of us."

"Steve had to understand," Anne Hayes says. "We worked very hard at that. I tried very hard to make sure that he understood his father. He would get mad at him about certain things, and he'd be disappointed sometimes. But I'd sit him down and say, 'I'm going to tell you all the good things your father does. It's perfectly all right to not like something about him, but you've got to see him as a whole man. You can't take part of a man.' Steve understood. He knew his father loved him and was proud of him."

"I would have liked to have spent more time with Dad," Steve concedes, "but I understood. I understood through Mom's offices. With him being away so much, she would say, 'It doesn't mean he doesn't care about us, or that he doesn't love us, because he does. That's just the way he is.' I was never bitter."

All those associated with Woody would confirm that he did indeed love his family and his home, although he may have given limited attention to some traditional expressions of that love. "I learned a lot from him by example," Steve attests. "He did what he said, he meant what he said. You watch that long enough and it's contagious. Another thing, you always got a straight answer—or," jokes Steve, "a straight left."

In fact, Steve remembers only one occasion on which his father found it necessary to correct him physically: "One time when I must have been 12 or 13, I was mouthing off to my mother at the dinner table. He warned me three times. The fourth time I did it, he grabbed me away from the table, stood me up against the wall, and let me have it with an open hand—the first and only time he ever did anything like that. It didn't hurt me, but I was sent to my room. About an hour later I came downstairs and he asked me, 'Do you know why I did that?' and I said, 'Because I was mouthing off.' There was no doubt I had done wrong. He said, 'Yeah, but you were mouthing off to your mother, and she's as good a friend as you've got in this world. If you had been mouthing off to me, I don't know if I would have done what I did. But it made me real mad.' I couldn't disagree. I got warned and warned and I got what I deserved. I didn't do it again."

Steve never felt deprived, either by the limited time with his father or by his father's aversion to personal wealth. The family had what in contemporary parenting lingo is called "quality time." Steve especially recalls the Sundays when Woody would take him along to Ohio State: "He'd be going over to work, and so I'd take maybe five friends, and we'd play basketball for a couple of hours while he worked," Steve explains. "Sometimes he'd come down and watch when he finished working, and then we'd all go swimming in the Natatorium. Then he'd drive everybody home. That was fun."

Steve also likes to remember going with his dad to a football clinic in Montana one summer. Vince Lombardi was also there. "He had just taken over the Packers," Steve explains, "and he and Dad were talking—they were real close—and Vince said he had a whole bunch of quarterbacks, but he didn't know who his starting quarterback was going to be. I piped up and said, 'Bart Starr is going to be your quarterback.' Vince never, ever forgot that. He always mentioned it."

As for Woody's outlook on finances, Steve says, "He wanted to have enough money so that we had a roof over our heads, we could eat, and I could go to school, and that was enough. If he had been concerned about money, in the sense of not having enough or needing more, it would have detracted from his effectiveness. He wouldn't have been able to concentrate on his job.

"He didn't want to owe anybody. If he did, then they had a hold on him. He had to do something as an obligation, not because he wanted to. He didn't mind them owing him. Mom was pretty much on the same wavelength, and I picked that up pretty quickly myself."

Steve was aware of Woody's feeling about law school and how he tried to steer many of his players in that direction. "He was big on law school, feeling that even if you never practiced, a law degree was a good thing to have," Steve notes. "But I got interested on my own, probably from watching Perry Mason on TV and reading books."

When Steve convinced his parents to allow him to live on campus, he remained under his father's watchful eye. "When Dad would visit football players in the dorms, he'd stop in to see how I was doing and if I was studying," the son says. "You never knew when he was coming by. The players didn't either!"

The summer after his first year on campus, Steve went to Alaska with several OSU football and baseball players to work and play amateur baseball. It didn't work out and he came home. "Dad met me at the airport," Steve relates. "It was unusual. I asked if something had happened to Mom, and he said, 'No, she's fine.' So we went out and got in the car. But I knew something was wrong. Finally he said, 'Your grades came.' I figured I was in trouble. I don't remember what I got, but I had a lot of fun that first quarter on campus. We sat there for an hour and he lectured me up one side and down the other."

If Woody was often an absentee father he seemed to find more time when the next generation of Hayeses came along, as Steve relates without a hint of jealousy. "When my son Phil was little," Steve says, "Dad would come out to our house on Friday night, and usually Phil would be in bed asleep. But we'd bring him down, and Dad would sit there and talk with him or just sit there and hold him. At times the two of them would be conked out in the big chair.

"Phil was born in 1976, so Dad was still coaching. That," Steve adds with a chuckle, "was more than I ever saw him on Friday nights!" After Woody left coaching, he and Anne would visit Kathy and Steve and the children—Laura was the second addition—for an evening or for dinner, mostly on holidays. Marvels Steve, "Nobody would have believed some of the scenes, with Dad on the floor in the family room, wearing a Darth Vader helmet and playing with the kids."

In 1986, Woody was inducted into the College Football Hall of Fame at the National Football Foundation banquet in New York City. Father and son made the trip, roomed together at the Waldorf-Astoria, and enjoyed the Big Apple. "It was a lot of fun, the first time we'd been together like that for maybe 15 years," Steve says, adding with unmistakable pride, "They asked Dad to be the spokesman for the Hall of Fame inductees at the banquet, and he did one of the best speaking jobs ever."

Another time the Hayes men, Woody, Steve, and Phil, enjoyed an entire day together at the family cabin in Noble County. It proved to be their last such venture.

Steve Hayes closed the 1987 memorial service for his father, held in Ohio Stadium, with a touching and revealing speech. Part of that speech was devoted to a father-son relationship that outsiders might have seen as incomplete, but which drew no complaints from the son. "People used to ask me how it felt to have a celebrity for a father," Steve related. "I never understood that. To me he was just Dad. I could recognize the other part, but he was just my father.

"I recall when I was in about the sixth grade, he came to me one summer and said, 'Well, you're going to play football, aren't you?' For two summers in a row, before they had organized football, Dad would take me out during the summer in full pads down at the open end of the stadium. I'd drive the charging sled 110 yards, I'd run the stadium steps, I'd do sit-ups, I'd do push-ups. And when Dad couldn't watch me, he'd have another coach watch over me—a coach named Bo. Those guys were tough. I was already through Marine boot camp.

"At the end of my first year in college, it was pretty apparent to me that I wasn't going to be an All-American. I said, 'Dad, what are we doing this for?' He threw out that chin, looked me in the eye, and said, 'You're going to learn to do it right so you won't get hurt.' That ended the conversation."

"I reflected on that because we were together off and on during that summer, probably the most time we ever spent in one sustained period. I wondered afterward what was the most precious thing I got from that. It took me a couple of years to realize that the most precious thing was his time. He was so busy, yet he took the time to spend with me, and I'll never forget that.

"There was a different side to Dad, and I've seen it. None of you have seen Dad on the living room floor with my family, with a Darth Vader helmet and a laser weapon playing with my son Phil. And then with his granddaughter Laura. He loved her, but I'm not sure he knew what to do with her! I cherish those memories.

"Not long before he died, Dad brought out a chapter from his book, which was a parallel between war and football. This particular chapter happened to be a parallel between the Battle of Britain and football, and he wanted my son Phil to read it to him. Phil's 11 years old and in the sixth grade. He got up on Dad's lap and read it to him, and you could see Dad beaming from ear to ear as Phil did a terrific job.

"My daughter Laura, who's seven, was out in the kitchen. She came in and wanted to know what was going on. Dad told her and she said, 'I want to read that to you.' He said, 'No, no.' Well, she's got more than a little Hayes in her and said, 'I'm going to read that.' So we figured we'd let her read a page and she'd give up. She read it all, 13 pages, and Dad sat there and grinned and grinned. I heard him tell people after that, 'She was great, she only missed one word—Luftwaffe.'"

No football players were involved, and it wasn't football season. But Woody Hayes never worked harder or gave more than when student riots struck Ohio State in 1970 and eventually led to a shutdown of the institution.

He stood among the students gathered on the Oval and other assembly areas of the campus. He listened to the speakers, some of whom appeared to be itinerant agitators. He made his own speeches, once even climbing on an overturned trash can to be heard.

The response? Tolerance sometimes, derision others. But, as Anne Hayes declared, "Woody tried. He tried!"

He roamed the campus and dormitories, hoping to calm down the students he believed were being led astray or were not thinking clearly. "They didn't want to talk to me, but I made them," he recalled some years later. Mrs. Hayes said, "He came home so tired those nights, I actually had to help him undress and get into bed."

"I wanted to test the reactions of the students," he explained. "And I felt that with older heads around, even with a generation gap, the older people might give at least some young people a sense of well-being they otherwise wouldn't have. If they've learned to respect their parents or grandparents or older people at all, we've got to be around at a time like that. I don't think any of us knows all the answers, but I'm not willing to believe youngsters know all the answers either. I'm certain they don't. I'm certain WE don't, but our experiences have been broader and deeper than theirs."

8

PRACTICE, PRACTICE

The late John Dietrich covered Ohio State football games for the *Cleveland Plain-Dealer* for many years. Once chided for not attending the team's Friday workout, he sardonically replied: "Why, have they found a new way to practice?" These rehearsal sessions did tend toward the routine—endless repetition of techniques, blocking, passing, running, kicking, all without the excitement of actual competition. The inevitable sameness marked most of Ohio State's practices, except for those moments when perfectionist Woody Hayes boiled over.

The practice field represented a classroom/laboratory for Professor Hayes (he held that faculty rank), but the atmosphere contrasted drastically with what might have been found in English literature, or music appreciation, or philosophy. This was, after all, where the physical merged with the mental, often on violent terms; where the professor sometimes instructed in a decidedly hands-on manner; and where students underwent mini-exams a hundred times a day.

An intense, uncompromising, volatile taskmaster was Woody Hayes for these two-hour-plus field rehearsals. "Woody was a demanding person," Gene Fekete acknowledges, "but he was most demanding during practice. He figured if you did it the right way in practice, you were going to do it the right way when Saturday afternoon rolled around. So he was more critical of everything that went on during the preparation phase."

Hayes' reaction to less-than-perfection ranged from a flare-up to falling on all fours and pounding the ground in frustration. In an early stage of annoyance, he would remove the black baseball cap with the scarlet O that he always wore for practices and games, run the fingers of his left hand through his hair, and slam the cap back in place.

In the second stage, the cap became the object of a one-man tug-of-war. He ripped it up and continued practice bareheaded, until a manager supplied a new lid. According to an oft-told tale, equipment repairman Phil Bennett once sewed the seams of Woody's cap as a gag. That way the coach, strong as he was, couldn't tear them—further fueling his rage.

But John Bozick debunks another Woody myth: "I would have known if Phil had sewed up the old man's cap, but I never heard anything like that," he declares. "What happened was that we used to buy caps made out of felt, which would tear very easily. Then we switched and started buying serge caps that were nicer looking and of very strong material. They wouldn't tear." Unable to rip the new caps, Woody turned to flinging them to the ground, and when the mood warranted, he tramped on them.

Watches took similar abuse. Woody recalled that one time at Denison, when practices lagged badly, "I threw my watch over some bushes along the practice field and told my players, 'By God, we're going to stay out here until dark!' They understood what I meant."

He set no wrist watch-throwing distance record at Ohio State, but he might snap the expanding band during mild displeasure and often hurled the watch to the ground in more agitated moments. In extreme cases he might plant a heavy, cleated foot on the ticking timepiece. According to Lou McCullough, one such watch-tromping episode prompted a quick-witted halfback to observe: "Hey, look, Woody's killing time!" Later Hayes would send Phil Bennett for another watch. The very inexpensive kind. He never risked wearing his Rose Bowl watches on the field.

He also vented his wrath on his steel-rimmed glasses, although being more essential, they were less vulnerable. But just in case, the equipment department kept an extra pair around—including on trips.

The players made a point of knowing where the coach was at all times, because a mistake, particularly one repeated, could result in a smack on the headgear or the shoulder pad or even a well-placed shoe—the side, not the toe—in the seat of the pants. Usually Woody hurt himself more than the well-padded culprit.

In the ultimate stage of frustration, Hayes might crash a fist, even both fists, to his own head. If he happened to be wearing one of his championship rings, the damage could be visible; even drawing blood. Eventually, coaches and players began referring to the more animated of these field explosions as "megatons." Said Esco Sarkkinen: "After players got to know it, we could almost tell when we were going to see a good show. As long as you weren't the guy who fumbled and you had to go back to the huddle."

The player who inspired a "megaton" typically suffered a withering stare on either end of a high-decibel tirade. Hayes had a remarkable vocabulary, and he never allowed ungentlemanly language to slip into conversation in mixed company or in his speeches or on his TV show. But the practice field was no place for tender, or sensitive ears.

Hayes posted paid guards at the practice field gate virtually every day, autumn and spring. He felt visitors would be distracting to the players—and, one suspects, confining for the head coach. He liked to keep those sessions "in the family." He wanted the freedom to be himself. And he particularly disliked having women present.

Bozick believed Woody's field antics were "90 percent psychological and 10 percent frustration." But Esco Sarkkinen makes a good case for their genuineness. "It happened too many times to have been for effect," Esco contends. "Some of it was for show, but for the most part it was natural reaction, Woody's personality. The way they happened, I don't think they could have been rehearsed. Woody wasn't that much of an actor."

Planned or spontaneous, Woody's outbursts were more effective than a reprimand. Causing the coach to wrench his wrist watch or break his glasses or drop to all fours and beat the turf in anger left an indelible impression.

Nobody escaped, not even two-time-Heisman winner Archie Griffin, a great Hayes favorite. "My first year, the freshmen scrimmaged against the first team," he recalls. "Toward the end

of practice, Brian Baschnagel, another freshman, and I were put
behind the first line. Brian carried the ball and fumbled, and on
the next play I carried and fumbled. That didn't sit well with
Coach Hayes—two freshmen fumbling on two plays in a row. He
hollered at us: 'You freshmen, you guys can't play!' It was his
way of making us get fired up and play better, but at the time I
didn't know that."

Archie, like every other object of a Hayes eruption, later
learned another element of the coach's philosophy: reconciliation. Explained Woody, "I learned from John Brickels at New
Philadelphia High School that if you ever have a run-in with a
player on the field, never allow him to leave the locker room after
practice until the situation is straightened out."

I've been a chance spectator at a few of those sessions. They
would start much the same, Woody asking the chastened young
man: "Do you know why I got so mad at you out there tonight?
Because you're a better football player than that. There's no
excuse for making mistakes like you did. Now, I want you to
come back out here tomorrow and I want to see you play like I
know you can play!"

"It's impressive," Griffin attests. "After practice, you have
to walk past his little cubbyhole office. He calls you in and talks
with you, and you come out of there feeling pretty good. As long
as you tell a player why you're doing it, he can understand.
Woody's whole reason was, 'I want you doing your best in every
situation. I don't want you to slack off, because if you slack off in
practice, you'll slack off in a game.'"

As a further step toward reconciliation, Woody would
trudge to the showers and as Bozick relates, "He'd have the kid
he'd chewed out on the field wash his back and he'd wash the
kid's back. It was something the kids were crazy about. It was
his way of saying, 'I wasn't on you because you weren't doing the
job, but I just feel you can do better.'"

Bill Myles watched the procedure at work many times,
including the second act. "The next day," he explains, "the kid
comes to practice and Woody will go out of his way to say
something complimentary about his play, like 'That's the greatest block I've ever seen' or 'We've never had a guard [or a tackle
or a halfback] practice like this!' The guy can do no wrong.
Woody lets him up off the canvas."

"He had a way of doing that," Griffin agrees. "All of a sudden, you go out there and make a play, maybe not a real big play, but he makes you think it's the best thing that ever happened."

One of Hayes' explosions nearly sent one of his greatest players packing, but the postpractice amends saved the day. Jim Stillwagon, twice All-American middle guard on the super teams of 1968-69-70, remembers the scene: "We were having a scrimmage in the spring of my freshman year; I tackled Rex Kern and he got hurt," he explains. Kern was the quarterback star of the freshman class, something like "the franchise." Hayes often protected his quarterback with a yellow "don't hit" jersey, but Kern wasn't protected that day. "Woody Hayes grabbed me," Jim continues, "and said, 'I want him out of here! I don't want to see him again. Take his scholarship; he's gone.' I thought fine, and went to the showers and said, 'I'm leaving.' I was going to West Virginia or someplace. I was leaving the training facility when Coach Hayes came in and asked if he could talk to me for a minute. We went in his little office and he said, 'You did the right thing. I was wrong. I'm not going to take your scholarship. I made a mistake. Another thing, if you leave Ohio State what will your mom and dad say? They're going to be heartbroken, and you don't want to upset your mom and dad, do you?' I respected Coach Hayes a lot. I stayed."

One of the most memorable "family" scenes concerned Tom Matte, a gifted but free-spirited halfback. Tom and Woody weren't an ideal mix. Matte thought football was just a game. In those days the marching band practiced in the parking lot west of the stadium, while the football team rehearsed south of the stadium. As the stirring strains of the band wafted around the stadium, Tom would do a quick-footed rhythm dance while waiting for his turn in the lineup.

One night, his antics touched off an explosion. Woody went for Matte. Tom ran. Woody ran after him. They ran around the field, Tom staying a couple of yards ahead. The other players and coaches laughed as much as seemed prudent. Woody tired first. But as usual, he left practice conflicts on the field.

In 1965, the Baltimore Colts lost Johnny Unitas and backup Gary Cuozzo before the season's final game with the Los Angeles Rams. They were desperate for a quarterback. Woody called

Colts Coach Don Shula and informed him that he had a fine quarterback among his running backs. Between halves of the 1959 Duke game—while 80,000 Ohio Stadium fans watched in amazement and amusement, Woody trotted erstwhile halfback Matte out onto a south practice field and converted him to a quarterback. The crash course paid off, because the talented Tom proceeded to lead the Buckeyes on a 63-yard TD march (14 tie with the conversion).

"Don't worry about a quarterback," Hayes told Shula. "Put Tom Matte in there. He's a winner." Shula laughed, saying he expected the call and that the staff had already decided to move Matte there. Matte's return to QB couldn't have been more spectacular. With Matte running, passing, and calling plays printed on his wristband, the Colts rolled over the Rams, lost to Green Bay in the playoffs on a disputed field goal in overtime, and ran all over Dallas in the Playoff Bowl in Miami. All of this happened on nationwide TV, and as a result Matte was suddenly the marvel of pro football. "I got letters and telegrams from all over the country," he reported, "but you know the first one I got? Woody's was the first."

The next spring, Woody brought Tom back to speak at the annual clinic for Ohio high school coaches and presented to him what he called "The Moment of Greatness" award. "It was Emerson, I think, who said a man prepares a long time for one moment of greatness," the old coach said. And Matte replied, "I've received a number of honors, but this one I really treasure."

I talked with Tom after he appeared on Woody's TV show that night. His comments sounded like a few others I'd heard from Buckeyes, thoughtfully reflecting on their playing days under Hayes: "Woody and I didn't see eye to eye when I was playing for him," Tom confessed. "But he had the biggest influence on me of anybody in my life. He made a man of me. He's got to be one of the great all-time coaches. He's not only interested in helping you become a better football player, but in your becoming a better man. It takes a long time for a guy to figure that out, but I did. That Woody! He's one heck of a man!"

Woody's all-time cause celebre occurred in 1958. Big Ten Commissioner Tug Wilson and a group of 35 sports writers known as the "Skywriters" arrived at the Ohio State practice field during their annual flying tour of the league's football camps. As the visitors watched the Buckeye scrimmage, Hayes suddenly stopped action and ordered "everybody out!" A disbelieving Wilson was ushered from the practice enclosure (along with the writers).

"I had sent the first team in," Woody explained later, privately, "and we were having a lousy practice [with the remaining squad]. I had to chew them out, but I wasn't going to do it in front of outsiders. It wouldn't have been fair to my players." He apologized to Wilson and the scribes profusely during the interview session that followed practice, but the writers spent most of their words on the "bum's rush," they'd received, particularly the fact that the Big Ten Commissioner had also gotten the heave-ho. When the Skywriters came to practice the next year, Woody had a bank of lounge chairs, umbrella tables, and pitchers of lemonade waiting. He lined up his offensive and defensive teams and introduced each player.

Jim Jones believes Woody's "singleness of purpose, ability to stay focused, and to keep everybody around him focused" were what set him apart from other coaches and other human beings. Bad practices—and there weren't many—threatened to disturb that focus, forcing the always-intense Woody to raise the intensity level several notches. McCullough and Sarkkinen have never forgotten a night that illustrated Hayes' ability to focus on the problem at hand and shut out all distractions. Baseball Hall of Famer Stan Musial visited practice and afterward came into the assistant coaches' room where Hayes was huddling with some of his offensive staff. "Woody was upset because something awful had happened in practice, and he was talking to the coaches about what had to be done," says Sarkkinen.

McCullough picks up the story: "I told Hugh Hindman to take Musial over and introduce him to the coach. Musial said, 'Coach, how would you like to have an old left-handed quarterback play for you this week?' But Woody had his mind on something else. He didn't want to talk to anybody, and he said, 'Nah, nah, I don't have time now.'" Adds Sarkinnen, "He brushed off Stan Musial! And Woody was a pretty good baseball fan, too. We were all astonished."

"You've got to understand," McCullough notes, "that on Thursday afternoon, Coach Hayes doesn't know Stan Musial from the president of the United States. He's interested in football! He never did know that that was Stan Musial standing there holding out his hand."

On the other hand, Rex Kern can testify that Hayes wasn't entirely oblivious at practice time, at least where his players' welfare was concerned. "I was going to class from 8 in the morning until I went to practice, without time for lunch," he relates. "Usually, I'd take a brown-bag lunch, but this one morning I didn't have time. Coach [George] Chaump noticed that I looked a little tired, and I told him I hadn't had any lunch. He said they'd check with Woody and send out and get me something. I said, 'Don't do that. This is the week of the Michigan game, and I gotta get out on the field.' We started practice, but not long afterward I saw a manager come through the gate carrying a McDonald's sack, and I thought to myself, it can't be! Woody pulled me out of practice and handed me the McDonald's sack. I sat over on a roll of tarp and ate my burger and french fries and watched the guys practice. After practice, Rufus Mayes, our offensive tackle, came over to me with that big smile of his and kidded, 'If that had been one of us linemen that was hungry, the old man would have made us get down and eat grass.'"

Buckeye players came to suspect that even a higher power would not intrude on Woody's sacred practices. "It wouldn't dare rain on Woody's practices," was the watchword, or "It won't rain today; Woody won't let it." One year, the squad's traditional preseason picture session had to be postponed because of rain. When 2:00 practice time arrived, the sun shone. At close of practice came a torrential storm. "He really does control the weather!" the players half-joked.

Even the fans began to believe. Granted, rain fell on some games, but Ohio Stadium did seem blessed with an unusual proportion of chamber of commerce-grade weather conditions. Lightning might chase Woody and his troops off the practice field, but little else did, not even snow. As far as Woody was concerned, inclement weather was just further preparation for game day. He observed: "As Admiral King said, if you're going to fight in the Atlantic, you train in the Atlantic."

After French Field House became part of the OSU facilities, practices moved indoors only if Woody felt no progress could be made in the elements. Before Rose Bowls, he had the field house temperature boosted to 72 degrees, simulating what the Buckeyes might expect when they worked out in California.

Woody hated the cramped French Field House quarters, partially because of injury risks. Among other perils were protruding steel beam roof-support girders. He would have appreciated at least one feature of the centerpiece of the new $10.6 million Woody Hayes Athletic Center: The magnificent indoor football building has no posts and 30-foot-wide safety areas on both sides and ends of the field. The Center was dedicated in November 1987, eight months after Woody's death. But would he have enjoyed operating in such a luxurious layout? Doubtful.

He once nixed plans to expand the spartan Biggs Facility, his home away from home. Among other things to which he objected was a proposed player lounge. "Too many comforts make you soft," he explained. The welfare of his players always held first priority, but he made a distinction between welfare and comfort. Too much of the latter, he believed, was not in their best interests.

Woody made his own dramatic statement about comfort. He spurned a jacket or a sweater at practices and often wore only a t-shirt, regardless of rain, frigid temperatures, or snow. Early in his OSU days, he wore a sport coat during games on good-weather days, or a raincoat or topcoat when conditions warranted. But for more than 15 years, his appearance in a short-sleeved white shirt and necktie became as traditional on the Ohio Stadium sideline as the yard chains and Brutus Buckeye. On some November Saturdays, he was a source of wonder for fans in the stands, who had great difficulty convincing themselves it really wasn't freezing or pouring.

"When I was coaching at Miami, I remember one cold day when we weren't practicing worth a damn," Woody once explained. "The players were standing around with their hands stuck in their sweatshirts and dancing around. All they were worrying about was the cold. I finally ripped off my jacket and threw it away, so all I had on was a t-shirt, and I said, 'There now, dammit, if I can stand it, you can stand it. Cold is all in your mind. Now let's forget about it and start concentrating on football!'"

As the years passed he hedged, slipping on a second t-shirt or a third. Players and coaches began rating late-season afternoons as "two-t-shirt" or "three-t-shirt days." He would also stand in the hot shower afterward until his blue skin resumed its natural tone.

When Tiger Ellison joined the staff as freshman coach, Woody needled him for wearing two t-shirts under a heavy jacket on cold days, sometimes a sweatshirt besides. "You say it's all in the mind," Tiger replied, "but dammit, Wood, MY mind tells ME I'm cold!" After his heart attack, at the urging of his doctors, Hayes finally bowed to the elements. He wore a finger-tip-length red jacket over the two t-shirts or the short-sleeved white shirt.

Woody concentrated so hard on practices—and all the other phases of coaching—because he felt failure in any degree would be an indictment. "Maybe it's vanity," he once mused. "I just despise getting beat. If I've got a good bunch of football players, and if we don't win I've got to blame it on me. When we lose a football game and I look at myself in the mirror the next day, I feel like taking a punch at myself." "He was harder on himself than anybody ever thought of being," suggests Jones. "He used to blame himself regularly when we failed."

Woody's "megatons" were the most memorable moments of his practices, but workouts weren't all bombast and bluster, nor hard-driving, chain-gang torture periods. Usually practices were smooth, unruffled, and businesslike—with an occasional light moment. Often Woody would be enthusiastic, encouraging; he would rub his hands in satisfaction, tug at the bill of his cap and commend, "Now that's the way!" or "Men, that's football!"

Worries about "tired legs" prompted easing of late-week field rigors, especially as the season wore on and its stress mounted. Says Bill Myles, "Monday, he's just driving you; Tuesday, he's driving you; Wednesday, he starts to let up a little bit; Thursday and Friday, the guys could do no wrong."

Friday sessions before a Saturday game were always accomplished in light no-contact, hurry-up style, both at home and away. Everything came under review, including the order of substitutions and bench seating.

Nor should Hayes' histrionics on the practice field be interpreted as abuse or as prelude to abuse. Players abused? "Absolutely not! Nothing like that!" attests Esco Sarkkinen, who participated in more practices than anyone but Woody Hayes himself. And as a reporter who has watched a few thousand practices during my 50 years, I'll add my testimony to Sark's.

Frank "Moose" Machinsky, a 1954 All-Big Ten tackle, reaches a similar conclusion about his coach: "I think everyone was a little afraid of him," Moose suggests. "He would rant and rave and at times kick and swear. But as you reflect, Woody

Hayes was one of those rare individuals that you only meet once in a lifetime, the dominant person in your life. My feelings were that I would do anything he asked me to do on the field. His players loved him, respected him, and wanted to be successful just because he asked us to be successful. I was afraid of him in my four years. But now, after many years of reflection, when you take away the hollering, the mean looks, the cursing, the locker room antics, there was a very warm, caring person underneath, and I believe every player he ever had knew it."

Red Grange, Illinois' famed "Galloping Ghost" of the 1920s, spoke at a luncheon in Columbus during one football season. After the program, Woody talked Grange into taking a later flight so that he could give a pep talk to the Buckeye squad that afternoon.

Excited about the impending visit by one of football's great early stars, Hayes stood outside his tiny office as the players came by on their way to the training room for prepractice ankle taping. He asked a number of them, "Who is Red Grange and what did he do?"

One youngster suggested that he had been a football player, but wasn't sure where or when. But the question inspired mostly blank stares and nervous silence. Obviously, their heroes were of more recent vintage, such as O.J. Simpson or Joe Namath.

Woody was shaken, but he vowed privately to give them a history lesson when he introduced Grange later on the practice field. Practice was in full swing when Grange arrived. Woody had a strict policy about visitors. The president of the University probably couldn't have cracked the security without prior arrangements.

The "no visitors" sign was always up, the gate to the enclosed field locked and guarded by a campus policeman. The latter checked with an assistant trainer, who said no arrangement had been made for Grange and his party. They departed.

When Hayes discovered that Grange had been refused entry, the eruption could have been measured by seismograph.

9

BY DEGREES

"If we bring a young man to Ohio State University and don't do everything possible to see that he gets an education, we are cheating him." In Woody Hayes' scheme of things, that commitment superseded winning football games, going to bowls and producing All-Americans.

"He was 100 percent committed," according to Jim Jones, who once served as "brain coach" and is now OSU's athletic director. "It was very, very important to him. Few people realize how much. And it was not a phony commitment. His dad set the tone early in his life about how important education was. I don't know if he was the first college football coach to hire a full-time academic counselor, but he had to be among the first. He believed in it."

During his first three years at Ohio State, Woody did his own tutoring, with help from Katie Hess, wife of assistant coach Bill Hess and a former teacher. He further expected his coaches to monitor students at their respective positions.

In 1954, he hired Tom Daly, an OSU professor as a tutor and extended his duties to full-time academic counselor in 1957— a first for Ohio State athletics. "Woody was one of the kindest, most intelligent men I've ever worked with," says Daly, who later taught at Walsh College and Kent State in Ohio, and now at West Liberty State in West Virginia. "He was totally dedicated to the education of the whole man, not just keeping him eligible for football."

"Woody insisted we get our players into courses that would move them toward a degree," says Jeff Kaplan, "brain coach" in 1973-74-75 and now special assistant to the president of Riverside Methodist Hospital in Columbus. "Once we had a kid here, whatever it took to get him through legitimately, in terms of resources, Woody was willing to do. He'd spend $10,000 on tutors because he felt that was an investment that was worthwhile, as long as it was all aboveboard and we made sure the kid was doing the work."

Woody never stopped selling, either. Jack Tatum, twice All-American defensive back on the 1968-69-70 teams, had already achieved stardom with the NFL's Oakland Raiders. He happened to be visiting his parents in Charlotte, North Carolina, when Woody had a speaking engagement there. "I went to the meeting where he was speaking," Tatum relates, "and afterward he jumped into my car and said, 'Let's go to your parents' house.' So we went over to the house I had bought for my parents, and we sat there visiting for a few hours. It was great. He made me promise that I would come back and get my degree, and he made me promise my mother I would. So I had them working on me from two sides. I couldn't turn either one of them down. The first year after football season I had to go to the Reserves, but the second year I came back and finished up. Yeah, I got my degree." Retired from the Raiders, Tatum is now involved in youth work in Oakland and is the author of two books.

Dick Schafrath, a talented OSU tackle/end in 1956-57-58, had established himself as an All-Pro with the Cleveland Browns when we renewed acquaintances at training camp. "When you see Woody," he requested, "tell him that I'm coming back to school in the winter quarter. Every time he sees me, he gets on me about coming back for my degree." Schafrath went on to become a state senator in Ohio.

It was pro baseball that detoured two-sport star Tom Perdue. "I should have graduated in 1962," he explains, "but all that mattered was professional baseball. I left Ohio State with two quarters remaining. Three years later, Woody called me in Hampton, Virginia, where the Cincinnati Reds had a farm club. He asked me about my plans for finishing school, and I told him that would be financially impossible. He asked if any other complication would prohibit me from returning and I said no. With that answer came a coaching job and eventually a college degree."

Dan Porretta played four years in the Canadian Football League after being a starting guard at Ohio State in 1962-63-64. He stopped at Hayes' office, and during a lengthy conversation the subject of his future arose. Dan, who hadn't graduated, said he was uncertain about his next move. "I'll tell you what you're going to do," Woody pronounced. "You're going over to the registrar's office and sign up for the classes you need to graduate. Then you're going to be my assistant freshman coach this fall."

Porretta hadn't been away long enough to risk defying a Woody order. He earned his degree and is a long-time teacher and football coach in the Holland, Michigan, school system.

Rex Kern tells about a visit to Woody's office, "Maybe four, five years before he got ill he asked me if I remembered a certain player that I'll call 'Joe', and of course I did. Joe went home for Christmas his freshman year. It was during the uproar over in Viet Nam, and one of his buddies had been killed there. Joe was in a bar, and there happened to be a lot of antiwar sentiments flying. Joe got hit over the head with a beer bottle and was partially paralyzed. He came back to school for a while but never played a down for us.

"On my visit to Woody's office, he said, 'Joe's had a lot of trouble, but by God, we finally got him graduated, and we got him a job, too!' Here's a guy who never actually played at Ohio State. Woody didn't owe the guy a thing except his commitment to get him to graduate from college. And this was probably 14 or 15 years later."

Mental mistakes on the practice field triggered some of Hayes' more volatile reactions, but lapses in his students' quest for knowledge touched off a few "megaton" eruptions too. One of Kaplan's charges, a senior who had completed his football eligibility, was skipping a class. "I warned him once and he ignored me," Kaplan explains. "Because of missing classes, he was in danger of failing the course. We had a warning from the professor. I told his position coach, but without results. So I decided to tell Woody. He sent out the order to track him down, and within the hour the player was in his office. Woody said, 'I understand you haven't been going to class,' and the guy finally admitted it. First Woody grabbed him and said, 'Don't you know the most important thing about your being at Ohio State University?' An animated lecture followed. Then he walked back to his desk, and was he mad! He picked up a metal film case—not a small one, but one of those 12- or 14-inch kind, filled with game films. He threw it like a frisbee. I ducked under a table, and the player jumped out of the way. I don't remember exactly what Woody said, but it was a clear threat. I think he made his point. The guy didn't miss another class and eventually passed the course."

Moose Machinsky, an All-Big Ten tackle on the unbeaten 1954 national championship team, caught Woody in a less menacing, but no less determined mood. "I was a very marginal student," he confesses, "and after several quarters of borderline passing, my grades deteriorated even more. One day Woody pulled up at my residence and said, 'Pack some clothes, get your books, and get in the car.' We drove in silence to his house, where he informed me this would be where I would live until my grades improved. I was virtually a prisoner there. He dropped me off at classes, picked me up after classes, made me study constantly, and would review my assignments and quiz me. I wasn't permitted to do anything—no dates, no movies, no TV, no beer, nothing but study. Needless to say, I worked my tail off to get out of there and not to return. My main accomplishment at Ohio State was not football, but graduating on time, in four years!" says Machinsky, now a highly successful Columbus businessman.

"Through the years, we kept quite a few boys in our home for the same reason Moose was there," Anne Hayes confirms.

One year a player chosen for the All-America team was scheduled to join other All-Americans on a weekend trip to New York, but Hayes informed him: "You're not going. Your grades are down, and final exams are coming up pretty soon. You're going to stay here with me and hit the books."

The study table was as much a part of Hayes' operation as the practice field. "You don't SEND them to the study table," he proclaimed, "you MEET them there." And he was THERE most evenings during his early reign. Even after academic counselors and tutors had assumed that responsibility, Woody dropped by regularly to check on who was at the study table, who wasn't, who should have been, what was being studied, and whether, in fact, studying was being done.

Larry Romanoff, a student football manager who became "brain coach," recalls, "Woody even had study table on road trips. Once we couldn't get a conference room, so he had the beds in the managers' room stacked in a corner, and each player brought a chair. It was jammed, but he had study table."

"His coaches had to know all about their position players," Jones says, "even though they had me: what courses they were taking, how well they were doing, what their cumulative average was, what they needed to make in their courses this quarter to keep progressing toward a degree." When Woody hired him in 1967, Jones says, "He talked about the importance of education and the importance of getting the freshmen off to a good start. He said, 'If we're still tutoring a kid when he's a senior, we're not helping him, we're giving him a crutch. Spend about 80 percent of your time with the freshmen.'"

Jones had no on-field responsibilities, but sat in on Woody's staff meetings. "He came into the staff meeting once," Jones relates, "and I was sitting at the opposite end of the table from him. He asked me if I read for pleasure, and I said that I did. He slid a general psychology book down the table to me, saying, 'Read this, because we have a great quarterback in that class who needs to do well.' I knew Rex Kern was taking psychology, but this was Woody's way of emphasizing to me what a great kid Rex was, what a great athlete he was, and how important he was going to be to the program. He wanted me to know that Rex was not doing well in psychology. He wanted me to keep after him, and he was right on all scores." Kern mastered psychology—and all his other courses, eventually earning a doctorate.

Hayes actually started grooming the freshmen academically long before they slipped into a scarlet and gray football jersey. He shipped a copy of *Word Power Made Easy* to every recruit during the summer, before they arrived at Ohio State. "We sent the book to every group of freshmen and told them to take the test," Jones explains of his pedagogic tenure. "We used to have them send their answers in weekly, then we had them come in with the answers completed in the fall. You could copy the test because it was in the back of the book, but Woody felt you were still learning something about vocabulary and word meaning. The name of the game was to convince kids they could be better than they were, and it usually worked for him."

In 1977 Hayes ordered renewed emphasis on *Word Power*. "We've eased up on it in recent years," the coach confessed, and as a result many freshmen had become lax about bringing in the completed tests. Furthermore, Woody complained he was "sick to death of hearing kids say 'you know' and 'it's like' in conversation. The clincher, though, was a news story Hayes read about the alarming national decline in test scores among enrolling college students.

"The book is 25 years old," he pointed out, "which attests to one thing: it's good. Some of the words may be a little out of date, but you still learn. You keep adding onto words all the time. That's the whole purpose of it. We're trying to help kids broaden their vision and their thinking with words. I don't want to sound pedantic, but the English language is a great language—fluid; it comes from many sources, and it's certainly not static. A vocabulary is extremely important. One year we had the kids study this book in the summer. We had 30 athletes, and 29 of them passed freshman English. The one who flunked was a guy who didn't do his summer assignments." Even while preparing his football varsity for its first game of the season, Hayes scheduled *Word Power* classes in the evenings and Sundays and taught most of the sessions himself.

No one was ever prouder than Hayes of the mark Ohio State products—football players or not—made on the world. Often in his speeches he would harken to this theme: "Who is the greatest track man in history? Why it's Jesse Owens! He won so many gold medals that Hitler left the stadium in Berlin because he didn't want to recognize that this great athlete from Ohio State was superior.

"And who is the greatest college football player? Why it's Arch [Griffin]. Nobody else in the history of football has ever won two Heisman Trophies.

"And who is the greatest golfer of all time? Why it's Jack Nicklaus. Nobody can touch him. He's the best.

"And who is the greatest in basketball? Why, it's John Havlicek. He's Mr. Basketball."

And, according to Woody's claim, of all OSU's students, the football players received the best education of any on the campus. Not only were they driven to fulfill the academic requirements, he reasoned, but as a bonus they acquired by practical application all of the game's values he held so dear—hard work, discipline, teamwork, respect for rules, sacrificing for a goal, and overcoming adversity, among others.

Some segments of academia might take exception to his claim, but as always he had evidence on his side. "For three straight years, the student who ranked number one in the first-year class in the Ohio State University College of Medicine was one of our football players," Woody boasted. "Arnie Chonko, an All-American defensive back for us in 1964, was the first. The next year it was Don Unverferth, who set a number of passing records as our very fine quarterback. And the following year it was John Derbyshire, who was on our freshman team but had to quit football because of a physical disability. Three straight years! The chances of that happening, I am told, are about one in 1,250,000."

Though a Denison University grad, Ohio State always came first with Woody Hayes even in retirement.

At lunch one day at the Faculty Club, a professor friend of his joined us at one end of the "long table." After brief pleasantries, the professor mentioned that he and his wife had visited their son, a Notre Dame student, and attended a Notre Dame football game the previous weekend.

He and I talked enthusiastically about the beauty of the Notre Dame campus and of the uniqueness of a football day and the game in the shadow of the Golden Dome. Woody listened to a point, then snapped: "Now, that's enough of that! To hell with Notre Dame. Let's talk about OUR OWN University!"

10

NO MIDAS TOUCH

J im Parker's two cogent sentences beautifully captured another Woody Hayes attribute.

"Woody never lusted for gold," he said. "He was not a greedy man."

Steve Hayes once suggested that his father was "perhaps the world's worst businessman. If they told him it would cost $20,000 to coach Ohio State football, he would gladly pay."

Jim Parker agreed: After an especially uplifting season, enthusiastic alumni proposed to give Woody a new Cadillac. But he declined, observing, "They give you the car one year and the gas to drive it out of town the next. Besides, I'm not the Cadillac type." He suggested instead that they help his coaches send their kids through Ohio State.

Insurance man Bill Wickes headed an evolving organization called the "Buckeye Boosters," which sponsored trips to several out-of-town games each season. He heard about Woody's suggestion and notes that, "That became the purpose of the Boosters." The education fund established then continues today. Over the years it has provided financial assistance for many assistant coaches' children to attend Ohio State, though naturally Woody did not tap the fund for Steve Hayes' education. "He never got a dime from us," Wickes says.

Woody did accept one car for a time: a four-wheel-drive, scarlet and gray Land Rover, a gift from players on his 1955 through 1965 Buckeye teams. "He'd been driving that old [Ford] truck, and we thought it would be nice to get him a new one with everything on it," explained former center Billy Joe Armstrong, who headed up the fundraising. "Woody's done so much for us."

"This is the best birthday present I've ever had," the coach exclaimed. The vehicle was presented on Valentine's Day 1978, his 65th birthday. But after a few years he worried that it consumed too much gas, and he traded it for an El Camino truck, not for financial reasons, but for ecological concerns.

That wasn't his first sacrifice on behalf of the environment. Years before, he had sold his car as his contribution toward easing air pollution and conserving fuel. He walked the 2.3 miles from his home to the Athletic Department and also legged it to the Faculty Club and other campus destinations. The gesture of conscience also paid physical and social dividends. "I feel better," he observed, "and I get to meet a lot of good people while I'm walking, especially on the campus. Maybe some of them aren't anxious to talk with me, but they do. You get some pretty interesting perspectives on things."

Obviously, though, a man of his many commitments needed transportation. Tired of depending on others, he bought a pick-up truck and began driving again. He asked equipment repairman Phil Bennett to line the bed with a scrap of AstroTurf left from the Ohio Stadium field installation. He planned to put a sleeping bag in the back for overnight stays at his plot of land in the Noble County hills. When Hayes attempted to pay for the turf, Athletic Director Ed Weaver refused to accept it. Woody, unwilling to take something for nothing, sent the check to the Ohio State Development Fund to salve his conscience. Later, the dealer who sold him the truck wanted to service it, but Hayes went to an independent campus-area garage, saying, "He does a good job and he needs the money. Besides, he lets me pay."

Shortly after the University raised salaries 14 percent across the board, Weaver stopped by the room where the football staff was meeting. "All of a sudden," he recounts, "Woody said, 'I just got my contract this morning. Hell, that's too much money. I've got to give some of that back.' In unison, the coaches said, 'Gee, Woody, don't do that!'" In the best interests of his staff, he accepted the raise.

"He and I always went over the assistants' contracts, but never his," Weaver adds. "The least of his interests was his own. He never made any pitch for himself."

Hayes was offered $25,000 to be the principal speaker at the national Elks convention one year and accepted on the condition that the check be made out to the charity of his choice. Along with representatives of the Ohio Elks, he presented the $25,000 check to Dr. Don Unverferth of the Ohio State University College of Medicine. As an OSU undergraduate, Don Unverferth had been the record-setting quarterback of Hayes' 1963-64-65 teams—a passing quarterback for a coach known for disdaining the thrown football. Don became research director of the Division of Cardiology in the OSU Department of Internal Medicine and a nationally recognized researcher in cardiomyopathy, the study of ailing heart muscles. Woody's check helped fund that research.

Woody's generosity, independence, and overwhelming passion for taking care of his athletes got him and Ohio State in trouble in 1956. Complaints about the jobs program caused Big Ten Commissioner Tug Wilson to launch a full-scale investigation for possible irregularities at Ohio State.

At about the same time an article in *Sports Illustrated* tipped Wilson that Hayes had used fees from speaking engagements and his TV show to assist players in need. "I questioned Woody," Wilson reported, "and he admitted to helping his players when they came to him in dire straits. I told him his help was laudable, but absolutely against the conference rule. He contended that these advances were in the nature of loans, but that he had not required athletes to sign notes because they were very small amounts."

I was an innocent participant in two minor episodes, though fortunately I wasn't called to testify during Wilson's probe. Woody sat on a training table one afternoon, waiting for the players to report for practice. A young man walked through the training room en route to the locker room. He had a glaring tear in a delicate location, the rear of his pants. "Hey, come here!" Woody yelled. "Your ass is hanging out. Haven't you got a better pair of pants?" The player said he was wearing his best. Woody rarely carried any amount of money and never in his coaching clothes. He asked me for a ten-dollar bill, gave it to the player, and said, "Go buy yourself a couple pairs of pants!" As usual, Woody repaid me. Always averse to debt of any sort, he would often ask, "Do I owe you any money?"

After practice another night, a player came to Woody, explaining that he and his wife had no money for groceries for the weekend; checks from their jobs weren't due until the next week, and their parents couldn't help. Again, Woody made the "loan."

He handled such emergencies—and others more serious— at his own expense, rather than calling a downtown business-man, a store executive, or a well-heeled alumnus.

Jim Parker's wardrobe was pretty skimpy when he arrived at Ohio State, he recalls. Woody sent him to J.C. Penney's to buy some clothes and Jim says, "I bought one pair of pants and two shirts. I guess that stuck in his mind, because I didn't try to overload him."

For offenses like that and violations found in the jobs program, Ohio State was placed on probation for one year, a penalty with which the NCAA concurred. Hayes at first refused to provide a list of players to whom he had given money, but University President Howard Bevis and Athletic Director Dick Larkins finally prevailed upon him to do so. Ohio State complied with all the terms of the probation, and the ban was lifted in 1957.

More typically, though, Woody's attitude toward money involved no such ethical or legalistic ambiguities. Instead, there was just this hard-headed, selfless code: Keep a meticulous account of what you owe and pay no attention to what others owe you.

Woody had three favorite eating places: the Faculty Club, where he often sat at the "long table" with professors and University administrators; the Jai Lai Restaurant; and the lunch counter at the Big Bear Supermarket, across from the athletic offices. He was an attraction everywhere, particularly among Big Bear shoppers and the counter habitués.

Dave Girvis, now the co-owner of the Jai Lai, discovered Woody's disdain for "freebies": "One day he called to order a dinner to go," Girvis explains. "I happened to be the one who answered when he called. A relative of his was in the hospital, and he wanted to treat her to some restaurant food. When he arrived to pick it up, he asked how much he owed. I told him there was no charge this time. But he said he wanted to pay. So I said, 'Coach, you're one of our best customers, and we've never given you a free meal. Besides, this isn't for you. I'm giving it to her.' He looked me in the eye, serious as I've ever seen him, and said: 'If you don't let me pay, I'll never be back!' Of course, I let him pay. So many public figures expect to be treated better than others. He not only didn't expect it, he wouldn't allow it."

Perhaps the most memorable billboard in Columbus history featured Woody and the Jai Lai. Beside a large picture of Hayes and a discreet mention of the restaurant was the legend, "In all the world, there's only one." Marvin Brown, president of Marbro Advertising, writes, "We knew that 'In all the world' slogan was not an original idea, but we'd proposed equating the Jai Lai to instantly recognizable man-made works, such as the Eiffel Tower, the Statue of Liberty, or the Mona Lisa. But Wes Sickles, an artist on the campaign, suggested instead using Woody Hayes, certainly a unique individual and one of the most popular and recognizable persons in Columbus. But we could not use Coach Hayes' photograph without his permission and a signed release."

Dave Girvis' father Ted and the late Ed Daugherty, then owners of the Jai Lai, reported to Woody's office, with Brown, who recalls, "At the time [Hayes] was rereading one of his many volumes on military strategy and philosophy. He proceeded to read us portions that he'd underlined as valuable lessons for anyone in athletics or even for life in general.

"Finally, the advertising campaign was mentioned, and Hayes was shown the range of layouts, with his the last. He laughed, commenting that he didn't think he was in a class with the great works of art we were showing," Brown continues. "Then he said, 'Sure you can use my picture.' I asked how much he would like to be paid, and with a somewhat pained expression he said, 'You don't have to pay me. I like the Jai Lai. I like Ted and Ed. I'll be glad to do it.'"

Hayes signed the release form. To seal the bargain, Brown handed him a dollar bill, "which he handed back. We argued a few minutes. Naturally, I was unable to budge him."

The billboard not only became a Columbus landmark, it also attracted national attention. It was literally a million-dollar promotion, and Woody wouldn't even let the Jai Lai punch his meal check.

Moose Machinsky recalls one testy episode with Woody over money when several former players refurbished the Hayes cabin in Noble County. "A bunch of us went down there in a caravan," Moose relates. "We did work around the cabin and had a great day with Woody. When we got back, he pulled out his checkbook and asked how much he owed us. Of course I told him to put his checkbook away. He actually got ugly with me! He grabbed me and said, 'You're going to take it!' I said, 'Wait a minute. We were going to put up a white picket fence around the cabin; you can pay for that if it makes you feel better.' So he had the fence put up."

The Athletic Department conducted a fundraising campaign in 1986 that eventually resulted in a magnificent $10.6 million training facility officially christened the "Woody Hayes Athletic Center." Woody was so eager to contribute beyond his finances at the time that he considered selling his land in Noble County, complete with the cabin. Fortunately, the fund drive hit the goal before he had to decide on that sacrifice.

As his fame grew, so too did Hayes' opportunities to cash in on that fame, and Woody was tempted to capitalize on some of those opportunities. But even a hint that his gain might turn out to be another's loss was enough to quash the deal.

Marv Moorhead coached the Upper Arlington High School football team before entering business. He received a call from "a guy who had been tremendously successful in making money and putting together deals and starting companies. He was going to put a company together and sell stock, and he wanted Woody on the board of directors. He said he was willing to give him a basketful of stock options, and if the thing flew, Woody would be a millionaire several times over. Would I get them together?

"I called Woody for lunch at the Jai Lai and proceeded to outline the proposition very briefly. I got about 30 seconds into it when Woody put that big hand in front of my face to stop me, and then he brought it down on the table so hard the silverware and plates jumped. He said, 'Hell, no! I'll have nothing to do with that. I don't know anything about that business. The only reason he wants me is for my name. If there would be one person that would invest in that company and lose $1 because of me, all the money in the world wouldn't be worth it to put my name on it.' The whole discussion took about 60 seconds, and then we went back to talking football."

"I don't believe Woody ever did one thing in his life for money," says Rev. Daryl Sanders, a former player and a sort of "spiritual adviser" during Woody's retirement. "I don't think I know anybody [else] like that. He had the greatest understanding of money of any person I've known, something that kept him free in his own life."

Gene DeAngelo, general manager of the television station that produced Woody's weekly in-season show, had a similar experience. With the kind of money available in TV, he believes "I could have made that guy probably half a million dollars. Woody was an authentic star. But he turned it down. He was that much of a man."

Gene adds that Woody paid an additional penalty for his generosity: "We gave him a gross check [for the TV show], and he paid taxes on it, and then he gave half of his checks away. That's a double whammy."

The same spirit characterized Woody's publishing and speaking ventures. He wrote books and made speeches not to make a fortune, but because he liked people and because he had ideas he thought people might learn from. "My dad wrote and published three books, and I would guess he gave half of them away," Steve Hayes said. The ratio for speaking engagements might be nearer 75 percent. Another head coach once complained: "Woody's the guy who makes it tough on the rest of us, making all those free speeches."

"Know where I got this tie?" Woody asked one evening after practice, as he tied a handsome striped number. "I gave a speech and they asked me what my fee was. Hell, I knew they didn't have much money. So I said, 'You know what my fee will be? A nice necktie,' and this is it."

Only six months before Woody died, one of his favorite players, Jim Stillwagon, talked with him about cashing in on his speeches, autographs, endorsements, and the like, as present-day coaches do. It progressed to a stage where Stillwagon submitted a contract. Resting on the big leather sofa in his office in the Military Science Building, Woody talked about his dilemma. "I'd like to make some money," he mused, in a rare confession. "My sister Mary needs an eye operation, and I'd like to set up a fund to help Steve's kids through college. Like Jim said, I've done all this stuff for free all these years, what's wrong with my making a little money?"

Several days later, I asked him what he had decided. "I'm not going to do it," he said. "I've been doing those things free all these years, I might as well keep on doing it the rest of the way. Suppose some little old lady came in and wanted me to autograph a book? I'd have to say, 'See my agent.' I could never do that. I think the world of Jim. I'd like to do it for him, but I can't."

Woody Hayes titled his last book, You Win With People, conveying his philosophy that the right kind of "people" can make a better football team than a collection of all-stars. He had the same philosophy toward the "team" of the human race; he respected, admired, and loved "just people."

"There are more good people in this world, more than there's ever been," he remarked one 1982 day as we chatted in his office overlooking Ohio Stadium. "So many great, great people. You go to a hospital and you see people who are dying, yet they won't talk about their illness because they don't want to get you down. They want you to talk about something funny.

"There are just unbelievable people! I went into a country store once and the lady there, whose husband had died long before, practically got mad at me because I asked her if she had really put eight kids through college. She wanted to know who I was, so I told her and added that I had a cabin down the road [in Noble County] . 'And everywhere I go down here they tell me that you put eight kids through school. How did you do it?' She said, 'I didn't do it. My oldest son started it. He got a summer job and put himself through college in engineering at the University of Dayton.'

"I asked where he had worked in the summer and she said, I wouldn't know, so I said, 'Try me.' She named Marietta concrete, and I said, 'Hell, I went to school at Ohio State with the president of that company, Len Christy.' She went on to tell me that after her oldest son got out of school, he helped the next one, and he helped the next one. The youngest daughter went to the Air Force and was in Europe for three years. She saved her money and went to school when she got back. All eight went to college.

"I've seen that in families literally scores of times, where one person helps the next, and they pass it on. It's a great philosophy. Yes sir, there are more good people in this world than you ever know about, great people!"

Anyone who knew Woody or heard him speak would recognize that philosophy: as he often said, "You can't pay back, but you CAN pay forward."

11

HIS FELLOW MAN

Phil Bennett followed his father's profession as a shoemaker until sidetracked by the lure of an association with Ohio State football. He repaired the Buckeye players' shoes and any other equipment that required fixing. He constructed special pads and harnesses, usually with no pattern but his own ingenuity. And he kept Woody's street shoes shining. "Phil was a talented guy with his hands, and Woody was quite impressed with that," John Bozick points out. "The old man genuinely admired and respected Phil, liked him very much. Phil? He just idolized Woody."

Woody would come out of his cubbyhole office in the Biggs training facility and shout down the hall, "Phil!" and Bennett would come running. Sometimes it was to fetch him a cup of coffee or a doughnut—Woody was a diabetic and wasn't supposed to eat sweets, but he loved them and ate them anyway—but sometimes it was just to talk.

Phil suffered a run of bad luck in the mid-1970s, including a severe stroke that confined him to a nursing home. Woody became a frequent visitor, but he was more than that. A friend of mine watched Woody sign over a $2,500 check he had received from a speaking engagement to help in covering Phil's medical care expenses. Those close to the situation knew the contribution to be only one of many. Phil wasn't one of Woody's players or coaches, but he was still in the "family." What Woody Hayes did for so many who weren't in the "family," how many lives he touched in tangible or intangible ways can only be guessed, but the number must be legion.

Dave Pavlansky wasn't in the "family," but Woody essentially adopted him. A successful football coach at Poland (Ohio) High School, Dave was diagnosed in 1976 with a brain tumor. The family naturally wanted him to have the best surgeon and the best hospital, but Mrs. Pavlansky recalls, "We had no idea where to go. We prayed about it one whole weekend."

As if in answer to those prayers, the Pavlansky family doctor called to say that Woody Hayes had set Dave up for University Hospital in Columbus. An OSU alumnus and recruiter had called Woody about Pavlansky's plight. The Pavlanskys had met Hayes at a banquet a year earlier, when Dave was honored as Class AA Coach of the Year in the Youngstown area. "But we just said hello and that was it," Mrs. Pavlansky recalls. "He didn't know us at all.

"We came to Columbus, and Dave was admitted to University Hospital on Tuesday. Woody came over on Wednesday. He was over every night, and this was during football season. On Thursday we walked over to the practice field. Woody took us out in the center of that huge stadium and told those kids [the OSU squad] about us. Then he had them bow their heads and say a prayer for Dave.

"After the operation and recuperation we stayed in Columbus. Woody would pick Dave up and take him to practice, and when he'd get tired, Woody had a student manager take him back. If it hadn't been for that, I don't know what Dave's spirits would have been." Hayes was the featured speaker at a benefit banquet for Dave the following winter. Over 900 attended. Dave Pavlansky died in 1978, two months before the Gator Bowl.

When I began this book venture, *Columbus Dispatch* columnist Jack Willey published a note on it and suggested I would welcome "Woody stories." A veritable avalanche resulted. Many of the stories, like Pavlansky's, have tragic endings—a young person's life cut short, but not before having his last days enriched by Woody's benevolence.

Many injured or ailing high school athletes from central Ohio and points more distant were brought to University Hospital. Often coaches, parents, or friends would contact Woody. He made every effort to visit the young man, sometimes more than once, maybe bringing along an autographed book.

·"Where the rest of us might hem and haw and fumble for something to say," Bill Myles points out, "Woody always knew what to say to people in hospitals. He always knew what to say to people at a wake or a funeral. I've never seen anything like him."

Jim Walker, a strapping 6-foot-3, 240 pounds, had been first-team All-Northern Ohio League offensive lineman/linebacker as a junior and was preparing for an even greater senior year for Bucyrus High School. However, according to a letter from Frank Fischer, "Just as football practice was to begin in late summer, Jim became ill. It was diagnosed as a form of lymph node cancer, and he needed treatment almost daily. Jim would attend morning practice sessions, jump on his small motorcycle, drive to Tiffin for treatment, and be back for evening practice. The treatments seemed to help. There was a gradual loss of weight, but Jim didn't miss a game."

At season's end, though, it was clear that any improvement was temporary. "By this time," Fischer continues, "he had lost 30 pounds and didn't look good. In November he entered Ohio State University Hospital and appeared to be losing ground fast. I had heard of Woody's many visits to hospitals to see people he had never heard of and thought maybe, since Jim was in Columbus, Woody might drop by."

Fischer talked with Anne Hayes, who assured him she would relay the message to Woody, as she had done so many other times. But when the coach went to see Jim Walker, he had been sent home for the holidays. "Early in the evening on Christmas Eve, Woody arrived at the Walker home, spent two hours with Jim, and left him one of his books," Fisher reports. "A round trip of 120 miles on Christmas Eve! For a kid unknown to the coach, so ill he could play football for no team, still Woody took the time before the most special family day of the year to see Jim."

The inevitable postscript: "Tom Walker, Jim's dad, believed Woody's visit so encouraged his son that he fought his cancer and seemed to beat it," Fischer concludes. "He went on to graduate from high school, was married, and enrolled at Ohio State. The remission was short-lived. The cancer took Jim in 1969."

Todd Alles, a former Ohio State player, tells of another time Woody went the extra mile for a youngster battling a terminal illness—and for the youngster's family after the battle was lost.

"When I was coaching at Dublin High School, I had a kid named Tim Patterson who had cancer," Alles reports. "He was in University Hospital and I called Woody, knowing he got over to the hospital quite a bit, and asked if he could stop in and see Tim. He said he'd be glad to. From December 1980 to July 1981, when Tim died, Woody went to see him twice a week, every week. I called Anne after Tim passed away, but she said Woody was down at the cabin, with no phone and no way to get hold of him. When I drove up to the funeral home the next day, there sat the scarlet and gray truck the Ohio State players had given Woody. Somehow, he had learned about Tim and came back."

Paul E. Thompson of Columbus contributes another story of a short life made fuller through Woody Hayes' kindness. Thompson's daughter, Tammy, an Ohio State graduate, was on the staff of the Mary Free Bed Hospital in Grand Rapids, Michigan. Early in 1986, another staff member asked her to meet a 15-year-old named Danny who was "a big fan of Ohio State and Coach Woody Hayes." Danny had lost a leg to cancer.

"To meet Danny was to love him," Thompson says, "and Tammy had a new friend almost at once. She called us to collect some Ohio State memorabilia and decorate Danny's room while he was in therapy one day. He returned from therapy to a party that involved the whole floor. But Tammy wanted to do more. We thought Danny might be able to come to an Ohio State game in the fall, but time was running out for him." Instead, plans were made for Danny's father and brother to drive him to Columbus for the OSU spring game.

"By this time," Thompson continues, "we had discovered why Danny was such an Ohio State fan and why, as a young quarterback, he had wanted nothing more than to play for Woody Hayes: His father, Dan Poretta Sr., had been an offensive guard for Woody's Buckeyes in 1962-63-64. We contacted Woody's office, and he immediately jumped on the bandwagon with both feet. He called Danny at his home in Holland, Michigan, inviting him to lunch before the spring game. Danny's strength was down from the cancer and the removal of his leg. But he went to work to build himself up to a point where he could use crutches rather than the wheelchair."

Game day arrived and at about 11:30, Danny, Dan Sr., and Danny's younger brother Steve left for Woody's office. "Danny walked all the way from the west side of the stadium to Woody's office on crutches, as he said he would, rather than in a wheel-chair," Thompson recalls. "As the parking lot filled with fans going to the game, around the corner came a Chevy pick-up and Dan, Danny, Steve, and Woody piled out. Woody wanted to meet the person—my daughter Tammy—who had started this re-union and had helped fulfill Danny's dream of meeting Woody Hayes. He thanked her endlessly for caring so much for some-one."

John Bozick, alerted to the situation by Ohio Stadium super-intendent Mike Dolan, had ordered a jersey with Dan Sr.'s old playing number, 78, on the front and "Porretta" on the back. Woody presented it to a speechless Danny. "Woody insisted that Danny, Dan, and Steve join him in the press box to watch the game," says Thompson. "After the game Woody returned to talk over old times. Later Danny's mother Debbie said of the day, 'It was like the illness was on hold for that space of time, and it was so freeing for all of us. A real light in the midst of it all.'"

Again, the inevitable postscript: Daniel John Porretta, Jr., passed away July 15, 1986. Adds Thompson: "In a letter from his mother, she told us the day he spent with Woody Hayes was the best day of his young life. Woody, a gentleman, had touched them all."

In 1977, Columbus policeman Tony Pecko III, a former Westerville High School athlete and veteran of four years in the Marine Corps, was battling pancreatic cancer. A fellow police-man alerted Hayes to Tony's terminal condition, explaining his love for the Buckeyes. On Wednesday before the big game of the year, against Michigan, "Woody called Tony and they had a nice conversation," according to Mrs. James Greiner, Tony's mother-in-law, "not only about football, but about life in general." Hayes promised to bring Pecko the game ball if the Buckeyes beat the Wolverines. But it didn't happen. Woody called Pecko again, apologizing for not getting him the game ball. "On November 27, Tony also lost," Mrs. Greiner adds. "Though the years have passed, I have always remembered that even though he was a loser in that particular game, Woody was a winner in our hearts."

As word spread of Hayes' visits and other kind gestures, requests from hospitalized patients' families increased. "People were always calling me because they had a hard time getting to Woody," Anne Hayes recalls. "I would take the messages and see that Woody got them. Many times they were people he didn't know, but he always went if he possibly could, bless his heart. And he often visited more than just the person he went there to see. When word got around, people would come from everywhere, asking if he could stop and just say hello to their son or father or mother, or some other relative or friend who was in room such-and-such."

Shelley Snyder of Columbus wrote about sitting in the lounge area at University Hospital when the elevator opened and Woody strode out and down the hall to see a former player. When he returned and waited for the elevator, she mustered the courage to ask for an autograph. "My father lay dying a short distance down the hall," she explains. "I decided to ask one more favor. Woody said he would be more than happy to step into Dad's room and say a few words to him. Woody was the best. Not only did he spend several minutes holding my dad's hand, having this wonderful conversation with this total stranger, but before entering the room he noted Dad's name on the door, so he could address him by name. At this point, Dad did not comprehend much, but he sure recognized Woody Hayes! The doctors were encouraged by the slight, but unfortunately temporary improvement in Dad's condition. Two days later he died."

Hayes' one-on-one in a hospital room might reinforce a patient's lagging will to go on. Hayes in front of a banquet audience is a better-known inspirational image. But in this role too, Woody was often inspired by selfless charity, certainly never by money.

Joan Frank of Marengo, Ohio, has a typical story: "My cousin's husband, John Delserone, was a high school coach in the Youngstown area. He had Lou Gehrig's disease, and we called Woody to see if he would be the speaker at a fundraiser. He never even hesitated. The day of the event, he showed up and gave a wonderful talk. We had a room at the hotel for him because it was a winter evening, but he drove back to Columbus, refusing to take a penny for all his efforts."

Frank Truitt, former Ohio State freshman basketball coach, asked Woody if he would be the speaker for a Kent, Ohio, Rotary luncheon honoring 150 seniors from the city's two high schools. Woody declined because on that day he was to host his annual Ohio State football clinic for high school coaches. Another Ohio State official accepted, but he canceled out the week of the event, leaving Truitt scrambling. "I finally called Woody," he relates, "and told him I was really stuck and embarrassed. If he could come it would be a great help and I would pay. He said he didn't need a cent—he couldn't be there for lunch, but he'd be there."

"About 12:36 he came through the door, and I was never more glad to see anyone. He spoke for about an hour. I had heard him at a lot of outings, but I never heard him better. He was inspired. When he finished, 300 people came to their feet. I've seen some standing ovations, but none like that! He left his clinic to help me out of a spot! But the more important thing, he gave those high school seniors a really worthwhile message."

As Truitt's story illustrates, Hayes' sympathies weren't reserved strictly for those battling life-threatening illness. Anyone in need could arouse Woody's generous spirit.

James V. Ross, a Columbus fireman, once lived across the street from a major shopping center in Upper Arlington, the suburb where Woody lived. "My son, Jeff, has had cerebral palsy since birth and used crutches to ambulate," Ross related. "There was a pedestrian crossing light that was visible from our picture window, and to help Jeff become more self-reliant my wife started giving him a list of two things to get at the Big Bear Supermarket. This required him to activate the pedestrian button, cross the busy street, walk to the store at the other end of the shopping center, make his purchases, make change, and return home. Unbeknownst to him, Mother watched from the picture window.

"One day my wife wasn't feeling well, and she sent Jeff over to get some things. She laid down and dozed off. When she awakened, she realized that Jeff had not returned. She ran to the window and saw this man helping our son up the driveway, holding Jeff's arm with one hand and his purchases with the other. She thought, 'Why, that's Woody Hayes!' Apparently, Jeff had become flustered at the light with the heavy traffic and all. Woody, who was driving by, recognized that, parked his car, and helped this young man of ours across the street and walked him up to our back door. When he got out of his car, he didn't know Jeff or whether he lived across the street or six blocks away or what."

Sister Angela of the Sisters of Notre Dame in Columbus wrote a delightful letter concerning another Hayes assist: "It was the first or second year he was coach at Ohio State," she recounts. "Two or three of our sisters lived at Maryhurst on Roxbury Road, but they taught at St. Augustine School. At that time we were not permitted to drive, so the sisters had to commute by cab. One morning the cab had a flat tire so the nuns, wearing full habits, got out of the cab and stood by it, looking quite distressed because they would be late for school. Woody was driving along, saw their predicament, and offered to take them wherever they were going.

"When he drove up to the school, the children came running to greet the sisters as usual. They couldn't believe what they were seeing. One exclaimed, 'Boy Sisters, you sure rate, having Woody Hayes as a driver!' Since at that time we didn't read newspapers or have radio or TV, the nuns had no idea that a VIP had chauffeured them to school. He had introduced himself, but didn't boast of his position. During the ride the conversation was about the importance of education and appreciation of what the sisters were doing for young people. As they talked about this incident later, they were as enthusiastic as those eighth-grade boys."

Remember when President Richard Nixon offered football advice to Washington Redskin coaches? Maybe it wasn't as funny as it seemed at the time.

"That man is more astute in watching a football game than any man I've ever seen," attested Woody Hayes, who got to know Nixon well. "You can't believe it. He'll ask, 'Why did you do this, why did you do that?' And you better have the answers."

Woody introduced the former president when Nixon made an appearance in Columbus in 1982, one of his early public appearances after he too had been forced from his job under regrettable circumstances.

Convinced that "the man needs friends now more than ever," Woody visited the banished Nixon in seclusion at his estate in San Clemente, California. Mrs. Nixon said afterward that Woody's visit did more than anything else to raise her husband's spirits.

12

MORE GOOD DEEDS

In 1971 the Phillips 66 Oil Company's district manager in Alamosa, Colorado received the following letter:

Dear Sir:

A few days ago I was traveling through Monta Vista, Colorado, and I stopped at a Phillips 66 station to get some gasoline. As I pulled up to the pump, a good, clean-cut young man came dashing out of the wash rack. He quickly started filling the tank, he just as quickly started washing the windshield. He was cheerful and mannerly in everything he did. Later when I asked for a receipt, he filled it out and gave it to me in a hurry. His whole manner was one of complete cooperation.

I was so impressed with his manner and attitude that I asked him his name. He told me it was David Vander Molen, and only then did I learn that he was a new [assistant] coach at Adams State, the college that I had been visiting that day.

My only purpose for this letter is to apprise you of the quality of this young man, for his appearance, manners, and obvious industriousness. He certainly stands out today, and I want to congratulate you on selecting a man of this quality. I just hope that we won't lose this man from the coaching profession, for we need them too.

The letter was postmarked Columbus, Ohio, and signed by one W. Woodrow Hayes, who had been in Colorado to speak at a coaching clinic at Adams State. Vander Molen sent a copy of the letter to Anne Hayes after Woody's death. It was the first she knew of the incident. In his own letter, Vander Molen told Anne he was coaching football and wrestling at Longmont (Colorado) High School. Of Woody's gesture, he wrote: "What your husband did for me in my younger years of coaching cannot be expressed in words. Your husband truly was an idol for me in the coaching profession. He was an idealist who believed in God, family, and country; one who believed the harder you work the luckier you get; a man who stood up for what he believed; a student first and an athlete second."

Frank Truitt coached Ohio State's freshman basketball team for a number of years. He recalls a day when his sister came to see him at the Athletic Department. "Woody was down the hall in his own office," Truitt relates, "and I asked her if she'd like to meet him. She said she would so I introduced them. Woody started talking, like he usually did. He asked her what she did, and she replied that she was a dental technician.

"He asked how long, and she told him ten years. He asked if that was what she always wanted to be, and she said, 'No, I always wanted to be a teacher, but I didn't have a chance to go to college.' He asked how old she was and learned that she was 39. Then he said, 'You're not too old; if you want to be a teacher, you get in there and go after it.' He gave her a real inspirational pitch.

"She quit her job—she was married, so her husband helped her—went to college, got her degree, got a master's, and was an elementary teacher at Worthington for 20 years, one of the top teachers they ever had. There's a memorial for her in front of the elementary school. Woody inspired her on the spot. It changed her whole life and that of a lot of kids."

In 1974, when Frank Truitt was head coach at Kent State, he was a candidate for the head job at Virginia. He asked Woody if he would be willing to make a call to the athletic director down there on his behalf, and Woody agreed. In a matter of days, however, Woody had his first heart attack. He was in the hospital, and the doctors had told him to rest and not to worry about anything. But he told Anne, "I never made that call for Frank. Call him and find out who the man was." Anne called Frank, but he said, "You tell Woody to forget about that. Don't worry about it." But she took the name and Woody didn't rest until he made that phone call.

But you didn't have to be connected with OSU athletics for Woody to touch your life. Fred C. Sweeney of Westerville wasn't a football player, but his fraternity, Alpha Tau Omega, did include a number of athletes. "It was Coach Hayes' practice to make frequent visits to his players' residence halls and fraternity houses to check on their study habits and academic progress," Sweeney recalls. "His unannounced visits to the ATO house usually occurred between 7 and 9 p.m. and lasted 15 to 20 minutes. The various fraternities operated a telephone hotline to warn of Coach Hayes' rounds, but he wisely varied his route, arriving unannounced and unexpected.

"He used this time to talk with his football players and nonathletes alike. At first Woody's presence was intimidating for us nonathletes, who had no other contact with him. But as his visits became more frequent, we all began to look forward to seeing Coach Hayes. It became a matter of personal pride that Woody Hayes knew us by our first names and actually cared whether we passed a specific midterm or not. We had more personal contact with Woody Hayes than with any other faculty member outside of the classroom. I know of no other faculty member than Coach Hayes who made personal visits to students in their residences in order to inspire their pursuits of academic excellence."

Woody was in Colorado for another coaching clinic in June 1960 when he noticed in the morning paper that 20-year-old amateur Jack Nicklaus of Upper Arlington, Ohio, was playing in the U.S. Open at Denver—and that he was among the leaders. Woody knew the Nicklaus family well. Once dad Charlie Nicklaus had asked the coach, whom he knew to be biased in favor of his own sport, whether son Jack should play high school football. No, advised Hayes: Jack's future was in golf, and a football injury could dim his bright promise on the links.

His stint at the clinic completed, Woody drove from Colorado Springs to Denver and paid his way into the golf tournament to join the Nicklauses and trail Jack around the Cherry Hills Country Club course. At 6:30 the next morning (Columbus time, that is—it was 4:30 a.m. in Denver), he called me at the *Dispatch* sports department and said: "I didn't see any Columbus writers out here, and this kid from Columbus is doing such a great job in the golf tournament that I thought people back home should know about it. I didn't start taking notes until the fifth hole, but I can tell you what happened from there on. Now, do you want it or not?" I took all his stroke-by-stroke, hole-by-hole notes and wrote the story. They were good notes too, although he knew little about golf.

Later I learned that Woody had made his presence known in other ways. Jack had played with Ben Hogan that day and consistently out-hit him, meaning Hogan would hit first on every fairway shot. The crowd came to watch the great Hogan, not the young amateur; when Ben hit, the crowd moved. Irked at their lack of consideration for Nicklaus, Woody became an unofficial but extremely persuasive gallery marshal. Charlie Nicklaus, a model athlete's father, usually remained in the background, but that day he had a place at the gallery ropes. Woody would say to the fans jammed ahead, "How about letting Jack Nicklaus' father up there where he can see?" And the galleryites would allow the reluctant dad to move up.

Woody's actions on behalf of both Nicklaus father and son at Cherry Hills were typical of his eagerness to direct the spotlight to others. He was equally skilled at dodging the limelight himself. One spring he delivered a speech in Philadelphia and learned upon arriving at the airport afterward that his flight had been canceled by bad weather. When an airline representative offered little hope of a late departure, Woody remarked that he probably would be forced to rent a car and drive to Columbus because he had an 8:00 staff meeting the next morning.

A serviceman next in line heard and asked whether Hayes indeed planned to rent a car. He explained that if he failed to connect with a flight out of Dayton for his home in Utah, he would lose a day of his leave. Could he hitch a ride?

Woody rented the car and pulled into Columbus at about 5:30 in the morning. He rousted freshman coach John Mummey out of bed and had him drive the GI on to Dayton, where he caught his flight home. Only on the drive with Mummey did the serviceman learn that he had ridden all night with Woody Hayes, the Ohio State University football coach. "He never mentioned it," the young man said. "I figured he was connected with the University, but I thought he must be a history professor or something like that."

Soldiers always occupied a special place in Woody's heart, particularly those engaged in the bloody, unpopular, and undeclared war in Viet Nam. One morning in 1987, two weeks before his death, Woody had a visitor from Texas at his campus office in the Military Science Building.

"He told me that he had been in a hospital in Viet Nam when I was there and that I had talked with him," Woody recounted later. "He said he was so impressed that I would come over there, and he even remembered what I had said. He said he made up his mind that if he ever came through Columbus, he'd look me up and say thanks. I told him it was the least I could do and, anyway, what he did over there was so much more worthy than anything I did. I didn't need any thanks. It was something anyone would do." Woody paused, then added, "But he said, 'I didn't see my coach over there.'"

Hayes made four trips to Viet Nam. He showed football films, gave speeches, but mostly just encouraged the young men whom he felt got too little support on the home front for their efforts. "They're over there serving their country, and the least I can do is go there and thank them the best way I can," he explained.

He left for one trip the day after his 1968 Buckeyes had captured the national championship by defeating Southern Cal in the Rose Bowl. He passed up the flight home with his triumphant team, the welcome-home celebration, rounds of interviews and TV appearances, and all the other perks attached to one of the school's greatest victories and greatest seasons.

Woody's presence in a battle zone half-way around the world inspired hundreds of troops. But for those who got the chance to meet him and talk with him, there was a bonus that meant even more. On his return to the States, Woody would spend many hours and considerable money making phone calls to the folks at home.

"I was stationed outside of Qui Nhon, South Viet Nam, in early 1969," recalls Stephen Stout of Columbus, "when news of an unexpected USO visitor spread through the compound. The conquering hero of the Rose Bowl was going to visit our camp! Although not popular with the USC Trojans and the Michigan Wolverines, the excitement of a celebrity flying into our small camp was met with great anticipation. As the helicopter approached at dusk, several GIs mentioned that he must have guts—evening landings and take-offs weren't recommended at that location in those days. Woody jumped out of the helicopter as several field officers attempted to keep up with him. He bellowed, 'Now men, gather 'round. We have films of our great victory in the Rose Bowl.'"

After providing commentary on the film, which was shown on the whitewashed side of the supply room, Hayes gave his audience a personal tribute. "He spoke from his heart," Stout continues, "He told of his separation from his loved ones during World War II; of stemming the Communist tide; and most importantly, he spoke of how much HE appreciated OUR efforts. Here was a man 10,000 miles from the mainland, watching grainy films on the side of a building, swatting mosquitos and discussing life, America, and democracy with 100 young men who would never catch a football, make a tackle, or throw a block for him! He was saying THANKS! He immediately won over the entire crowd, including the Trojans and Wolverines!"

While he didn't realize it at the time, Stout's story didn't end there. "Within two days of arriving back in Columbus, the very busy coach dialed my parents' phone number and spoke first with my father (not a football fan), then my mother (definitely a worried mother), and lastly to my very impressionable 12-year-old brother about the importance of a great education. He gained an entire family of loyal supporters. He was bigger than life in Columbus, but with a little known but very compassionate heart as big as Ohio Stadium."

Michael Camboni of Grove City, Ohio, tells of having a brother in Nah Trang, Viet Nam, in 1968. "It was a hard time for my mom and dad, running a family business and having the day-to-day worry of a son in a war zone," he recalls. "The holidays were the hardest for our family that year. Shortly after the holidays the phone rang at our family business. As he answered, my father's face began to glow with happiness, and he called my mom to the phone. After the call was over, my mom and dad told the family that Woody Hayes had called to tell them he had met their son in Viet Nam and that he was healthy and anxious to come home. That call was a great gift of love from a total stranger to worried parents. Until then Woody was a character in the sports pages. On that day he became a family member. If you spoke against Woody Hayes in my mom and dad's presence, you would have been asked to leave. My mom and dad have a special love for a man they never met."

Ed and Evelyn Gillespie of Bellefontaine, Ohio, knew that their oldest son Bo had departed the West Coast on a troop ship for Viet Nam, but had heard nothing for two months. While Mrs. Gillespie was visiting a neighbor, her 11-year-old son came running to say that Woody Hayes had called. She wondered if it might be a prank. When Mrs. Gillespie reached the Hayes residence, Anne confirmed that Woody had indeed called, and he came to the phone. "Mr. Hayes assured me that he had met and talked with our son in Cu Chi, Viet Nam, and that Bo was just fine." she recounts. "Later we learned that our son had met Woody, and that they had had a one on-one discussion for more than a half-hour, not just talking about football, but home, education, etc. Needless to say, Mr. Hayes' time and effort to make that call to us helped greatly in our coping with the stress of having a son in a war zone. We've never forgotten his kind gesture—and never will."

Mike Jones, a Columbusan now living in Chillicothe, Ohio, boasts that he was "recruited" by Woody Hayes. "I met him in Viet Nam," Jones wrote. "During the height of the 1969 recruiting season, he toured Viet Nam with Ohio University coach Bill Hess. What a treat! We were going to see two football films and get to talk with a legend. Many of the soldiers swarmed Woody after the viewing. I wanted to meet him, but I knew I couldn't get close. A few of us joined Coach Hess. I told him I grew up in Columbus, attended South High for a year, and graduated from West Jefferson High. Coach Hess, a South alumnus, said I had to meet Woody and introduced me, saying I was from Columbus. Woody promptly asked me what I was going to do after the Army, and I said I was considering college. He began talking about the opportunities available at Ohio State University. He showed love for the school, the community, and the people of central Ohio. I was elated. A legend was recruiting me! But not for football. I was only 5-foot-1."

Bob Hope came to Columbus to play in Jack Nicklaus' Pro-Am golf tournament during the summer of 1974 while Hayes was in University Hospital recovering from his first heart attack.

"How's Woody?" he wanted to know, after finishing his round. "Is he having visitors?" I checked with Dr. Joe Ryan, Woody's heart specialist, who instantly approved Bob's visit and made all arrangements with the hospital staff. What followed left me with several indelible recollections, not the least of which was the privilege of sitting in on a fascinating conversation between these two giants of their respective fields.

Bob arrived at the hospital that evening unannounced, at least as far as the patients and their relatives and friends in the lobby were concerned. But when he walked through the door, there was a swell of immediate recognition— shouts of "It's Bob Hope!" and "Hi, Bob!" rang out. Alert autograph-seekers quickly assembled as he waited for the elevator.

Hope and Hayes talked for more than an hour, until it was time for Bob to head for Port Columbus and a flight to Cincinnati. He spoke of experiences on his trips to entertain U.S. servicemen in locations around the world; Woody talked of his four trips to Viet Nam, which had a similar purpose.

Inevitably, the name of General George Patton—one of Woody's heroes—was mentioned. "I never met the General," Woody confessed, "but I had a chance to talk with his son in Viet Nam." Bob in return recalled the time he was about to return to the States from Europe after doing a show for Patton's troops. He was summoned by the General, who had just been accused of slapping an over-wrought soldier, which stirred negative public opinion back home. "Patton said, 'I want you to do one thing for me,'" Bob related. "He said, 'When you get back to the States, I want you to tell the American people that I love my men; I care about my men.'"

13

DRUGS AND REDEMPTION

I'm sure Woody's probably looking down from somewhere and saying, "Dammit, Leo, I told you you could do it!" Leophus Hayden is a sort of prodigal son who not only returned "home" from much-troubled wanderings, but with the helping hands of his former Ohio State football teammates and his old coach, he put his life back together.

When drugs first raised their ugly heads on college campuses and threatened to invade his own domain, Woody Hayes reported: "I tell my players there are two things you don't do: no drugs and no haters. I won't tolerate either one on our squad."

"Woody was violently opposed to drugs," attests OSU's long-time team physician Bob Murphy, who has headed the Athletic Department's drug testing program for the last ten years. But in Woody's time, the head coach assumed responsibility for the prevention effort. "He did the lecturing," explains Dr. Murphy. "He'd take a 45-minute period and talk to the football squad about drugs. He took the direct approach to it, which I think is better than the indirect approach—drug testing and all the other things. He was really on top of it."

Dr. Murphy feels that Hayes' closeness with his players and his unquestioned interest in them off the field fostered mutual respect and steeled their resolve to resist temptation. "The best way to manage drug use in young people is through their parents, their teachers, and dealing with them directly, and he did that," Dr. Murphy concludes.

Hayes' primary enemy in the '60s and '70s was marijuana. That might seem incongruous now, cocaine and crack having become far more destructive to society, but Woody may actually have been ahead of his time in perceiving the dangers of the "milder" drug. "It took 'em only 12 years in Washington to come out with the truth," he once observed. "They're politic as hell over there. But we've known for years; anyone working with kids knows that marijuana destroys a kid. You can fool yourself if you want to, but if a kid's making Cs, he'll go to zero; if he's making As, he'll go to Cs. He'll be running play 28 when he should be running play 29. Sure marijuana will help 'em graduate," he added sarcastically. "Graduate to cocaine!"

He considered football players less susceptible because "they have to take a full schedule, besides practice and all that. They say, 'Who needs it? I'm too doggone busy. I've only got one head, and I've got to keep it straight or I'll flunk out.'" Hayes felt that players also spurned drugs because "they don't want to disappoint their parents, and that's a damn good reason." Players at Ohio State had another "damn good reason" too: fear. "I was so scared of the old man, the thought [of using] never even crossed my mind," recalls Leophus Hayden, a tailback on the 1968-69-70 OSU teams.

"That's exactly the point," Murphy acknowledges. "I think Woody had a very positive influence on those kids. They knew he'd run 'em out. If he had any suspicions, he would call them in and ask them directly."

Hayes warned, "You have to make sure you have the evidence, and if you do, you get rid of him [the drug offender] right away."

Woody Hayes recognized the power of peer pressure— "the tyranny of peer pressure groups," he called it. The few problems that arose among the Buckeyes were dealt with quietly, within the "family," with more compassion than vindictiveness.

Though his denunciation of both drugs and liquor was rigid and dead-earnest, Woody preferred to exorcise the demons and salvage the young man, assuming the subject had demonstrated qualities worthy of redemption. "I never saw him get rid of a guy if the guy wanted to straighten up his act," John Hicks points out. "The guy really gets rid of himself. If he genuinely tries to straighten himself out, the old man would cheer for him."

And as was the case in other regards, Hayes' cheering went on long after a player left his team. An All-Ohio fullback ranked one of the ten best high school athletes in the country, Leo Hayden became part of Ohio State's greatest freshman football class in 1967. Hayes already had a sufficient supply of fullbacks, so Hayden was switched to tailback and started for the 1968 national championship team. The extra-fleet 6-foot-2, 205 pounder's headline accomplishments included a 90-yard, two-touchdown day in the 1969 Rose Bowl and 769 rushing yards as a senior, second-best for the 1970 Big Ten championship season.

The Minnesota Vikings picked Hayden in the first round of the NFL draft, and he played sporadically in the next three years. During that time, he was introduced to drugs. Hayden was traded to the St. Louis Cardinals, "where everything began to peak," he says. "Divorce, much heavier drug use. Then the World League came along and it looked like salvation, an opportunity for a real new start for me. I could put the problems I had created for myself in the NFL behind me. But I hadn't dealt with the real issue, and the real issue was my using and the behavior it created. Whether it was the NFL or the World didn't make any difference until I dealt with that."

By the time the Chicago Fire and the World League folded a year later, Hayden admits, "I was pretty much a full-blown addict. Not wanting to come back to Ohio, where people knew me and I would have had to face the music, I moved to Kentucky and started working in insurance. That's when I began getting into trouble. That also began the turning point. I finally wound up with bad checks and forgery, which is why I went to prison. I had a judge who was real tough, kind of reminded me of the old man. He said, 'I think you need a taste of this [prison],' and he sent me up."

At that low point, the bonds forged during his football career at Ohio State under Woody Hayes began to tug at Leo. "At the time I was incarcerated, I was in contact with Jan White [OSU All-American tight end in 1968-69-70], my college roommate at Ohio State. When you're using, you lose a lot of friendships, but one thing that had stayed fairly constant was the fact that the friendships I made playing football at Ohio State University and with Coach Hayes remained very supportive. Even though I had pretty much severed those ties, all I needed to do was ask, and it began to happen. Jan contacted John Hicks, and John got to Woody, and Woody said, 'There's probably something I can do for Leo, but I can do a hell of a lot more if he comes back to Ohio.'

"That played very heavily with me. I was sick and tired of being sick and tired. I was ready. I came back to Columbus in 1986. But no matter how much you profess to folks that you've changed, they need to see that behavior in you. But I think that I was able to start showing people that old Leo's back, and that it's time to put those things behind me and go on. Woody gave me that opportunity. He put me in touch with [State] Senator Dick Schafrath and other people, and it began to work from that point."

After selling cars for four years, Hayden ran a drug treatment program for the city of Columbus and is now with the Ohio Department of Alcohol and Drug Abuse, coordinating policy and procedures for treatment within the criminal justice system. "Being a recovering person myself, I'm getting involved in the treatment community, taking some courses, and getting my certification."

Harking back to his old Ohio State days, he believes that "Woody Hayes and Ohio State brought a flavor to my life that possibly wouldn't have been there otherwise. I was very fortunate to be playing football at Ohio State at the time I did, and probably more fortunate to play under Woody and be exposed to his leadership, although it was hard to realize at the time. The old man was tough. Everybody caught hell one time or another."

He talks with pride about his rehabilitation because "a lot of people have not accomplished the things in life I accomplished. But to lose all that and then regain something even greater— the ability to help other people who are down and out—that only comes when help comes to you. I knew I had reached that crossroads. I asked for help."

When Hayden returned to Columbus, he stayed with Hicks, and John urged him "to make peace with the old man." Hicks adds, "I called Woody and he asked if Leo was off that stuff. I told him he was and asked Woody if he would meet with him. The old man was mad at Leo, but I don't think he could ever stay mad. He said he'd meet Leo."

Hayden and Hicks went to Woody's office, and Leo brought along a picture he wanted autographed for his boss. "I began to go through this long story," Leo explains, "and Woody asked,

'What is it you need, Leo?' I mentioned the autograph, and he kind of chuckled and said, 'Is that all?'"

"Right then, the old man wasn't mad at Leo anymore," Hicks recalls. "We sat there and talked, the three of us. A great experience! If we hadn't had Woody in our lives, who could we have gone to?"

Hayden picks up the story: "Woody told me, 'Leo, you were a darn good football player. I enjoyed coaching you. Without you we couldn't have won.' I never heard Coach say that before. I thought that was a heck of a thing to say. That statement wiped away whatever misunderstanding existed. We were both much older and had seen a lot of adversity, and I think we saw that in each other. We developed a relationship where I would call Coach on the phone, and that's something you never did when you were in school.

"It's kind of a realization that 'the Woods' was more human than anybody could have realized. Down deep inside, he had the player's best interest at heart. The only thing he asked was that you give him the same type of commitment that he gave you. You see it but you don't when you're playing because you're thinking, 'Boy, this is tough!' But because of that toughness, he took a bunch of green sophomores and turned us into national champions. That in itself is a spiritual peace.

"The session I had with Woody did a lot toward bringing me full circle. I began to understand that there is frailty in all of us, that we all have to answer one day, that we're not without faults. But we have to live with them and learn from them. That's what impressed me most about Woody. Shucks, we all knew the old man couldn't live without that whistle and baseball cap, but in the end he proved to be much more than that."

Hayden reaches a conclusion of which Hayes would have been cheering proud: "One of the things I want kids and other athletes to understand," Leo specifies, "is that I'm a very, very fortunate man—fortunate in the fact that I played football at Ohio State; fortunate that I played with the group of guys I played with; fortunate that I had a coach like Woody Hayes who was forgiving and has the type of power he had; fortunate that I didn't die; and fortunate that I was able to come full circle. It's not a scenario where you do what you want, all these bad things, then put your mind to it and recover. It doesn't work like that, and I don't want to give that message. The message is that I'm here by the grace of God and the faith of a lot of people who knew who I was and what I was and could be. That's the fine line between my being here and somewhere else."

As for any past ill will toward Woody, Hayden considers it a "misunderstanding" on his part. "Lots of times, in Woody's quest to get the best out of an individual, misunderstandings developed. I didn't know that. I felt I should have gotten the ball more. But there's a heck of a lot more understanding of life in me now than there was in the young kid I was when I left Ohio State."

As for Woody's peeve at him, he figures, "The old man believed that when people have opportunities, they should make the best of them. I guess he was kind of upset that I didn't. I'm trying to do that with this second chance."

Could Woody Hayes, with his rigid discipline, his military tactics, and his total demand, be a successful coach with today's young football players? Many observers seriously doubt it. All-American tackle John Hicks takes exception.

"Today a lot of people would love that," he contends. "I think he would be much better today than when I played [1970-72-73], by virtue of his organization and discipline. I think the kids would love him even more. I find today that people want that kind of discipline and leadership."

14

PROFESSOR HAYES

On the day after Woody Hayes died, a visitor to his office could find these titles between the book ends on his University-issue metal desk: *Allies* by John Eisenhower, *Landscape Turned Red* by Steven Sears, *Counting Our Blessings* by Daniel Patrick Moynihan, *Short Stories* by Irwin Shaw, *The American Newness* by John Gunther, *The Miracle of Dunkirk* by Walter Lord, *Small Town America* by Richard Lingeman, and *Famous American Statesmen and Orators*. Close by lay a smallish, red-covered book, titled simply *Essays* by Ralph Waldo Emerson, so worn that a rubberband saved its underlined, check-marked pages from spilling out in disarray.

Behind the empty chair—a stern, upright metal variety— stood a floor-to-ceiling, 15-foot-wide bookcase. There were, of course, some football books and teaching manuals, but in surprisingly limited numbers. Actually, with office space at a premium, the bulk of Woody's literary collection was stored in boxes that crowded the basement, garage, and upstairs bedroom at 1711 Cardiff Road. The office shelves were lined with such titles as *The Timetable of History: Churchill, Roosevelt, Stalin, Patton* (three volumes); *At Dawn We Slept; History of the Romanian People; Krushchev Remembers; The Third World War; Jimmy Carter, the Man and the Myth; Memoirs of Richard Nixon;* and *Superstars*.

Visiting the office, you'd swear Woody would be tramping in at any moment. He'd reach for a book and begin reading a thought-provoking passage to his visitor. The scene seemed to fix an instant in time, recalling a moment 14 months earlier when the morning mail brought an official acknowledgment that Woody would treasure, acknowledgment that his contributions to the University—and to his fellow man—had gone far beyond mere football victories.

Sandy Trelay, Woody's secretary, read it to him; his eyesight had failed to the point that he could discern only the largest of type. The letterhead: Office of the President; date: January 31, 1986; addressee: Professor W. W. Hayes;

Dear Woody,

In conversations about excellence at The Ohio State University, your name is invariably mentioned. The achievements and honors that have brought you national recognition and respect over the years also have brought great credit to Ohio State. Your long record of outstanding accomplishment and your well-known dedication to the academic enterprise are symbolic of this University.

For these reasons, you have been chosen to receive an honorary doctorate degree to be conferred upon you at winter commencement exercises on Friday, March 21, 1986.

It is with special pleasure that I also invite you to honor the University community by delivering the Commencement address.

Edward H. Jennings, President, The Ohio State University.

The old coach had always been a closet softie. He diligently shielded his sentimental side from all but those closest to him, and even those intimate few saw only brief flashes. As John Bozick put it, "He liked to have you consider him an SOB, and he was disappointed if you didn't." But in his last years, weakened by a succession of physical ordeals and tormented by frustrations of continuing ill health, he became easily emotional, though he always made a quick recovery. President Jennings' letter loosed unabashed emotion: "I've never had a greater honor!" he choked. Then, remembering a scholarly Newcomerstown High School principal, long gone, he mused, "My dad would have gotten a great kick out of this! He had such a great influence on my life."

Receiving an honorary degree and being selected as a Commencement speaker—some thought it a surprising twist for one who had been dismissed by the University—meant so much to Woody because he admired the teachers, the scholars, the thinkers, the researchers, the academicians. He frequented the Faculty Club because it was a sort of core of the academic community, and it gave him an opportunity to exercise his intellectual curiosity. He mingled with professors in various fields and enjoyed engaging them in discussions of their specialties.

"I felt he wanted to be with us to get away from football," suggested Harold Shechter, professor of chemistry and for six years Ohio State's faculty representative to the Big Ten. "He wanted to deal with us on intellectual subjects. One thing about Woody, he could ask questions. He was enormously well-read, and he was interested in what various members of the faculty were doing. He knew a lot about a lot of us and what our function was with the University. The fact that the University gave him an honorary degree tells you an awful lot about what we thought of him."

Hayes' favorite dining spot was what was once called the "bachelors' table." With the advent of the women's movement, it was renamed the "long table." As many as 20 could be seated there, a heterogeneous, always-changing assembly: deans, professors, administrators; sometimes President Jennings, sometimes an off-campus visiting dignitary.

"Woody made very close personal relationships with faculty members, whether it was mathematics, engineering, law, you name it," says Esco Sarkkinen. "And it wasn't just word-speak. He believed in participation with the faculty in many ways. He didn't care to talk football, he wanted to know about other things. In a way, it was an ego thing with him. He was proud he could step into the Faculty Club and sit at a table with members of different departments and discuss things."

Sometimes, perhaps on the recommendation of a player, Hayes would visit a Faculty Club colleague's classroom. Greg Lashutka, his 1964 tight end and captain, told him about Professor Rhea Foster Dulles, chairman of the History Department and cousin of former U.S. Secretary of State John Foster Dulles. Hayes accompanied Lashutka to a Dulles lecture, and as always in those circumstances, he approached the professor afterward to thank him and extend his congratulations. "I got the impression he wasn't too happy about my being there," Woody suggested, "but I heard later that at lunch that day, he told some friends at the Faculty Club that I'd sat in on his lecture, and he seemed delighted. Maybe he didn't resent me after all."

Faculty members would often alert Woody to a lecture or a discussion class in which they felt he might have special interest. School of Music Professor Paul Hickfang once mentioned at the "long table" that he was bringing Sherrill Milnes to the campus for a master class and concert. "Sherrill who?" Woody asked, and Hickfang explained that Milnes was an internationally known baritone, a regular with the Metropolitan Opera who had sung all over the world. When Milnes arrived, Hickfang took him to the Faculty Club for lunch. Woody dropped by their table and Milnes, an enthusiastic football fan, invited him to the afternoon workshop. "And Woody came," marveled Hickfang. "There was a hush immediately and then whispers as people remarked on Woody attending a music class! He stayed for two hours, came down to shake hands with Sherrill, and said he was impressed." That night, he attended Milnes' concert.

Woody's range of musical appreciation spanned considerable territory. One of his all-time favorites was Billy Maxted and his Dixieland jazz band. He stopped at Grandview Inn many nights when the band appeared there, and Billy became one of his close friends. Maxted had been a Navy flyer in World War II, another common bond.

In short, Woody admired excellence wherever he found it—and people who worked hard to achieve it. And his quest for knowledge was not confined to the campus of Ohio State University. On a stop-over in Albuquerque, New Mexico, he went to the Sigma Chi fraternity house and asked for the name of the outstanding history lecturer at the University of New Mexico. He found the class, heard what he considered "a magnificent lecture" on the history of the Compromise of 1850 and its aftermath, and spent several hours afterward talking with the professor. In San Francisco he attended a meeting of the American Historical Society to hear a lecture, and during a visit to Cornell he sought out a class taught by a recognized authority on the American presidency.

Woody gave as well as received. He spoke for a score of different University groups, from the College of Medicine to the

College of Agriculture to a class in philosophy. Someone once said, "If you don't want to like Woody Hayes, don't hear him speak." He captured audiences, made them think, and charmed them whether or not they entirely agreed with everything he said. No subject seemed beyond his reach or his ken. He had strong opinions and voiced them eloquently. His ability to deliver an absorbing, "meaty" speech, usually without preparation and often under the most difficult circumstances, continually amazed his coaches and players and others around him.

On the morning of March 11, 1987, the day before he died, he spoke to an Army ROTC class a few doors down the hall from his office in the Military Science Building. Because of his failing health, arrangements had been made for him to sit during his talk. "But you know Woody, he insisted on standing up through the whole thing," recalls Mrs. Trelay. "Then he was so tired he had me drive him home."

Hayes accompanied Jim Stillwagon to Houston in 1970, where the Buckeye middle guard was to become the first recipient of the Lombardi Award, named for Woody's great friend, the late Vince Lombardi. But something happened to arouse Hayes' ire toward the organizers. As Jim tells it, "They came to me a few hours before the banquet and said, 'Coach Hayes isn't going to speak tonight. He won't even answer his door. Can you do something?' I went up to his room and banged on the door. I found Woody in a bad mood. He wasn't even going to go, but he finally said he would, but only for me: 'As soon as this thing is over, you come and get me. I don't want anything to do with these people.' I helped him take his insulin, gave him my suspenders, and he yelled at me all the way. He went down there and he gave the greatest speech I ever heard. He was really on, and the people went crazy, giving him a long standing ovation.

"He'd been so worn and tired and out of sorts, but when the crowd responded, he became like a new Woody Hayes. Afterward, I went up and asked him if he wanted to go to our room. But he said, 'NO, I'm with my friends. We're going out and have some white wine.' He wanted to be appreciated, in his own way. But he wasn't a glory seeker."

The Quarterback Club had an annual "ladies night" meeting to which members brought their wives. One such night, during dinner, Woody claimed, "I don't have a thing to say to those women tonight; what can I talk about?" I penned a half dozen possible topics, he glanced at them, and put the paper in his pocket. He went into the meeting room, talked for more than an hour and simply wowed 'em—and never touched one of my suggestions.

Another night he arrived late, having stopped at the Main Library to check out a volume of poems by James Whitcomb Riley. He read, "When the frost is on the 'punkin' and the fodder's in the shock," a poem obviously known and appreciated by the Quarterback Club members. They cheered when he finished that classic from the Hoosier poet's collection and clamored for more. He wound up reading eight or ten Riley poems.

W.W. Hayes had a sharp mind, a rich store of knowledge, amazingly ready recall, surprising breadth and depth, and a vocabulary worthy of a professorship on the University's academic side. He always considered himself a teacher, in the tradition of his father. "I can teach history as well as any of 'em," he once boasted. "Woody Hayes WAS a truly superb teacher," attested Shechter. "Sure, he liked to win; sure, he liked national championships; sure, he liked publicity. But he was more of a teacher than a football coach—although he was an outstanding football coach. He taught football, but he also taught English, he taught character, he taught all sorts of things about improving oneself as a person."

Woody was an informal academic counselor to the students who served his table at the Faculty Club, constantly quizzing them: Where are you from? What are you taking in school? What's your best subject? Are you studying enough? What are you going to do after graduation? What's the best book you've read lately? Are you writing your parents?

Hayes' one active teaching assignment was an off-season football class, which normally would have been populated by physical education majors. But he made it attractive enough that a number of other students heard about it and elected it. Disappointed in the existing textbook, he wrote his own.

Woody also wrote a book specifically for high school and college coaches, baring his football soul in generous detail. So thoroughly, in fact, did he describe his philosophy and strategies, that some opponents devoured the contents of *Hot Line to Victory* and believed they now had the secret to overthrowing their tormentor from Columbus. But the book was published in 1969, and Hayes' record from then through 1978 suggests that his rivals needed more than a book to beat him. Ohio State's ledger for that period was 88 wins, 19 losses, 3 ties, 8 Big Ten championships, and 5 Rose Bowls.

Woody spiced everything from books to squad meetings with classical allusions, colorful versions of historical moments, and wise utterances of famous men, and some not so famous but nonetheless wise. Every player and assistant coach associated with Ohio State football between 1951 and 1978 heard the inspirational message of Leonidas and his brave 300 at the battle of Thermopylae, as told by Woody Hayes. The lesson was not only one of bravery, but disdain for the odds: "Xerxes of the mighty Persian force said, 'We will fill the air with our spears and they will blot out the sun,'" Woody related. "And brave Leonidas replied, 'Good, then we shall fight in the shade.'"

Mentioning a historical subject in Woody's presence invited an enlightening discourse. One of his rival head coaches casually referred to Thermopylae during his speaking turn at the Big Ten football preview luncheon. When he had the podium, Woody elaborated: "The Persians got in the back door at Thermopylae, you know. A traitor showed them a new path through the mountains and they outflanked Leonidas."

Another favorite object lesson concerned the "Young Turks," students who led an 1890 uprising against an oppressive sultan. "As soon as they would kill off the leader," Woody explained of the rebels, "a new leader would spring up from the ranks to take his place."

A gratified Hayes once returned from a hospital visit with a veteran player who had undergone a season-ending operation. "Do you know what he said to me?" the old coach mused, fairly glowing. He said, 'Well, one of the young Turks will just have to take over.'" The message had hit home. Most of Woody's messages did.

Hayes' heroes were many, and from many fields. He delighted in recalling their expressed wisdom, especially as it might be applied to football. He loved to repeat Winston Churchill's lines upon becoming prime minister of England during World War II: "I have nothing to offer but blood, toil, tears, and sweat." Or Churchill's commendation to the British flyers who valiantly dueled the German bombers: "Never was so much owed by so many to so few." Or Lincoln's "Let us have faith that right makes might, and in that faith let us to the end dare to do our duty as we understand it." Or Franklin D. Roosevelt's "The only thing we have to fear is fear itself." Or Napoleon's "Things are never as good as they seem, nor as bad as they seem."

Harvard University recognized Woody's intellectual side on April 25, 1982, inviting him as one of three principal speakers on the career and works of Ralph Waldo Emerson for an observance of the 100th anniversary of the famous scholar's death. Officials at Harvard knew of Woody's great admiration for Emerson, how he frequently quoted from Emerson's works, and how thoroughly he had studied Emerson's life and writings.

But Hayes acknowledged a possible incongruity: "I'm sure you're wondering what a football coach is doing here tonight," he suggested to the select audience of 200. "It's simple. I've come to pay back something I owe. Emerson has been an inspiration to me all of my life. He wrote about how important spirit and attitude were. He was an enormously positive man." The audience broke into laughter when Woody added, parenthetically, "He would have made a good football coach.

"Emerson said that the more you give, the more you get in return. I was charmed by the fancy of this endless *Compensation*. And doggone if it isn't true. It became the cornerstone of my coaching philosophy." After he finished his discourse, the audience acknowledged with hearty applause Coach Woody Hayes' status as a genuine disciple of Emerson and a worthy participant in the anniversary tribute. "It has to be one of the highlights of my life," he said after returning from Harvard. "I couldn't have been treated any better. Of course I didn't imply that I was a great student of his, but I have studied his *Compensation*, and I wanted to tell how I used it. I wasn't going to talk about transcendentalism."

Recognized as a scholar by the nation's foremost university, Hayes inevitably turned his thoughts toward the man who taught him to love learning, and who introduced him to Emerson. He recalled asking his dad one time what transcendentalism meant, and he was told: "Oh, pshaw, Wood, you took Latin: 'trans' means over; 'scandere' means 'to climb.'" Woody felt that his father gave him credit for more intelligence than he had. "But that was Emerson's motif, and I tried to stress that in my lecture.

"He could speak to anybody," Woody recalled of Emerson. "He was a great communicator. Great men can do this. The greater they are, the easier they are to approach. He was brilliant enough that he could make the Phi Beta Kappa address at Harvard on straight-out scholarship, then he could cross the Midwest and get in a skiff on the Mississippi River and go over to Iowa and talk to farmers in a one-room schoolhouse and make sense to them. He could go to Nebraska where they were laying railroad tracks and talk to those railroad workers and make sense to them. He always marveled at man's ability to think. Here's the essence of a democratic education."

Hayes' Harvard experience showed him another example of "a democratic education." Woody was invited to lunch at the home of Harvard President Derrick Bok the day after his speech, and he was amused that "the one thing President Bok bragged about was their last All-American, Pat McInally, who was playing with the Bengals at that time." Woody had had 58 All-Americans at OSU. During lunch Woody told him that when he was a kid, his dad had read him a book called *The Americanization of Edward Bok*. "That was my grandfather," said Bok. And said Hayes, "Isn't that something? From a Dutch immigrant boy to the President of Harvard in three generations. You can't beat that. That's America!"

OSU equipment chief John Bozick remembers Woody Hayes humming to himself as he moved about the training facility during quiet times when few people were around. "He couldn't carry a tune in a bucket," John notes, apparently explaining why Woody hummed.

The old coach always conceded that his sister Mary had the musical talent in the Hayes family. After studying classical piano, she chose to go on the stage and once was George Jessel's leading lady in a play.

But Woody did achieve one triumphal—and unlikely—musical moment in 1982. On Saturday night following Ohio State's home game against Michigan, he appeared with the Columbus Symphony Orchestra at a concert, reading the lyrics to "America the Beautiful" and taking the baton to lead the orchestra in "Stars and Stripes Forever."

15

TALENT FOR
TALENT

Many coaches consider recruiting a necessary evil. Some dislike it, some even hate it, but Woody Hayes loved it. He relished getting into the homes, meeting the parents, brothers and sisters, grandparents. He liked to sample the atmosphere in which the prospect had spent his early years. He felt he would have a better football player if the young man "grew up knowing he was WANTED in that home."

"He was so great in the home," declares Bill Myles, who as a one-time recruiter of Ohio high school talent for the University of Nebraska, has seen Hayes from the perspectives both of friend and foe. "Maybe the father was a plumber. Coach would mention something about a particular wrench used in plumbing. He may have read about it in a book. Maybe that's all he knew about plumbing, but now the father thinks Woody knows something about plumbing.

"He's got the guy on his own turf, and the next thing you know, he's got the kid. He was an amazing man!" Myles recalled going with Woody to recruit an athlete who lived with his mother in obvious poverty. As the coaches entered the clean, neat, one-room walk-up apartment, they discovered the mother had baked a cake. Woody's diabetic condition notwithstanding, he devoured a generous slice. "He really made a big deal about that cake," Myles recalls, "and he did it in such a sincere way; nothing phony-sounding." The football-playing son became a Buckeye.

Woody's ways weren't always orthodox. While other coaches might rave nonstop about a recruit's athletic ability, Hayes always had other concerns.

Jim Stillwagon grew up in Mount Vernon, Ohio, but was attending a military school in Virginia when he got a call from Lou McCullough, inviting him to make a recruiting visit to Ohio State. "My dad had gone to Notre Dame and I never liked Ohio State," Jim admits. "I really came home to see my parents, but I went over to Ohio State and was sitting in the lobby when Woody Hayes came by. He said, 'You must be the boy from military school.' I guess my hair was really short! But Woody remarked that I looked like a football player, and asked 'What's the last novel you read?' I had never read a novel to that time, but I said *Moby Dick*. I had seen it on TV and remembered it. He asked me into his office and for about 30 minutes, he talked about what a great American novel *Moby Dick* was.

"Then he said, 'I'll bet you're a football player; let me see your ankles.' So I pulled up my pants and he said, 'You've got thin ankles; you ought to be quick, you should be a good football player. I can promise you two things: if you're good enough you'll play, and if you aren't you won't. Your mom and dad would probably like it if you came up here and played well. Would you like to come to Ohio State?' I said yes." That's how Hayes recruited the two-time All-American middle guard/linebacker who won the Outland and Lombardi Trophies and in 1991 entered the National College Football Hall of Fame.

The recruitment of a three-time All-American running back and football's only two-time Heisman Trophy winner followed an entirely different pattern. Archie Griffin not only didn't commit to the Buckeyes in his first recruiting talk, he didn't get an offer. "The first time I really met Coach Hayes was when I came to Ohio State to watch them play Colorado during my senior year in high school," he relates. "After the game, he invited all the high school players up to a room in Ohio Stadium, and he came around and shook hands with everybody and talked to them. The thing that impressed me most about Coach Hayes was that he knew a little bit about everyone. He knew what I had done in my high school game the night before, and that was pretty doggone impressive for an athlete meeting Coach Hayes for the first time.

"During wrestling season, he called me on the phone. We had a good conversation and he asked me to dinner. We went to the Jai Lai, and I had the first big sirloin steak I'd ever had. But during the conversation, probably more than an hour, he didn't mention one thing about football. I was disappointed. He talked about education and the importance of education and what an education can do for you. When we finished dinner and dessert, he shook hands with me, said he was glad to meet me, and that he'd get back to me.

"When I got home, my dad asked me how it went with Coach Hayes, and I said I didn't think he wanted me to play football for him. My dad asked why and I told him that he never mentioned it. My dad asked me if I didn't think Coach Hayes was more interested in me as a person and not just as a football player."

Rudy Hubbard, an assistant coach and former Buckeye halfback, kept close touch with Griffin, assuring him that Hayes was interested in having his football talent at Ohio State. Later Griffin received another dinner invitation, enjoyed another steak dinner, and announced to Woody's delight that he would enroll at OSU.

Pete Johnson, who blocked for Archie and became Ohio State's all-time leading touchdown scorer, liked Hayes' non-football approach. The big fullback from Georgia (via Long Island) had committed to West Virginia before Assistant Coach Chuck Clausen and alumnus Jerry Brondfield talked him into visiting Ohio State. "I had never even heard of Ohio State," Pete recalls, "but then I met Archie and the guys and Coach Hayes. He really impressed me. Other coaches didn't talk anything but football. But Coach Hayes and I sat down and really had a long talk. I don't recall what all we talked about that day, but it wasn't football. It was everything. After I saw the school and talked with Coach Hayes, I really wanted to go there."

Johnson still felt an obligation to West Virginia, but he recalls a talk with his mother. "She was really impressed with Coach Hayes, and she asked me if I had a son, where I would send him. I said to Ohio State. She said, 'Don't you think you deserve just as much as your son would?' That did it." Pete scored 56 times in 1973-74-75-76, nine more than any Buckeye before or since, and made the Academic All-American and Academic All-Big Ten teams as a senior.

Hayes always weighed factors besides sheer athletic ability in evaluating a prospect. Dwight "Ike" Kelley, a muscular linebacker/center, catapulted high on the list because of an off-field decision. "When I was in high school, Harvard wanted to put me in a prep school," Kelley recalls, "I think because of both football and academics. But I rejected it because I wanted to stay with my class [at Bremen High School in Ohio] and graduate with the kids I started school with." Woody rated few attributes above loyalty, and Kelley had demonstrated that quality. He also could play football. He twice became an All-American linebacker at Ohio State and then a regular with the Philadelphia Eagles.

Incidentally, the Buckeyes unknowingly helped their own recruiting cause. "I was trying to decide between Ohio State and Michigan," recalls Kelley, now director of corporate personnel at Worthington Industries. "When Ohio State beat Michigan 50-20 [1961], that's when I decided. Woody offered me nothing but 'a great opportunity to get your education at a great University.'"

Hayes liked the face-to-face, one-on-one approach. "Woody never could get over the fact that Wes Fesler used to talk to a bunch of recruits at the same time," Esco Sarkkinen notes. When the prospect and his parents came to the OSU campus, Hayes would take them into his office, close the door, and the talk was on, sometimes for hours.

"When Coach Hayes came to recruit me, my father and mother were there," says Jan White, the prototype tight end of the 1968 national champions, "and by the time he got done, my father was asking where to sign up. My dad wanted that scholarship himself. Coach Hayes just had a lot of charisma."

But Hayes' foremost recruiting assets were his forthrightness and his ability to communicate on a range of subjects that intrigued and impressed young players and their families. "He sold Mom, Pop, and apple pie," says Larry Zelina, smooth-running wingback on the 1968 team, "but he was honest. He didn't just talk football, he talked grades, family, honesty. . . . He talked less about football than anybody that recruited me. He promised me nothing but a fair chance."

That promise from Woody Hayes was sufficient to convince a lot of fine high school athletes to entrust their futures to OSU. Hayes' integrity, in fact, was so well known that that quality in itself became a prime recruiting tool. "When I went into a home, I could sell Woody Hayes," says Lou McCullough, who reorganized the recruiting system when he joined the staff in 1963. "He was great at recruiting because of his name and his perseverance."

"He was a charmer when it came to talking with parents and kids," attests Gene Fekete. "A great recruiter." "He was very impressive," agrees McCullough. "The mothers always seemed to like him. Of course he always knew what to say. He made a great speech. The only thing was," Lou chuckles, "sometimes he'd get wrapped up in history or something and talk for two hours and never get around to offering the kid a scholarship."

The campaign to bring fresh football talent to OSU knew no holidays. "Coach Hayes was a tireless worker," McCullough declares. "One year he called about 10:30 on Christmas morning, wished me Merry Christmas and said 'This is Woody.' I said, 'Dang, I was hoping it was Santa Claus.' He said, 'You know who it is. Why don't you come over here.' I went over to the office and we called our 25 top prospects and wished them a Merry Christmas. That took us three or four hours. I worked with him seven of the nine Christmases we were together."

One of Woody's hospital visits even paid off with a surprise recruiting bonus. "Richard Nixon sent me 24 roses after we beat Michigan in 1975," he related. "I took them over to the University Hospital and gave one to each patient I could. An older gentleman in one room told me, 'I've been watching Ohio State football for a long time, long enough to know that we have a kid down in Ironton that can make your team. He can play.'

"We had pretty much passed him over, so I went back to our coach who scouted that area. He said he had seen the kid but didn't think he could play at Ohio State. I told him to give the kid a closer look, and we eventually tendered him. Do you know who that kid was? Kenny Fritz, who made All-American guard in 1979. You gotta listen to old people!"

Nor did Woody always confine his recruiting to football. John Havlicek had been a promising quarterback in high school, as well as a standout basketball talent. He let recruiters know from the beginning that he would concentrate on basketball in college. But Woody persisted, telling John's mother: "I don't care if your son ever plays a minute of football or not, he's the kind of young man we want at Ohio State." Havlicek didn't play that one minute of football, but he helped Fred Taylor's OSU basketball team to one NCAA championship and two runner-up finishes.

Woody continued to attend Jack Nicklaus' Memorial Tournament after leaving coaching. One year he was standing outside the Muirfield Village clubhouse, shaking more hands and signing more autographs than most of the golf stars. A gentleman approached with a husky, blond young man in tow, advised that his son had recently graduated from high school, and added almost apologetically, "Coach, he didn't play football, but he was a straight-A student."

"You're coming to Ohio State, aren't you?" Woody demanded of the son, who was noncommittal. "Now, you come to Ohio State. Doggone it, we need young men like you." Quality was the key for Woody, whether the recruit was a basketball player, a nonathletic scholar, or a blue-chip prospect on the offensive line.

Hayes' philosophy differed from many coaches' in that he rarely signed the maximum number of recruits permitted under NCAA or Big Ten rules. He believed you chose recruits carefully, kept them, and pushed them toward a degree.

Even before the NCAA set recruiting limits, he usually brought fewer than 30 scholarship freshmen to the campus. More often, the number would be in the 20s, or sometimes even the teens. "Rather than numbers," McCullough recalls of his tenure, "it was a matter of (recruiting) quality to fill positions where we needed the help." Archie Griffin was among only 16 scholarship freshmen in 1972. "And," Woody boasted, "they won 11 games as seniors. All you need is good ones: get 'em and keep 'em.

"There was a 17th recruit," he joked with one audience, "but he didn't last long. At the end of the quarter, he had four flunks and one D. I called him in and said, 'Jim, what went wrong?' and he said, 'I don't know, Coach. Maybe I spent too much time on that one subject.'"

Another favorite Hayes story concerned a potential recruit who had a taste for the barley and hops. As an object lesson one night, Woody claimed he drove the young man past a large Columbus brewery, which was obviously in full production. "See, son," he suggested, "no matter how much beer you drink, you can't drink it all." To which the recruit replied, "Yeah, but you can see I got 'em working overtime."

Hayes' "hands-on" approach to recruiting led him to adopt a cautious stance toward well-meaning outsiders who wanted to help the Buckeye program attract high school stars. Ohio State had an active recruiting organization in place when Woody became head coach. In 1947 Ed Weaver, then field secretary of the OSU Alumni Association and later the school's athletic director, had put together the "Frontliners," a group of well-heeled alumni, businessmen, and professional leaders in Ohio and elsewhere. With guidance from freshman coach Ernie Godfrey, the group bird-dogged Ohio high school talent and did everything possible within the rules to steer the best of the breed to Ohio State.

"When Woody came in, he pretty much took over the recruiting," Weaver recalls. The Frontliners continued to exist, but to a diminished degree. When McCullough joined the staff, the organization underwent a facelift that included a new name, the "Committeemen." Big Ten Commissioner Tug Wilson had long objected to the Frontliners, although no hint of impropriety had ever been raised. But increasingly stringent NCAA rules and Woody's philosophy so eroded the activities of the Committeemen that it became little more than a social club. The members came to Columbus each summer for a golf outing, a dinner, and Woody's speech, but that was the extent of their involvement.

It wasn't just stubbornness that made Woody want complete control over the recruiting process. He was well aware that, innocent though the Frontliners may have been, other schools' programs had been laid low by violations committed by boosters who were simply unfamiliar with the complex and uncompromising NCAA recruiting rules. Woody Hayes had what might be called an immaculate conception of recruiting. He was scrupulously honest. Players voiced a unanimous chorus: "He never offered me anything but an opportunity to play football and get a degree." An assistant coach ran greater risk of summary dismissal for bending a recruiting rule than for inadequacy on the job. Hayes fretted about anyone other than his staff being associated with recruiting for fear of innocent or over-enthusiastic missteps.

He held foes to the same strict standards. "I think the Big Ten was especially clean over the years because of Coach Hayes," suggested Archie Griffin. "People knew that if they cheated, he'd turn them in. He made no bones about it." In fact, Hayes boasted at the 1976 Big Ten preseason luncheon in Chicago that he had done just that: "I turned in Michigan State, you're damned right I did!" he thundered, as the audience buzzed.

But he was surprised—and a little miffed—when it was later revealed that his complaint had not been the first. In fact it had ranked no better than fifth or sixth in line. But he enjoyed the satisfaction of doing it and being the first to announce it. Michigan State was placed on probation for three years by the NCAA and the Big Ten. "I don't want any damned cheaters around me," he vowed. "If a man will cheat, he'll break his word. The first thing I want is character."

Tom Skladany was the first punter ever offered a scholarship by Hayes, and he was also Ohio State's first and only three-time All-American kicker. He recalls, "I already had the scholarship, and Woody told me to come a week early. So I came to Columbus and I'm out there every day, practicing my kicking. This one day, a real hot day in August, I came into the squad room, and Coach Hayes said, 'I'm as thirsty as a camel, let's go get a soft drink.' So, we get in his truck and drive over to McDonald's, and when we walk in, he says 'You know I can't buy you anything,' and I said 'Why not?' He said it would be a (rules) violation. I told him, 'Don't worry about it, Coach, I'll buy you a coke.' You talk about the letter of the law! That's how honest he was. He couldn't buy me a soft drink and he wouldn't."

*Bob Ferguson, a two-time All-American, repre-
sented the prototype Woody Hayes fullback: powerful,
durable, determined, a short-yardage machine that
could kick into long-range gear. Ferguson and Hayes
were not totally sweetness and light. But he thinks back
to the relationship and finds "I didn't have too many
problems with Woody, and my parents really got along
with him very well. If he liked you as a person, and you
did what he asked you to, he'd go that last mile for you.
If you teed him off, he could be your worst enemy. But
he didn't seek things."*

*Bob laughs about one minor exchange, which he
figures he won: "About my junior year, I had grown a
little moustache," he says, "and Woody told me, 'Quality people don't wear moustaches.' I asked, 'Are you
saying my dad isn't a quality person?'"*

16

A NIGHT AT THE MOVIES

A "date" with Woody Hayes was not your stereotypical evening on the town, his wife Anne can attest."We hadn't been anyplace together for so long," she relates, "and one night he asked me out to dinner and a movie afterward. We went to the Jai Lai, had a nice dinner, and when we got back in the car, he said he wanted to stop by the office and make some telephone calls. That wasn't anything unusual. We got to the office, he made a few calls, and then said he wanted to get a film out. We sat there the whole blessed evening! They were Michigan State films, and they were split into offense and defense. You know how they reverse them and how badly they flickered in those days. I don't know how many hours we watched, but when we were ready to go home—I think it was 1:00 in the morning—my eyes were spinning! Later Woody asked if I didn't think it was a pretty good evening and a good movie as well. To which I said, 'Yeah, and damn cheap, too!' That's a true story. He couldn't imagine anybody not liking football films."

An unfortunate omission in *The Guinness Book of World Records* is the category, "Most Football Films Watched." If such a listing existed, it would surprise the assistant coaches on the Ohio State staff between 1951 and 1978 if the record holder wasn't one W. Woodrow Hayes. "No coach ever watched that many movies," declares Lou McCullough. "He saw 'em on Saturday night, every day, in the summer, on the Fourth of July, his birthday. . . ." Esco Sarkkinen, who was on the staff for 26 of Woody's 28 seasons, agrees.

Anne Hayes, of course, knew better than anyone of Woody's love affair with the whirring projector and flickering football images on the screen, but I once got a first-hand glimpse of that myself. One blizzardy night in the middle of February, I suddenly needed information on an Ohio State football player. With the Buckeye basketball team playing at Iowa, I could expect no answer at the Publicity Office. On a million-to-one shot, I dialed the football office. After a half-dozen rings, Woody answered. "What are you doing in the office on a night like this, and in February at that?" I asked, incredulous. "I'm looking at the Ohio University-Bowling Green films," he replied, as though that shouldn't be considered out of the ordinary. "It's a hell of a game! You ought to come up and watch, you'd enjoy it."

Woody didn't care much for the real movies. But within limits they did figure in his philosophy for preparing a football team for battle. The squad watched a theatrical movie early every Friday evening before a Saturday game. The responsibility of selecting the Hollywood film fell to one assistant coach, but as in all matters, Woody established the parameters: no sex, no comedy, no violence, and in later years, no drugs. He thought any one of those elements might adversely affect the mental approach of his young men with a kickoff only 20 hours away.

McCullough remembers a trip to Michigan State when the movie wasn't a problem, but arrangements were. "Coach Hayes looked at the paper," McCullough recounts, "and found a movie he thought would be fine. It was a John Wayne Western. But it was at a drive-in about 17 miles away. I reminded him that we didn't have any transportation. Hugh Hindman called the rental place, but the only thing they had was a 36-passenger bus. So Woody called the Oldsmobile people, and within about an hour later, he'd lined up some cars. He planned to put a coach and four players in each car and leave at 7 p.m."

Shortly after the evening meal, Woody decided to change the routine on the postmovie football film; the offense would meet in one room and the defense in another. He wanted the film already loaded on projectors so no time would be lost changing reels. "That's about a 90-minute job, and we had 25 minutes," McCullough points out. "We got the motel manager to find us two rooms, and Hugh and Larry Catuzzi set up the offense while I did the defense. At 7:02 we reached the front of the motel, about the same time Woody came out the door. All the cars had left without us. Woody was really upset—'You SOBs have lost the game. Why aren't you with your team?' I said, 'Coach, we don't have any transportation. Hugh checked earlier and the only thing available was a 36-passenger bus.'

"Coach Hayes said, 'Get the damn bus and get out there.' At about 7:30 the bus picked us up. When we got to the drive-in movie, the girl at the ticket window wouldn't let the bus in. I told her to forget the bus, I just wanted three tickets. But she wouldn't sell 'em to me because we didn't have a car. I finally got the three tickets, and here we were in this big drive-in theater looking for new Oldsmobiles. It was about 28 degrees, and the cars were fogged over. I yanked open one door, and a boy and girl were making passionate love. I excused myself and went on. Finally I found an Oldsmobile, and when I opened the door I found some of our players. I got in and I told them in short order that I'd kill the first guy to ask where I'd been! Woody was right. We lost the game to Michigan State."

Earle Bruce, who succeeded Woody at Ohio State in 1979, was "fired" from the movie scouting assignment after a miscalculation at Minnesota. "The night before the game," he explains, "there were two movies we could go to at 7:30—we always had to be back at the motel by 9:30. One was a Disney movie and the other was *Easy Rider*. I didn't know anything about movies, but the players said that if we went to the Disney movie, they wouldn't play the next day. So I picked *Easy Rider*. It was a terrible movie. I didn't even understand it, to tell you the truth, but it was full of drugs and violence.

"As we got off the bus after the movie, Woody was waiting for us. [Assistant coach] Dave McClain was the first off, and Woody asked how the movie was. Dave told him it was the worst movie he'd ever seen. I said to myself, 'Thanks, Dave,' because he didn't know Coach Hayes like I did.

"This was 1969 and we were averaging something like 47 to 48 points a game. We beat Minnesota 34-7, but didn't look too good. On Monday Woody asked what was the matter with our team. He always said you never stay the same, you either get better or worse. 'We're getting worse. There's gotta be a reason.' He stopped talking for five minutes, then he put his head up and said, 'I know the reason, it's that damned movie. Earle, you didn't do a good job taking us to a movie. You're fired. Rudy Hubbard, you got the movie job!' Rudy never forgave me."

On a trip to Michigan one year, the squad reported for Friday lunch in our motel at Ann Arbor. Assistant coach Max Urick sniffed the salad and crinkled his nose. That was an alert for the head coach. Hayes quickly called everyone to attention, reports McCullough: "All right, men, don't eat the salad. They're trying to poison us." McCullough recalls that they didn't eat the salad, but they ate the lunch. Hayes then insisted on having the evening meal at another establishment, much to the chagrin of Athletic Director Dick Larkins, who still had to pay for the meal at the motel. But it was the Michigan game, and nobody dared deny Woody's wishes.

If the Buckeyes lost a road game, Hayes usually changed motels the next time around. Fortunately, road defeats were few; otherwise, suitable motels in some locations would have been in very short supply.

Home games were easier. The "movie coach" had all week to scout local theaters, and often films would be made available by the state censor board, which was well aware of Woody's specifications. One time Woody rented a theater for the squad to see the first half of *How the West Was Won*. The following week they would see the second half.

Another Friday night tradition, home and away, was hot chocolate and cookies in the players' rooms after the movie and just before curfew. For a game with Southern Cal in Los Angeles, the Buckeyes headquartered at the plush Ambassador Hotel. The players were assigned to cottages away from the main building. They returned from the movie to their rooms, but there were no hot chocolate and cookies. Woody immediately discovered the oversight and went looking for Floyd Stahl, who handled travel arrangements for all football trips. Stahl had already been to the hotel kitchen to speed up room service and was on his way back to the cottages when Woody caught up with him. Floyd, a spunky 5-foot-8, 148-pounder, absorbed Woody's initial verbal blast, which included veiled threats of unemployment. But then he waved a finger in the face of the much larger coach and snapped: "Dammit, Woody shut up! I was here at OSU before you came and I'll be here after you're gone."

Such confrontations notwithstanding, Hayes and Stahl shared a warm admiration and respect. Incidentally, contrary to his prediction, Stahl retired in 1970; Hayes left in 1978. Stahl turned 91 in 1990.

Home or away, Woody fretted every detail, no matter how seemingly insignificant, if it could have any bearing on the outcome of a game. But traveling, being in a strange environment and away from the usual routine magnified the possibility of glitches.

On the other hand, the junkets often represented an opportunity for Woody to enrich his football players in nonfootball matters. If a historical attraction existed in the area, the Buckeyes saw it. On a trip to Iowa, Woody decided to bus the squad to the birthplace of President Herbert Hoover on Friday afternoon. As the tour of the home proceeded, Woody became more and more restive. Finally, he took over. "Woody said that what the curator had told us wasn't right," recalls Greg Lashutka, a 1965 tight end/co-captain, now a Columbus attorney. "He got up and talked extemporaneously for 45 minutes about Herbert Hoover. It was amazing. The curator sat down and never challenged anything Woody said."

Trips to Illinois were always special to Woody, because it was the land of Abraham Lincoln, about whom he had read extensively and for whom he had the highest of praise. He usually gathered his troops about him after their Friday warm-up and spoke of "Honest Abe," observing that he would have made a good tight end but a lousy football coach.

Ohio State's fabled 1968 team led Illinois 24-0 at the half, and Hall of Fame middle guard Jim Stillwagon recalls, "Woody came into the dressing room and started talking about Lincoln: 'This is the greatest land in the country, where Lincoln was born. . . . . Here we were number one in the nation and in the middle of a Big Ten game—and he was talking about Lincoln. We went out in the second half and almost got our asses beat. He never did that again."

The Illinois stadium also called to mind a Hayes football hero, Red Grange, the famous "Galloping Ghost" of the Fighting Illini. This was hallowed turf, Woody often told his players.

It was in Champaign that Hayes herded his squad into a University of Illinois class on astronomy. After monitoring the lecture, Woody approached the professor and said, "My name is Hayes. I want to thank you for letting us sit in on your class." The professor laughed, "My name is Hayes, too."

"One Friday at Illinois," Stillwagon remembers, "Woody urged me to come with him to a chemistry class. We sat down and people looked at us. Pretty soon the prof recognized Woody and asked if he was indeed Woody Hayes, the football coach from Ohio State. Woody said yes, and 'I got a question to ask you.' He went down and started talking with the professor about chemistry theories and other related things. When he finished, the class applauded. He blew their minds! I thought to myself, 'This guy is unbelievable.'"

On many of the Illinois trips, the Ohio State party stayed at the Urbana-Lincoln Hotel, a place Woody rated highly. One year the hotel featured a singing waiter in the dining room where the Buckeyes had their evening meals. Woody was so delighted that on succeeding trips he insisted on having the singing waiter at Friday night squad dinners—even after the waiter had retired. "He sang songs like 'Autumn Leaves,'" Stillwagon remembered. "I loved it."

Stillwagon gets a bigger charge in recalling a 1969 trip to Seattle for a game with the University of Washington. The squad headed for the hotel dining room for its Friday evening meal. As Jim tells it: "We had just walked into the room to eat when Woody had a great idea, 'Something the boys would remember for the rest of their lives—a trip to the Space Needle.' He ordered Mr. Stahl to get the buses immediately, but Stahl reminded him that dinner was ready and waiting.

"Woody said, 'Hell with it! These boys will never be here again, and this is something they'll remember the rest of their lives. Get the buses!' Well, we went to the Space Needle. The whole team walked in, and everybody stared at us. They finally got us big steak dinners. Well, you know how Woody was about desserts, so he ordered sundaes on top of that. They brought us the most enormous mounds of ice cream I had ever seen. After we finished, he got up and said, 'Boys, this is something you'll never forget. But now we're going to have to walk off those big sundaes'—and he really walked us. I love to remember that incident. He was neat."

Usually on road trips, Woody had the team buses drive through the opposing team's campus, either en route from practice to the hotel or after lunch. During one trip in the turbulent 1960s, Ohio State played at Wisconsin. Many believe that Wisconsin has the most beautiful campus in the Big Ten. Naturally, the OSU buses toured the campus. Woody decided to stop at the student union, allowing the players to look around.

Woody, age 14, as a high school freshman. ▶

◀ *Hayes offers encouragement to his team from the sidelines.*

Photo by Chance Brockway

Woody, in 1953, early in his 28-year reign as Ohio State football coach. ▶

Photo courtesy of The Ohio State University Photo Archives

◄ **W**oody with two former assistants who were Big Ten head coaches at the time, Bo Schembechler, at Michigan (left), and Earle Bruce, at Ohio State (right).

Columbus Dispatch Photo

An ailing Hayes poses with his three Heisman Trophy winners, (left to right), Howard "Hopalong" Cassady, Archie Griffin, and Vic Janowicz. ►

Columbus Dispatch Photo

Columbus Dispatch Photo

◄ **R**ichard Nixon joins Woody in a Victory salute during a campaign stopover in Columbus.

◄ **W**oody performs his coaching duties in the style for which he was famous.

Woody in a rare ► moment of silence on the sidelines.

◄ **C**omedian Bob Hope dotted the "i" during the OSU Marching Band's halftime show, and old friend Woody Hayes escorts him from the field.

Woody emotionally delivering the 1986 Commencement Address, where he received an honorary doctorate degree.

▼

But the place turned out to be loaded with long-haired hippies and peaceniks: Hayes hustled his troops out of there and back onto the buses.

The Rose Bowl expeditions—eight of them—could justify a chapter in themselves. But two incidents further illustrate Woody's unpredictability and his human side. One morning, while the 1972 Buckeyes were in Pasadena for a New Year's date with Southern Cal, television and the morning papers brought word of the death of President Harry S. Truman. That also was the day of the annual country club luncheon for the media, officials of the competing schools, and business and civic leaders. The traditional highlight of the luncheon would be interviews with the rival coaches.

As a visiting journalist, I was designated to interview USC coach John McKay. As expected, it was football talk exclusively. But when Woody's turn came, he strode to the microphone and delivered a stirring 15-minute eulogy on President Truman. The audience, surprised at first, became more and more impressed with Hayes' oratory and obvious knowledge of the subject. They accorded him a standing ovation, although he totally ignored the Rose Bowl.

On the drive back to the Huntington Hotel, OSU headquarters in Pasadena, I feigned surprise that Woody, a staunch Republican, had so eulogized a Democratic president. "I was sitting there listening," he explained, "and I realized that a former president of the United States had died that morning, and not one word had been said about it. NOT ONE WORD! I made up my mind I was going to do something about it."

One day on another Rose Bowl trip, Woody table-hopped after lunch with the squad and stopped at a table in the Huntington dining room where Anne was seated with a Columbus couple. An adjacent table included eight adults and, at the end where Woody stopped, a baby in a highchair. He smiled, nodded hello, and waved to the little one, who was clutching a toy that he promptly dropped. Woody picked it up and handed it back, and then asked an attractive lady nearby how old her son was.

"Son?" she said with a pleased smile, "I'm his grandmother!" Everybody laughed and the youngster dropped the toy again. And once again the big man retrieved it. The baby seemed to realize that this was fun—and promptly dropped the toy a third time.

Woody returned it genially and warned: "You drop it once more, young fellow, and I'm going to think you're a fumbler. And you know what we do with fumblers at Ohio State? We put 'em on the bench!" A look of recognition spread over the adults' faces. "Coach, this is a USC table," the grandfather volunteered, almost apologetically. "That's all right, " Woody nodded, placing a large hand on the baby's shoulder, "as long as you send this little fellow to Ohio State someday." But the baby apparently didn't want to become a Buckeye recruit and dropped the toy again. Woody picked it up, shook the tiny hand, and went off to his ever-consuming world of Xs and Os.

Woody took no chances that New Year's Eve revelers might disturb his warriors' sleep the night before the Rose Bowl. Although the Huntington Hotel headquarters was among the most staid and least boisterous places in town, he secreted his squad on that special night at the Passionist Fathers Monastery outside Pasadena, where abundant quiet prevailed. But Woody finally relented before the 1973 game, allowing the players to remain in their assigned rooms at the Huntington on that and future game-eves.

Although he insisted that the team was a family, indicating that trust and common bonds should preclude unacceptable conduct, he was a realist and enforced stringent training rules. Probably the most convincing deterrent was fear—of him.

During their stay at the Huntington, all the players occupied rooms on one floor of the hotel. Woody's room faced the elevator, and his door was always open. He might be asleep, or he might be watching movies; it didn't matter. There were also the inevitable bed checks by the old man or the assistant coaches.

However, on one early bowl trip, a player managed to beat the system for a late-night adventure, only to be confronted on his return by threat of disastrous punishment—though not from Woody. Sneaking through the bushes of the Huntington's back yard, he was suddenly set upon by the hotel manager's Doberman, a suspicious, long-toothed watchdog. The transgressor needed all of his athletic prowess to reach the safety of the nearest hotel entry.

17

THE Xs AND Os

"Three yards and a cloud of dust" was Woody Hayes football, right? Recruit big, strong linemen; recruit big, strong fullbacks; recruit quarterbacks adept at handing off; and power over the opposition like the Patton tank corps Woody so admired.

Of course the "three yards" premise is wanting from the outset, because three plays wouldn't add up to a first down, and Hayes' 28 Buckeye teams bagged more than 6,000 of them. Nor does it account for the defensive units, a substantial component of his 21 two-platoon teams. Nonetheless, the ground-hugging, ultra-conservative image of Woody Hayes football persists. As is the case with the man himself, the reality is not as simple as the image.

As defensive coordinator for eight years, Lou McCullough became an authority on Woody Hayes' offense. One of the treats for the few privileged spectators at Buckeye practices, and for the players as well, were the times Woody's "Red I" (first offense) squared off against McCullough's "Bucks" (first defense). "I always said some of the greatest football games ever played at Ohio State were played on the practice field," claims Jim Stillwagon. "Man, that was war!"

Thus McCullough knew the problems that Buckeye opponents faced, and several years after leaving OSU for the athletic directorship at Iowa State, he contends that: "The biggest misconception of Woody Hayes-type football is the thinking that he is conservative, won't take calculated risks, and won't pass. He has used all types of formations and plays and will beat you with the pass about 40 percent of the time. One year, we won every game but two by passing. He just uses the pass to supplement the running game, as do most consistent winners. In practice, he spends as much time—if not more—on the passing game."

Maybe the conservatism was more evident in the types of passes Hayes employed to supplement the precision power of the foot soldiers. When he sent in a pass play, it was usually of the high-percentage variety. Passing, Woody insisted, "must be complementary to the running game" and "must show at least 50 percent consistency and a low interception rate." Not many "bombs" exploded over enemy secondaries. Buckeye quarterbacks never suffered from arm fatigue.

Woody often said that "Three things can happen on a pass play, two of them bad." And statistics show that bad things didn't happen to Hayes' teams very often. In the 1968 national championship season, with Rex Kern and Ron Maciejowski quarterbacking, OSU averaged 18 passes per game (and scored 10 touchdowns through the air, compared with 34 by rushing). The 1954 national champions passed 12 times per game (8 TDs); the 1955 Big Ten champions passed 5 times per game (2 TDs); the 1957 national champions passed 7.8 times per game (4 TDs); and the Big Ten champions of 1972 through 1975 passed 11.0, 7.9, 8.4, and 10.4 times per game, respectively. "Wide open" was not a term applied to Hayes football.

Some fans complained. So did some sports writers. Characteristically, Hayes responded, "I don't care how they react. I'm only interested in one thing: how my players react." The guys in the uniforms were more often satisfied than any of their counterparts in the league. Hayes football produced 205 victories, 13 Big Ten championships, 3 national titles, 58 All-Americans, and 4 Heisman Trophies.

Woody often quoted one of his heroes, Vince Lombardi, who said, "The name of the game is running." The off-tackle play, Hayes granted, is "the trademark of our offense." Quite a successful trademark: a dozen Ohio State linemen made All-American during Woody's years, as well as four fullbacks in an 11-season span.

To the fan in the stands, and others as well, Woody's system looked simple. After losing another game in Columbus, a Big Ten coach once mused, "That's the easiest offense in the world to stop on the blackboard, but just try it on the field."

"People didn't recognize the subtle nuances of those plays that looked so simple, " says Michigan's Bo Schembechler, who played for Hayes, coached under him, waged a ten-year annual battle against him and remained a devoted friend. "Take the off-tackle play. Truth of the matter is, probably more than any other coach, he refined everything involved in that play to make it successful, no matter what you did [on defense]. The line splits had to be exact, and the blocking adjustments just as exact. The ball handling looked the same, which is what the public sees. But the innovation was up front. As you looked at it and got ready for a certain blocking scheme, all of a sudden another blocking scheme hit you. The old man was very astute and as a coach, he was the greatest teacher of them all. He absolutely taught his team that when the play came in, no one could stop them."

Earle Bruce, Hayes' successor and another former assistant, agrees that WHAT the Buckeyes did became subordinate to HOW they did it: "Coach Hayes was a great, great teacher. When I was a high school coach, I used to marvel at the teaching that went on at Ohio State. I once heard Coach Hayes talk for an hour on the off-tackle play (numbers 26 and 27). It was the greatest lecture I ever heard because he was so thorough. The fundamentals were always taught. His teams executed like you couldn't believe. Sure, he had good players, but other people had good players too. The strength of Woody Hayes was the strength of any good coach—blocking, tackling, fundamentals, and elimination of mistakes."

Hayes abhorred fumbles, interceptions, and penalties. He harped on them and demonstrated his displeasure with the guilty. He hired high school and college officials to work every practice and yelled at them if they tended to be too considerate of players. Buckeye teams usually ranked among the most mistake-free nationally.

"But he really didn't get mad about physical mistakes," notes Fred Pagac, a rugged tight end in 1971-72-73 and currently the Buckeyes' outside linebacker coach. "He got mad at you for mental mistakes. Make a mental mistake a second time, and he'd really go off." Against Northwestern Fred once "made a good one-handed catch on the sideline, and I thought I did something great. But I came up the sidelines and he punched me in the stomach, openhanded. I hadn't gotten out of bounds to stop the clock." Ohio State teams seldom beat themselves.

But Hayes football was more than Xs and Os. "The thing you have to do is go back each year and review what actually wins for you," Woody once said. "You'll find it's the discipline on your squad and your morale and how you handle your players and how well you bring them along. Those are the things on which you win, rather than all the technical ideas that all of us have." Hayes teams rarely gave less than maximum effort and avoided more than most the peaks and valleys, the elation after a big win or the letdown after a jolting defeat. Because, he insisted, "they've got a mean old coach who won't let 'em."

It was a given: he was a motivator. "There are two things I know about motivation," he once suggested. "I've read a lot of books on it. If you want to motivate a person, give him personal attention; secondly, show him improvement. When he sees that, he's going to stick with it." Another time he said: "I don't motivate the players. I get them to motivate themselves. That's the only kind of motivation that's worth a damn."

He thought about it, worked at it, and jealously guarded against any outside influence that might subvert his careful preparations, whether it be a suspicious salad in enemy territory, a travel foul-up, or girlfriend problems on the home front.

Notre Dame's Lou Holtz, a roundly hailed motivator himself, came to appreciate Woody's effect on Buckeye football players. "When I was an assistant coach at Ohio State [1968]," Lou declares, "it became obvious to me that our athletes weren't that much better than what other people had, but they thought they were super."

Pre-game speeches were Woody's finest motivational moments. Jeff Kaplan hid a tape recorder in his trench coat before most 1975 games, thus preserving some absolutely classic orations—without the coach's knowledge, obviously. "Several years afterward, I got up enough courage to tell him about it," Jeff recalls, "and of course he said, 'Why, you SOB!' A little bit later he said, 'Let's listen to one.' Then he said, 'Let's hear the rest of them.'" The contents qualify as "family" treasures—Kaplan played them at the 1975 team reunion to the delight of the players. Maybe it would be permissible to loosely recreate the pre-Michigan message:

Men, this is war! I don't care anything about the national championship or the Big Ten championship [voice cracks], but if we win this game today and afterward, if the Good Lord says, "Woody, it's your time" I'll say [shouting], "Lord, I'm ready! . . ." I'll have time to take it easy up there—or down there—but I know where I'll go. . .so let's pray no one gets hurt today.

"Or down there" may have been an intentional tension-breaker. In that regard, he often cited the World War II experience of General Dwight Eisenhower on a muddy hillside in France: "The General accidentally slipped and fell on his back in the mud," he recounted, "and the men laughed so hard that even those who assisted him to his feet could scarcely do so for laughing. He felt it was a great morale-booster for the battle-weary soldiers." Woody never took a pratfall in the mud, but when he sensed that his squad was too tight or too high before a game, he considered it essential to say or do something to break the tension.

One of Hayes' most effective motivational tools, of course, was his own volcanic personality. "Talk about love and hate motivation," says Pagac, "he had FEAR motivation. He scared the hell out of you."

Three-time All-American punter Tom Skladany agrees, "You were very, very scared of him early on—I was still scared of him as a senior." But he recalled another facet of Woody's motivation: "The thing that was great about Woody," says Tom, "was that he never complimented you on something you did great, because that was expected. If he wasn't talking to you, you knew you were kicking ass. He never would say 'great job.' You'd know you were doing a great job by reading the papers or hearing him at a banquet. I loved that because I was brought up the same way by my father. You don't ask for thanks; that's what you should be doing anyway."

After Hayes spoke glowingly of Skladany at a squad banquet once, Woody told him afterward, "You should be kicking me in the shins." "He always told us, 'if somebody gives you a compliment, kick him in the shins, unless the compliment is from a lady over 80. Compliments make you soft.'"

The erudite Esco Sarkkinen has the best credentials for an overview of Woody the coach, based on 26 years of close association. "There are three or four areas where a coach shows his mettle, his worth," he suggests. "There are the marvelous blackboard coaches, there are the innovative coaches who come up with innovative things that are way ahead of the game. Woody admitted he was a great borrower. He felt he could do it better by outworking everyone. He liked Wes Fesler's theories on zone pass defense, for instance, but he felt he could do it better. Whenever he borrowed, he did it as well or better than the guy who invented it. Give Woody a plus on that.

"Then you have the practice coach who works on basics, the fundamentals, the techniques. Woody was superb. He would go over the clinical approach to fullback plays 26 and 27 in a marvelous way that would inspire and rejuvenate us coaches. Bill Hess [Ohio University head coach] would come up every year just before fall practice and bring his whole staff to hear Woody's 30-minute lecture on 26 and 27. I asked Bill once, why he did that, since he'd heard it 100 times. He said it inspired him and got his juices flowing. Woody did it better than other folks, but woe if you ever tried to change any of those well-established theories of his.

"In a staff meeting once, Woody was explaining plays 26 and 27 from the full-house backfield: quarterback, fullback, and two halfbacks. [Quarterback coach] George Chaump asked why 26 couldn't be run from the T-formation with one of those backs out on the flank. 'If you don't accept this, you're fired,' Woody said. Nobody was going to move those people around and take away all those factors of blocking on 26 and 27. It had to be run from one formation only, Woody's way.

"Finally, there's the game coach. As Woody said, strategy is the plan you have before the game and tactics are the changes you make in your strategy during the game. Woody tried to be a battle coach, a coach that would make those changes. That's why he liked generals and the way they reacted.

"Woody was a student of the game. A lot of coaches let someone else make decisions, let the game play itself out. But Woody wanted that emotional control of the game, and he did it simply by virtue of his competitive nature. You couldn't beat him on competitiveness. I don't know how you measure it, except by the actions and reactions he showed on the sidelines during the game. He just had to immerse himself completely in that competitiveness. That was the biggest plus of all, although it got him into trouble at times because of his antics and reactions on the sidelines."

The old coach stacked up well in all three categories, and a good many others. Hayes was a winner in more ways than any scoreboard ever showed. "The thing I always respected most about Coach Hayes was the integrity he gave football at the college level," Earle Bruce says. "He loved the game of football. I recently talked with former Washington State coach Jim Sweeney, whose team played Woody's. Sweeney recalled a play that went on to score a touchdown, but the touchdown wasn't allowed: Jim said, 'Woody was out there yelling and ranting, and I wondered what the hell he was doing. He was out there saying, 'Give the man his touchdown, give the man his touchdown, it was a touchdown.' I wasn't used to that kind of stuff.'

"When he told me that story," Bruce concludes, "I thought, now that's the integrity of Woody Hayes!"

Sports writers toiled over their hot typewriters in the press box, reporting Ohio State's rather undistinguished 7-0 triumph over Michigan in 1960. The crowd had departed Ohio Stadium. As the first hint of darkness crept over the giant horseshoe, three figures emerged from the southeast portal and proceeded to the practice field. One figure—one FULL figure—was easily recognizable as Woody Hayes. Binoculars soon identified team members Paul Warfield and Matt Snell as the others.

Woody proceeded to conduct a workout until the light became too dim. Warfield and Snell were freshmen running backs (freshmen weren't eligible for varsity competition at that time), but he had them throwing passes à la quarterbacks, while he played center.

"Tom Matte was graduating," Woody explained later, "and we were going to have to come up with a quarterback for 1961. Both of them were such fine athletes, I was hoping one of them would be able to pass, but I could see it wasn't going to work."

He conducted the after-game tryout because "to work them out later would have been a rules violation." As a reward for their extra time and effort, Woody treated them to dinner at the Faculty Club.

Warfield played running back, flanker and defensive back at Ohio State, Snell halfback, fullback and defensive end. Both followed with great pro careers, Warfield with the Dolphins and Browns, Snell with the New York Jets.

18

ON CAMERA

Today's football coaches spread themselves generously over the airwaves and the TV screens—call-in shows, pregame shows, postgame shows, radio and TV commercials. Woody Hayes never had any of those. He kept too busy otherwise, and extra money didn't matter. But he did have—and loved—a weekly 30-minute television program that he had for years on Friday evening, then on Sunday before the NFL games, and finally on Saturday night.

"Woody's show ran for 28 years," points out Gene DeAngelo, president and general manager of WBNS-TV, Columbus. "His program started when the station was only two years old. As far as I know, other than a newscast like "CBS News," for instance, that's the longest run by the same person on the same station in the history of television. The show was number one in its time period. I don't ever recall that anybody beat that show in the ratings. But, of course, it was more than a coach's show. Woody was the star of the show for as long as he coached Ohio State football. He became a legend!"

I wasn't a raw television rookie when I was called upon to host Woody's show. I'd done sports reports on WBNS-TV during a couple of strike shutdowns at the *Dispatch* and one 15-minute stint that apparently was meant to be an audition (obviously unsuccessful; they didn't ask me back). But the prospect of hosting a half-hour of live TV created some fright pangs, even though I knew Woody Hayes would carry the show. Channel

10's Carl Papai and Paul Yoakum outlined my role at considerable length, including oft-repeated pleas to "move your lips,"
"enunciate," and "project."

After football practice on Wednesday before my first Friday night on the air, I suggested to Woody that we sit down and
plan the TV show. With a blithe flip of the hand, he said,
"Surprise me!" It was the last time we mentioned it until he
hurried into the studio about five minutes before air time. Considering the uncertain state of the host, all went well. I learned
quickly that it was called the "WOODY HAYES Show" for good
reason. All my fears had been wasted. Woody was never at a loss
for words—and charming, engrossing, interesting words at that.

As my predecessor Earl Flora and I both agreed later, the
host's chief function was to start Woody off with questions most
likely to evoke pertinent comment, respond when appropriate,
stay loose, elbow in the commercial cues, and say good night.
Woody was the star. In all my years on the show, we never had
a script and only the vaguest of formats (or "floormats,"as
assistant coach Ernie Godfrey once said). Woody rarely appeared more than five or ten minutes before the show; sometimes
he arrived as the theme music played. He had, after all, a football
team to prepare, game films to watch.

Many times I stood in front of the Channel 10 building,
scanning all traffic southbound on Olentangy River Road—and
panicking at the thought of doing a solo. But somehow, when the
little red camera light came on, he always managed to be in his
seat to say an unhurried and cordial, "Good evening, fans!" In
light of slick present-day production, artistic sets, and strict
formats, we were pretty primitive—but with very high ratings,
thanks to Woody.

But things did happen. One year, WBNS-TV organized an
Ohio network. Papai and Yoakum drummed into me that each
local station would sell its own commercials; when I gave the
commercial cue, they would cut off immediately. Previously, I
threw the commercial cues only after menacing gestures and
sign-flashing by director Wally Strathern, or when one of the
crew threatened to become violent.

In one segment of the first show, Woody explained the
triple-option offense using blackboard diagrams. When he
reached what I considered a stopping point I said, "That's very
interesting, Woody. Now we'll be back, right after these mes-

sages." But Woody wouldn't have it. "Now wait a minute, Paul," he protested, "I'm not through." We stayed on in Columbus, but viewers along the network never did fully understand the triple option!

Woody's player interviews were a point of amusement to some. Most of his questions could be answered with brief agreement: "That's right, Coach." One night he talked with a sophomore who had started in his first game the previous Saturday. "Were you a little nervous before the game?" Woody asked. Replied the player, "I sure was, Coach. I had to go to the bathroom three times." Today that would be innocuous, but at the time it shocked everybody—except the other players waiting in the studio, off camera. They literally rolled on the floor, as did their teammates watching back in the dorms and apartments. The kid later took a terrible ribbing, which was exactly what Woody's interviewing style was designed to prevent. By asking questions that could be answered briefly, almost automatically, he was doing his best to protect a young man from embarrassing himself, or Ohio State football in any way on television—particularly on HIS show.

Woody surprised me sometimes. In 1959, Ohio State had been highly ranked before the season, but they started slowly. While the theme was playing, Woody whispered: "Ask me why we haven't done very well, after being highly rated." I opened the show with that question, and he delivered the explanation he'd obviously wanted to make public. When I walked into the press smoker later, my colleagues hailed me for hitting him with such a hard question. Little did they know.

In 1963, the Buckeyes had lost at Southern California 32-3, and Woody's show was to air at 12:30 Sunday afternoon. The team had flown home immediately after the game, but I doubted that the coach had slept much. Because I'd had to do my story and column for the *Dispatch*, I'd stayed over and caught the "red-eye" from Los Angeles, going directly to Channel 10 from the airport.

It figured to be a dismal day and a dismal show. Yoakum suggested that maybe this was the day for the "Buddy Dial film." He screened a film clip in which Dial scored a TD for the Cowboys. Somebody shoots off a miniature cannon behind him, just outside the end zone. Dial then leaps into the air, looking like he's been shot, grabs his chest, and falls flat.

I decided to use it to open the show, although it had nothing to do with Ohio State football. It was a gamble. With the loss, the long plane ride, and a morning of suffering through game films, would Woody be amused or angered? Fortunately, he arrived in time for one look at the Dial antic before air time. He laughed. When it ran at the start of the show, he laughed and asked me to play it again. Thanks to Buddy Dial, the mood brightened, Woody hit his usual stride, and the show was OK.

After the fateful 1978 Gator Bowl incident, DeAngelo did a rare on-air editorial to mark the "end of one of the greatest college football coaching careers of all time.... Woody brought pleasure to hundreds of thousands of television fans each week of the football season. . . . While we occasionally had our differences with the coach over how the show was put together, we discovered that Woody frequently knew more than we did.... He knew what his fans throughout central Ohio wanted, and he fought to give it to them. It wasn't always good television, but it was always good Woody."

Legend has it that Woody damaged his own cause in the 1956 Big Ten probation case by innocently mentioning on his TV show that if a player came to him in dire financial need, he would provide monetary assistance. Strathern insists it didn't happen on camera, but rather in a casual conversation Woody had with a *Sports Illustrated* writer in the studio after the program.

Either way, the *SI* quotes were part of the reason Big Ten Commissioner Tug Wilson slapped Ohio State with a one-year probation. Neither the magazine nor its representatives enjoyed cordial relations with Hayes for some time after.

One controversy—Woody's feud with Jack Fullen—did break out on camera. Their discord began after Ohio State's appearance in the 1955 Rose Bowl. Fullen, the able but outspoken secretary of the OSU Alumni Association, conducted a train tour to the game. But later, in the monthly alumni magazine, he blasted the Rose Bowl for "overcommercialization" and questioned the propriety of Big Ten involvement. Hayes took exception. He also felt Fullen had been too cooperative with *Sports Illustrated* in the magazine's "nosing around" that led to the 1956 probation. And later, when the Faculty Council turned down the 1961 Rose Bowl invitation, Woody blamed Fullen's continuing criticism of the Rose Bowl and possible "politicking."

On his TV show the following fall, Woody took the feud public, criticizing Fullen for such offenses as his anti-Rose Bowl stand, his alleged part in the 1961 Rose Bowl rejection, and his negative effect on recruiting. Hayes was abetted and supported by the program's host. WBNS-TV deemed it necessary to grant Fullen's request for equal time for rebuttal, although football fans reportedly backed Woody.

Several years after Hayes left coaching, Channel 10's program director, John Haldi, approached him with an idea: hosting a series of war movies in prime time. "I told him he could front [introduce] the movie and do bridges leading to the commercials," Haldi explained. "He could also add to the movie's history, add dimension to it." It wasn't a tough sell, considering Woody's love of history, especially military history. He eventually appeared with six of the World War II film epics, and the station gave the project big-time treatment.

"One of the movies was *Patton* with George C. Scott," Haldi recalls. "We flew Woody down to Fort Knox, where there's a tank museum with Patton's original car and all that. Then I got in touch with Patton's daughter, who lived outside of Boston. We flew Woody up there, and he and the lady got along marvelously. She made lunch for us and talked about traveling with her dad all over the world. Her brother, who was himself a general, also lived there."

The next stop was West Point, where, Haldi attests, "They were very attentive to Woody. He talked with the cadets at a breakfast, about 2,000 of them, and he gave them hell and high spirits: 'Goddam, war and life are similar and you've got to fight,' and so on. Then he spoke at a luncheon for faculty, wives, and anybody who could crowd into the place to hear him. West Point's football coach had had several disastrous seasons and Woody said, 'Now, I want you to do one thing: doggone, you've fired too many coaches up here lately. You hang onto this guy, he's good. You can't develop a program in less than five years.' He pointed the finger and scolded them and they loved it."

For the film *Midway*, Haldi says, "We got hold of a guy who had been in the cleanup squad for the *Yorktown*. The ship was listing 20, 30 degrees, and their job was to go aboard and strip off the armor and all the weight so they could tug it back to Pearl Harbor. We flew to Florida for the shoot. This guy was an eyewitness to what happened, and Woody kept interrupting: 'My sources say the Japanese weren't even in the area.' The guy responded that, 'They came in and the torpedoes came and they hit. . . .' Woody stayed firm, 'No torpedoes.' The guy retorted, 'But Woody, I was there.' And on they went: 'But you couldn't see the torpedoes.' 'Yes, they laid them in about on a level, and I could see them coming. I knew my ship was going to get hit. They hit us four times.' 'No, it was six times.' I finally said, 'Hold everything.' We gave them privacy, and they went into a little huddle. They did the scene again and the guy who was actually there was finally allowed to tell what happened."

On a shoot at Jacksonville, Florida, all the arrangements had been made in advance. Woody was to stay in the admiral's suite, but Haldi was informed after they arrived that that would not be possible. "I found out that the admiral's nose was out of joint," Haldi explained. "This was Jacksonville, where Woody hit the guy [in the Gator Bowl incident]. I made an excuse to Woody that they were doing something to the admiral's suite, and he would have to stay with us in the seamens' quarters. That night after dinner Woody realized the connection: 'Clemson, eh?' and I nodded. You couldn't put anything over on him.

"We filmed on the *Yorktown*, Woody sitting in the captain's place on the bridge, all very Hollywood. Everybody just adored him. A female ensign even came up to say that the ensigns, particularly the ladies, wanted to give him a gift. It was a cap, and the colors were maize and blue. Obviously, he never put it on. I mean, Michigan colors? But he honored the lady. He thanked her and said, 'John, you take good care of this. I want to take it back to Columbus.'"

Traveling around with Hayes on two- or three-day shoots, the Channel 10 crews came to appreciate his celebrity. "Every place we'd go," notes Haldi, "somebody would recognize Woody Hayes.

"Something in particular impressed me as being typical of Woody: we all ate together on company expenses. I made sure when I signed the bill that I had left enough [tip] to honor Coach Hayes, so we didn't look like a bunch of cheapskates from Columbus. But every time, after the lady came with the bill and they got autographs all around, he always left his own tip, $10, $15, sometimes $20. I asked him what he was doing, since I'd already added 25 percent. But Woody would say that the lady was particularly nice, or she looked like she could use it."

Hayes' association with WBNS-TV followed his usual pattern of trust. "We never had any paper with him," Haldi attests. "A handshake was all." But his loyalty required no contract.

Michelle Gailiun had attended Ohio State's weekly football press luncheons during her fledgling days as a reporter/assistant to Jimmy Crum at Channel 4 and later moved to Channel 6 as evening news anchor. She was hard to miss, even for the usually oblivious Woody. She was very attractive, and she asked Woody to give her an interview. Said Woody: "She's such a dandy girl, and I'd like to do it. But I can't. She's on ANOTHER station."

After his retirement, Woody enjoyed seeing the halftime band shows he had always missed while coaching, although his halftimes as a spectator were interrupted too—by a steady stream of visitors to his booth above the press box. But he enjoyed that.

If he missed being center stage for these stadium dramas, he never showed it. He was content and once confided, "I coached long enough." He enjoyed the games, rejoiced in the victories, and was downcast over defeats. But he accepted his new and different perspective.

Even failing health didn't keep him away. The Athletic Department paid him deserved respect by assigning him the number-one parking place next to the press elevator—closer than the governor or the University president—thereby minimizing his walking distance.

Unfortunately, the distance from the radio booth to the field proved too much for his failing eyesight in the last two or three years. Images on the stadium floor were fuzzy. I sensed it from his questions and began to do a virtual play-by-play account. He eventually thanked me for that assist, but proud and so long self-sufficient, he generally resented help of any sort. One time I let him struggle with his topcoat, but he grew frustrated, so I helped slip it into place. "I'm not worth much anymore," he groused. "Can't even put on my own damned coat."

All-American Jim Parker got a brusque reminder of Woody's independence: "The last time I saw him, we were going over to the Holiday Inn," Jim relates, "and when we crossed the street, I went to help him onto the curb because he was gimping a little bit. He said, 'Get the hell away from me! I can do it myself.'"

19

THE FOURTH ESTATE

The West Coast media was part of "them" in Woody Hayes' "them against us" Rose Bowl scenarios. Coming to Pasadena, he once warned his OSU squad, "They'll be bothering you all the time. Be damned careful what you say. Not a one of them wants you to win. But I don't expect you to carry a chip on your shoulder like I do."

The general perception that Woody Hayes and the media did not represent a mutual admiration society is reasonable and accurate, at least regarding the national media. He wasn't much concerned about his public image, and Woody's relationship with both the print and electronic representatives hinged on a word, "trust."

Hayes frequently cited an experience during his coaching stay at Miami University: "This writer came in one day," he related, "and I talked with him and let him come in to practice. The next day I read in his newspaper everything we were doing. Of course, our next opponent read it too."

Woody realized that this did not indict all sports writers, most of whom prided themselves on adhering to the profession's unwritten code of ethics. But it made him wary, especially with those he didn't know or those he knew and didn't quite trust. Being badly burned twice in succeeding years reinforced his caution.

Depending on his mood, he was generally "good copy." He could be expansive, engrossing, controversial. Liberal in expressing his strong opinions, he had a reporter's sense of the "colorful." He tossed historical, classical, military, and political references into a variety of fields. And even when he began in restraint, he usually gained momentum. With rare exception, he enlivened the weekly Monday press luncheons during the football season. His traditional preseason press gathering regularly produced a headline or six, and he always highlighted the Big Ten football preview in Chicago. But never was providing "good copy" for the media high on Woody's list of priorities. In fact, it wasn't on the list at all. "I never knew of a newspaperman winning a game for us yet," he once suggested.

He kept his postgame audience waiting, sometimes for almost an hour, while he met with his squad and shook hands with recruits and players' moms and pops. Press interviews ranged from marathons to brief to nonexistent. But even in the case of the latter, the writers had a "hinge" for Sunday stories.

Hayes steadfastly refused to allow his players to be interviewed, a sore point with many writers. It was not an insult to his players' intelligence or good judgment, he insisted, but "in the heat of the moment, right after a defeat, or even after a victory, a young man might say things that would be embarrassing later or that could adversely affect our squad morale." Local writers had access to the players during the week, although "outsiders" seldom managed to gain an interview or even a comment, particularly on the road or on bowl trips.

Much Hayes-bashing came from writers or broadcasters who didn't know him, or those who came looking for confirmation of their preconceived dislike. Unfortunately, he supplied some ammunition, such as his on-field eruptions—most of them televised and rerun often. Word-of-mouth sometimes treated Hayes unfairly as the stories grew with retelling. Before the 1973 Rose Bowl, a photographer reported that his camera had been pushed back in his face by an angry Hayes. He apparently suffered no significant injury: he returned from a check-up at a first aid station to continue working the game. Several years later, however, I read in a West Coast column that "Hayes smashed the camera in the photographer's face with such savage force that the poor fellow was sent to a hospital for two weeks and nearly lost the sight of his eye."

For all the adversarial relationships, Woody had a number of friends among sports writers. Dayton's Si Burick was one. Si's last column, before cancer claimed him, was an account of watching the 1986 Michigan game with Woody in the stadium radio booth. Though weakened and ailing, Woody attended a memorial service for Si in Dayton two months later.

John Dietrich of the *Cleveland Plain-Dealer* and Jack Clowser of the *Cleveland Press* were journalistic rivals. John would write a story extolling Woody's conservative football, Jack would rebut with a demand for more passing. They argued in person, as well as in the papers. But they came to OSU home games together and ate together on Friday nights—after arguing where dinner would be—as well as on road trips, and even on Rose Bowl trips. Woody delighted in telling this story: Clowser missed one Rose Bowl trip because his paper, owned by Scripps-Howard, was on strike. After a few days, Dietrich suggested to Woody, "You know Roy Howard, don't you? Why don't you call him and see if he can get Jack out here?" Woody made the call but never located Howard.

Some of his fellow scribes claimed Dietrich liked Woody's football because, without all that passing, he could finish his game story and make the 6:00 train back to Cleveland. Longer games meant a layover in Columbus.

Paul Brown happened to be one of my closest friends. At the time Woody was hired in 1951, I wanted Paul back coaching at Ohio State. But it didn't work out. I then cast my lot with the man my alma mater did pick as its coach. Woody said in many banquet introductions that my reaction to his hiring, under the circumstances, paved the way for a close friendship. It may have been awkward for each of us at times, but it never wavered—and it served both of our interests well.

There were other writers who got along well with Woody over the years, including Dick Otte, Wil Kilburger, and Lou Berliner of our paper; Kaye Kessler (my able and respected competitor on the Ohio State football "beat" for many seasons) and Tom Pastorius of the *Columbus Citizen* (later *Citizen-Journal*); Earl Flora of the *Ohio State Journal*; Ed Chay of the *Cleveland Plain-Dealer*; the UPI's Gene Caddes; and Pat Harmon of the *Cincinnati Post*, to name a close few. There were a number outside Ohio, too, including Paul Zimmerman of the *Los Angeles Times*; Dick Cummum of the *Minneapolis Tribune*; and Bert McGrane of the *Des Moines Register*. Even acerbic Jim Schlemmer of the *Akron Beacon-Journal* became a convert.

Most writers were capable of seeing Woody's best side if

they gave him a chance. The Tournament of Roses thought up a new wrinkle prior to the 1976 Rose Bowl: a press breakfast. Woody Hayes was "Mr. Congeniality" on this trip. One West Coast writer, overwhelmed by the transformation, referred to him as "a genteel old philosopher"—although the old coach announced that very afternoon, "I've been 'good old Woody' long enough!"

At the breakfast, though, he won over the press. Marveled one L.A. writer, "How are you going to fight a guy who mentions Plato, Khrushchev, and Lana Turner in the same sentence?"

"You're doggone right, I'm an idealist," Woody had said, espousing one of his favorite philosophies. "I've been looking up all my life. I've been a hero-worshipper from way back in the 1920s. When I was in Viet Nam seven years ago, Lana Turner was there, too. While I was talking with her, all of a sudden she looked up and I said, 'You're more beautiful than ever when you look up.' I know of no one who isn't more beautiful when they're looking up."

Hayes once set forth a blueprint for young coaches in dealing with the media. "Tell the truth, or say nothing," he counseled. "To mislead the press is neither ethical nor sensible." He advised them to follow his own strict policy of "taking the blame for a loss" and "carefully avoiding any comment that can be construed as criticism of a player or an assistant coach."

As for "reading your press clippings," he quoted his favorite chapter from Ralph Waldo Emerson's essay, *Compensation*:

> The wise man throws himself on the side of his assailants. . . . Blame is safer than praise. . . . I hate to be defended in a newspaper. As long as all that is said, is said against me, I feel a certain assurance of success. But as soon as honeyed words of praise are spoken for me, I feel as one who lies unprotected before his enemies.

Retired Ohio State freshman coach Tiger Ellison studied oratory, wrote a book on the subject, practiced what he preached, and impressed audiences. Woody brought him back as the speaker for the OSU clinic banquet for Ohio high school football coaches. Ellison related a conversation he claimed to have had with Woody:

Ellison: When are you going to retire?

Hayes: I'm never going to retire. I'll probably die right there on the 50-yard line in Ohio Stadium.

Ellison: But, Wood, what if the score is on the wrong side?

Hayes: Then I won't go!

The coaches laughed and laughed. "Of course Woody didn't say those things," Tiger attested later. "I just made it up. I thought the coaches would get a kick out of it."

I related it in the next day's Dispatch, again as a joke. Unfortunately, as the story circulated, the quotes were mistaken as genuine and serious. After the Gator Bowl incident, one writer cited the "I won't go" kicker as an example of "the incredible arrogance of the man."

20

DOTTING THE "i"

I called it a "love feast," the halftime events I watched in Ohio Stadium during the Ohio State-Wisconsin game on October 29, 1983. Other patriarchs of Buckeye football agreed that it was five minutes of the most delicious emotion ever experienced during these intermission spectaculars.

Applause and shouts of "Hi, Woody!" and "Yea, Woody!" had begun when Woody Hayes emerged from under the stands and walked onto the running track, a few minutes before the Buckeyes and Badgers concluded a wild opening half. The first great swell of excitement, applause, and cheering blossomed when Hayes moved to midfield to receive a framed certificate signifying his election to the National College Football Hall of Fame. Ohio State's 192-piece marching band blared "Auld Lang Syne," while 25 of its members unfurled a huge caricature of the old coach, providing a backdrop for the ceremony.

Even with the stadium sound system on high volume, the presentation speeches could barely be heard over the excited roar of the multitude. Woody then silently executed one of the much-advertised basics of his football, the hand-off: OSU President Ed Jennings accepted the certificate on behalf of the University and shouted into the microphone, "Coach Hayes, you do us great honor!" As the group left the field, the 89,000+ crowd, already standing en masse, poised for the real dramatics.

Hayes retired to the sideline where the band was assembling. A score of the young musicians dashed over to shake his hand and say "Hi, Coach!" or "Thanks, Coach." Then they took the field and played "Across the Field," followed by the first strains of "Le Regiment." The Ohio Stadium faithful knew what that meant: Coming up was the band's signature maneuver, the "Incomparable Script Ohio," climaxed by one of the hallowed traditions of Ohio State football—"the dotting of the i."

Drum major Bruce Hart paced the fast-stepping musicians through a script O, then an h, then an i —without the dot— and finally o. The stadium faithful, already making an ear-pounding din, went berserk as Hart came to the sidelines and grabbed Woody by the arm. Ushered to the i spot normally occupied by a senior tuba player, Lieutenant Commander W.W. Hayes, U.S.N. Ret., drew himself to attention and smartly saluted the American flag at the south end of the stadium. An ocean of sound— applause, cheers, screaming, foot-stomping, and whistling— swept down out of the stands and engulfed the field. It must have been heard as far away as Toledo. The demonstration continued for minutes, and no matter how old-time melodramatic it may sound, there weren't many dry eyes in the house.

As Hayes walked around the west side of the stadium on his way back to his seat in the press box, a strong-voiced fan leaned over the rim 98 feet above and yelled, "Hey, Woody we love ya!" It summed up the most moving halftime tribute in memory.

Director Paul Droste said earlier that band members had originated the idea of this salute to Hayes. It was nostalgia at its thickest, yet the student section and "Block O" may have been the loudest—who could judge degrees at a moment like that? And most of them would have been in high school when Woody finished coaching.

Woody, frankly touched and still savoring that outpouring of appreciation and affection, talked about it the next day. "Those fans made me feel very, very good," he attested. "It makes you feel good to see fans get as enthused as they did yesterday. I thought it was wonderful."

He said that on the way down to the field he had thought about saluting the flag, especially since that national symbol he loved and respected so much flew that day at half-mast to honor the Marines who had died in a terrorist bombing in Lebanon. "Here was this small flag[it was actually a huge flag, but Woody's eyesight had begun to ebb] at half-mast because of those Marines who lost their lives a week ago," he mused, "and I worried about seeing the flag. But I made up my mind I had to salute."

He credited the professors at the Faculty Club for his appearance in the trademark black baseball cap with the scarlet O. He explained that "they had asked me last Friday if I was going to wear the baseball cap. I hadn't thought of it, but they said I had to do it, so I went down to John Bozick and got a cap and wore it."

But the nostalgia overtook the physical incidentals. "When you get recognition like that, or any reward," he said, "you start looking back at all the people who have had a part in it, your players, your coaches, the administration, the University, the fans. I found that I did become emotional out there yesterday, because I thought of all the great victories we've had and all the great people we've had. It makes you realize how doggone lucky you are."

Some years earlier, I had asked Hayes to discuss some of those great victories for a magazine article, but he declined. "I hate to reminisce," he reasoned. "That always softens people. You think about the good things and forget the bad."

But once out of coaching and past the Gator Bowl aftermath, he was free to savor some highlights. "In 1952, my second year, we beat Illinois, which had been the Big Ten champion the year before," Woody recalled. "John Borton threw three touchdown passes in 20 minutes. Then we beat the team up north [Michigan] the next Saturday, and that helped both the team and me. It was the first victory Ohio State had had against them in eight years. Fred Bruney intercepted three passes in the first half! Not long ago, he called me up on the week of the Michigan game and said, 'Do you know what happened on this date 30 years ago?' and I told him, 'You're doggone right I do!' He's coaching with the Atlanta Falcons now.

"In the 1954 game, we stopped them on the six-inch line and marched the length of the field. They had first down on our four, but we held 'em out of the end zone. Pictures of that goal-line stand still resemble the Marines' goal-line stand on Mount Sarubacci, except for the flag. Jim Parker, Hubert Bobo, Hop Cassady, it looked like just about our whole team was in that pileup. Then we marched 99 yards and six inches for a touchdown to go ahead. Cassady had a big 61-yard run in there.

"Jack Gibbs, who was substituting for Bobo, intercepted a pass and took it down to the 11-yard line late in the second quarter, and Dave Leggett threw a pass to our right end in the end zone. That end was Fred Kriss, who is an outstanding doctor up in Madison, Wisconsin, now. Fred tightened up his shoelaces and kicked the extra point to tie the game 7-7. Gibbs' interception was a real, real big play, because in the first half Michigan had outgained us terribly. That turned it around. We won the game and the first Big Ten championship I ever had.

"Then we went to the Rose Bowl and won there for an unbeaten season and a national championship. We won seven straight Big Ten games, and only one team had ever done that in one season: the University of Chicago in 1913 under the great Amos Alonzo Stagg.

"In our fifth game of the season, we beat Wisconsin for a great victory. They'd come to our stadium number two in the country. We were trailing 7-3 in the third quarter when Cassady picked off a Wisconsin pass and got some good blocks on the way to a great 88-yard touchdown. I said it was the most spectacular play in our stadium in 20 years. It sure was a big one for our team, and for me. After that, we scored three more times in a 20-minute period.

"The morning of our game with Southern Cal in the Rose Bowl, I looked out and saw that it had started to rain. I emphasized to the quarterbacks that the team that avoided fumbles would win. Leggett handled the ball 82 times in that rain and mud and never fumbled once. We got a big win.

"In 1955, we had lost a lot of players from the year before, but we still had Cassady and Parker. We started by winning two, and then we lost two. But then we went to Wisconsin and started another winning streak. We fell behind 14-0 right away. I learned later that when our trainer Ernie Biggs went on the field, the players asked him how I was taking it, and he said not very good. They said, 'Tell him not to worry. We're still going to win.' And they were as good as their word.

"In our final home game, against Iowa, Cassady ran 45 yards on the belly play for a touchdown on our first play from scrimmage. It was his last home game, and the crowd gave him a well-deserved standing ovation when I took him out in the fourth quarter.

"Up at Ann Arbor, their team only crossed the 50-yard line once against our defense. But Parker made a tackle in their backfield on the next play, putting them back where they belonged. We only scored 17 points, but they didn't score any. I had never seen one good team so dominate another good team."

Michigan had been favored for the Big Ten title and the Rose Bowl bid that year, but the loss to Ohio State meant that the Wolverines' hated rival, Michigan State, would get the trip to Pasadena. They didn't take it well. "When some of their players showed their frustrations late in the game and incurred penalties, some of our players pointed to the scoreboard and shouted, 'UNPACK!'" Hayes recalled with a chuckle. Ohio State thus reigned as champion for a second straight year, although at that time the conference did not permit a team to appear in the Rose Bowl two years in a row.

"Our Iowa game in 1957 is one that many people still remember as one of our greatest games." Woody claimed. "They had great personnel and a great record, and they led us 13-10 in the fourth quarter in a hard-fought battle. At 7:51 on the clock, we started a drive. Our fullback Bob White proceeded to carry the ball seven of eight times and took us 68 yards to a touchdown. We held on to clinch the title and the Rose Bowl. He was going so well we just kept calling his number."

Iowa coach Forest Evashevski told writers after the game, "It was fantastic! We knew what was happening, knew how it was happening, but couldn't stop it. One boy carrying seven of eight times for 68 yards, I never expect to see it again in the Big Ten!"

Woody liked to recall that the vice president of the United States, Richard M. Nixon, was in the stands at that game, and that he called it the "greatest game I ever saw."

Ohio State edged Michigan in the season-ender and beat Oregon in the Rose Bowl on Don Sutherin's field goal to rank number one in the final United Press poll.

In 1961 the Buckeyes were tied by Texas Christian in the season opener, but they finished the season with a historic 50-21 romp over Michigan, the most points ever scored by OSU in the torrid interstate rivalry. "The last game was one of the most explosive we had played up to that time," Woody declared. "Bob Ferguson's touchdown put us ahead 14-0 in the second quarter, but their punt returner scored on a 90-yard run. Paul Warfield broke a great run for an 80-yard score. We had everybody blocked on the play but the safetyman. Paul put a move on him into the sidelines and broke inside. The kid fell on his behind. The crowd laughed, which I didn't like. Paul also ran 70 yards with a pass and Bob Klein scored on an 80-yard pass play.

"After our great victory, we heard on the bus to the airport that Wisconsin had upset Minnesota, giving us the undisputed Big Ten championship and presumably the Rose Bowl. Later, the Football Writers Association picked us as national champions."

Because the Pacific Coast Conference had disbanded, the agreement between the Big Ten and the Rose Bowl was no longer technically in force, but it was the general understanding that the Big Ten champion would again be the visiting team. Ohio State received the invitation, but the administration lateraled the decision to the Faculty Council. On Tuesday, after a round of oratory on both sides, the ballots added up to 28 against accepting the bowl bid, 25 in favor.

"I was in Cleveland to speak at the OSU alumni dinner," Hayes remembered, "when Dick Larkins called me. I was so upset that I left the hotel and walked around for maybe an hour. I didn't want to go before an audience and say some things I might later regret. I finally went back to the banquet and made my speech. I guess I still couldn't keep from showing the anger I felt, not for myself, but for our team. They got cheated out of a Rose Bowl trip.

"I learned afterward that back in Columbus, students had marched to the Statehouse and later started a protest rally on the campus. Our co-captain, Mike Ingram, heard about it and went there to help the police. He grabbed a police bullhorn and told the crowd that no one was more disappointed than the football players, but 'If we can stand it, you can stand it. Go home!' I was proud of that example of leadership outside the football field.

"But we still didn't go to the Rose Bowl, even though we had earned it." Although Woody had many friends among the faculty and was admittedly well respected in academia, campus opponents had apparently seized an opportunity to deal a blow to "big-time football."

"We didn't win the championship for the next six years, although we finished second three times," Hayes pointed out.

"Our recruiting definitely suffered because of the 1961 Rose Bowl turndown."

The Faculty Council reversed its vote the following year, after a contract between the Big Ten, the new Pacific Eight, and the Rose Bowl had been negotiated.

By 1967 recruiting had recovered. Recalled Hayes, "We brought to our campus in that fall the finest group of talented football players we had ever recruited, maybe as good a freshman class as anybody has ever recruited. Thirteen of them would break into the starting lineup as sophomores, and seven of them would become All-Americans, two of them twice. And several others deserved that recognition as well.

"In 1968, when this group joined the varsity, we had several truly great games. Purdue came into our stadium with pretty much the same players who had embarrassed us the year before, 41-6. They were number one in the country, led by All-American Leroy Keyes and highly rated quarterback Mike Phipps. We went through them for 73 yards early in the game, but missed a field goal. Later in the first half, we missed another field goal. This was our first big test and we were tight, making mistakes, and getting penalties.

"In the third quarter, we got our big play. Jack Tatum had just played tremendous defense on Keyes. Phipps saw Tatum go with Keyes deep on a pass play, so he felt the out-cut would be open. But Teddy Provost stepped into it at full speed and sprinted 35 yards to the end zone. Later in the quarter, we worked the ball to the Purdue 15, where Rex Kern was hurt. I put in Billy Long, a senior, because I wanted the more experienced man in that situation. Some of the crowd booed, apparently feeling Ron Maciejowski, another fine sophomore, should go in. We called a delay pass to Jan White, but he was covered; so Long ran up the middle and scored. Now the crowd cheered. Our defense was out of this world. We shut out this strong Purdue team 13-0, and it was a great boost for the confidence of our young team."

The Illinois game two weeks later may not have been as big as the Purdue game, but it was crucial. The Buckeyes rolled to a 24-0 lead in the first half, but the host Illini did an amazing turnaround, scoring three touchdowns and three two-point conversions for a 24-24 tie in the fourth quarter. On the first play after we got the ball back, Rex Kern got hurt. This time, I put

Maciejowski in because of his scrambling ability. He hit a 44-yard pass down the middle to Larry Zelina on the four, and Jim Otis took it in to give us a hard-earned victory, 31-24."

With a capacity crowd jamming Ohio Stadium, the Buckeyes finished the 1968 season in an appropriate manner, beating Michigan and scoring 50 points against the Wolverines for the second time in eight years. "We scored twice in the first half, but they pulled even," noted Woody. "Just before the half, we went 84 yards to put us up by 21-14, and in the second half we made a rout of it. That gave us another unbeaten season, another undisputed Big Ten title, and the Rose Bowl."

The Rose Bowl couldn't have been bigger. It was for the national championship, with Ohio State at 9-0 and number one in the polls; Southern Cal was 9-0-1 and number two. The game had the greatest buildup of any Rose Bowl. That was partly due to the Buckeyes' spectacular sophomores and that Southern Cal was powered by one of the greatest backs of all time, O.J. Simpson.

Hayes recalled, "O.J. soon showed us why he was the Heisman Trophy winner. We contained him on a sweep at our right end, but he cut back against the grain and outran everybody 80 yards for a touchdown. That put them ahead 10-0 early in the second quarter. Rex Kern passed 17 yards to Ray Gillian to the four and Otis scored. Jim Roman kicked a field goal to tie at 10-10 as the half ended. I still felt we would win, and we started to take command in the third quarter. Roman kicked another field goal, Kern passed to Leo Hayden for one touchdown and to Gillian for another, so we led 27-10. In the last minute, they threw a pass into the end zone. One official called it an interception by our Mike Polaski, and another official called it a touchdown for Southern Cal. I went out on the field to get the ruling, and they charged me 15 yards. But it didn't matter. We still won 27-16 for the undisputed national championship and another unbeaten season."

For sheer drama, few games in Ohio Stadium matched Ohio State-Oklahoma in 1977. The Sooners ran up a 20-0 lead early in the second quarter, but the Buckeyes mounted a magnificent comeback to go ahead 28-20. A pair of late fourth-quarter fumbles proved their undoing, but a last-second field goal decided it for Oklahoma. Asked if it was the most thrilling game he'd ever seen, Hayes ruefully replied, "I'd rather have it dull and win."

Bo Schembechler had been immersed in Michigan football from early August of 1985 through the Ohio State game on November 22. Then came recruiting, preliminary planning for the Fiesta Bowl, and Thanksgiving. Finally he had a day off. How did he spend it? In Columbus, visiting Woody Hayes, who at the time was battling back from the double body-blow of a stroke and a mild heart problem. The visit tacitly confirmed Bo's deep-down feelings about his former coach, former boss, and former sparring-mate in the Big Ten's most storied and intense coaching rivalry.

He brought along a cherry pie baked by his wife Millie as her personal contribution to boosting the old coach's spirits. Woody's taste for pie often overpowered his diabetic's diet. Cherries ranked high on his list of temptations.

Bo drove Woody to the Jai-Lai for lunch. They stayed for almost three hours. The coaches finally adjourned to 1711 Cardiff Road, where Woody stretched out on a couch and Bo picked a wooden rocker.

They talked about a range of subjects, and I was fortunate to have been privy to the conversation. I don't remember any discussion of the classic football games that climaxed each season of the incomparable "Woody vs. Bo" decade. This time it was just friend to friend, up close and personal.

I kept thinking that here was a bona fide historic meeting: the two most dominant figures in Big Ten football for the last 30 years, sharing a day, a lunch, and a conversation in an atmosphere of mutual admiration—and love.

I kept marveling at how alike they were: cast from the same mold, cut from the same cloth, whatever cliché came to mind. In his early years at Michigan, Schembechler had been tagged "Little Woody," which he sharply resented and rightly so. He soon proved that he was a major personality and a superb coach in his own right.

But the similarities were undeniable—the intensity, the work ethic, the dedication, the from-the-hip outspokenness, the unpredictability, the volatility on the sidelines, the plain-talk good sense off the field, the commanding drive, and the almost religious fervor for the best IN college athletics and the best FOR college athletics.

21

THE "TEN-YEAR WAR"

T he 1969 game at Michigan stuck in Woody Hayes' memory, but not in the "great times" section. The Wolverines' rookie coach, Glenn Edward Schembechler, proved that he'd learned his lessons well from the old master.

"They beat the greatest team that ever stepped on a college football field, best team we ever put together," declared Hayes. "We were so far ahead in the polls it wasn't even close. We'd beaten everybody we played by four touchdowns or more [low margin of victory, 34-7; total points 371-69]. That team would have been national champions without a doubt. We went into the last game with an 8-0 record and a chance to break our own record of 17 straight Big Ten wins. But Bo beat us! We scored the first time we had the ball, but they got a couple of long punt returns that helped them get ahead by 24-12 in the first half. And that was all the scoring.

"Rex Kern was hurting. They wanted to take some pictures after we worked out on Friday, and he stood outside sweaty and caught a chill. The next morning his back was so stiff he couldn't get out of bed. I shouldn't have played him, because Maciejowski could have done a better job. But I'm not going to alibi. Bo had his team ready and beat us. That was Bo's first year of coaching the team up north."

For one full year, through spring practice, fall practice, and even during the season, Hayes and the Buckeyes—and their fans—had one mission in mind: REVENGE! "We got them in our own stadium and beat them good, 20-9," Hayes pointed out. "I expect there was as much emotion in the stadium as there's ever been. We had been waiting for this day for a year, and so had our fans. We were ready."

Michigan came to the showdown 9-0 to Ohio's 8-0, with the Big Ten championship and the Rose Bowl at stake—just the conditions the Buckeyes wanted. "We got a field goal from Fred Schram and a touchdown pass from Kern to Jankowski to lead 10-3 at the half," recalls Hayes. "They scored early in the third quarter, but Tim Anderson blocked the extra point. We got another field goal, and Leo Hayden scored on a perfectly executed option from Rex Kern. I called that game 'our greatest victory.' WE had avenged our defeat of the year before and were again undisputed Big Ten champions, going to the Rose Bowl.

"That Rose Bowl was another great disappointment, because out there, we were beaten by Heisman Trophy winner Jim Plunkett and an underdog Stanford team. It cost us a virtually certain national championship, and it was only the second time our seniors had lost in 31 games. We came back from an early 0-10 to lead by a touchdown, but Plunkett hurt us with his passing and even some scrambling."

The monumental 1969 upset by Michigan and the satisfying Ohio State revenge in 1970 started what came to be called the "Ten-Year War" between Hayes and Schembechler. Ohio State-Michigan had been an intense football rivalry for half a century. The dominant, irrepressible personalities of Woody and Bo in conflict raised these annual stadium spectacles to a level never before experienced—and never again to be duplicated.

In eight of the ten years, "The Game" settled the Big Ten championship. Six times they shared the title. Each team represented the Big Ten in the Rose Bowl five times. Schembechler, billed as the "pupil," won five; Woody, the "teacher," won four; and they played one tie. With one exception, the ten were tough, close, dramatic battles in which defenses usually dominated, partially because both coaches played it "close to the vest." The Wolverines devastated Ohio's defense in the second half for a 22-0 final in 1976; but other point margins were, in order: 12, 11, 3, 3, 0, 2, 7, 8, and 11. Obviously, other games in those ten years were important, but Woody—and undoubtedly Bo—always remembered "The Game."

"We never lost to the school up north in the four years we had Arch." Hayes pointed out. But the defense rated top billing in 1972, Griffin's first year. "We played super defense," Hayes agreed. "In effect, that's what changed the ball game, those two great goal-line stands." The Buckeyes held for downs after Michigan had first down on the Ohio State one and then on the OSU five. So charged were Buckeye fans that several hundred swarmed out of the Ohio Stadium stands to attack the south goal posts with seconds remaining and Michigan again threatening.

Hayes sprinted down to the end zone to help the police restore order, but not before the goal posts fell. He explained the sprint: "I was afraid the officials might let Michigan try a field goal at the other end of the field; then they would have had the wind at their backs and might have tied us." But they didn't, and Ohio State thus qualified for the first of four straight Rose Bowl appearances.

Woody wasn't aware that the Athletic Department kept an emergency set of goal posts under the stands. "If I'd known that," he grimaced, "I could have saved myself a pulled [calf] muscle."

Hayes fielded some fan flack for the 1973 10-10 tie at Ann Arbor because he didn't call a pass play until the final minute of a struggle in which Ohio won the first half, Michigan the second. "Our quarterback [Cornelius Greene] had a thumb swollen to twice its size and could barely hold the ball," he explained. "We couldn't use him at all that week [in practice]. We tried to pass him a little bit on Wednesday, but he couldn't do it."

Since the teams had identical records, shared the championship, and had played a tie, Big Ten athletic directors voted for the Rose Bowl representative. Hayes was pessimistic, explaining, "I wasn't very popular, didn't try to be. They [Michigan] stood very strong in the conference politically. I thought the directors would vote for them." But about noon, Hayes received a confidential message. Sworn to secrecy until the official announcement, he called Anne, hummed "California Here I Come," and hung up. He also tore up his "concession" speech.

Ohio State proved its right to the Rose Bowl appearance by giving the old coach what he hailed as "the greatest victory I've ever had," adding, "It may be the greatest victory WE'VE ever had. The best game we've ever played." Green's thumb was healed, and he covered 129 yards with six pass completions, figuring in four of the six touchdowns in a 42-21 rout of USC.

The 1974 game with Michigan was more unusual than outstanding. "Bo had a great defensive team, and they did an enormous job that day," Hayes conceded, "but we moved the ball enough to get within kick range four times. Ordinarily, you wouldn't make all four field goals in four tries, but Tom Klaban kicked them all." Klaban's four field goals edged the Wolverines 12-10, the first time Woody had won without scoring a touchdown in 81 games. Mike Lantry, Michigan's All-Big Ten kicker, missed a field goal by a fraction in the last minute.

Woody's last great game of the "War" came in 1975 at Ann Arbor. "For two quarters, they controlled the game [14-7]," he said. "But in the second half, we went 80 yards to tie it up. Bo had said before the game that they weren't going to settle for a tie, so they started passing. Ray Griffin intercepted and ran it back to their three, and Pete Johnson took it in."

That 21-14 win meant Woody's last of eight trips to the Rose Bowl. He recalled: "I said after the game that this was our greatest comeback, so it had to be the greatest game I'd ever coached."

One often-told story claimed that Woody Hayes disliked "the school up north" so much that when his car ran out of gas near the Michigan-Ohio border, he pushed it into Ohio to avoid contributing to Michigan's economy.

He never confirmed that to me, but I know for certain that he once ran out of gas twice on the same trip. Lou Berliner of the Dispatch *staff was a passenger that night. They walked to the nearest filling station, returned with a can of gas, and went on because Woody figured there was another station ahead. There wasn't. This time a kindly motorist came to the rescue.*

22

IN HIS FOOTSTEPS

L ou Holtz coached Ohio State's defensive backs in 1968, before embarking on a trail of head coaching jobs that eventually led to Notre Dame. When a Columbus organization planned a "roast" for Woody in February 1987, Hayes was accorded the right to choose the "roasters." He wanted Holtz, among others. But Holtz explained that he would be in Arizona for Notre Dame alumni meetings. "To hell with that, I want you here!" Hayes said.

Holtz flew to Columbus by private plane, arriving after the roast had started. He wowed the audience, as he always does. He shook a few hands, then hurried back to the airport for his return to Arizona for the next day's meetings.

Asked why he had made such a whirlwind round trip, Holtz said simply, "Woody said he wanted me here! And here I am!" He joked with a friend later, "I got to thinking about it. Here I am the head coach at Notre Dame, I've been away from Ohio State for 19 years, and I'm still taking orders from Woody Hayes!

"Woody had more of a positive influence on my coaching career than any other single individual, perhaps all of them put together," Holtz insisted. "He was a legend in his own time. He taught me football, but more importantly, he taught me more about life than anybody else."

Call them "Woody's disciples." The 42 assistant coaches who served Ohio State from 1951 through 1978 bore—with pride—the unmistakable mark of Woody Hayes. He chose them well and they served him well. All of them benefited by exposure to the old master's words and deeds. Fourteen became college head coaches, four of them NFL head coaches, and six served as NFL assistants. At one time, 1984-85, half of the head coaches in the Big Ten were graduates of Hayes' staff: Bo Schembechler at Michigan, Holtz at Minnesota, Bill Mallory at Indiana, Dave McClain at Wisconsin, and Earle Bruce at Ohio State.

Holtz worked for Hayes for only one year, but it was long enough to assimilate career-shaping knowledge. "I don't think you can possibly be around Coach Hayes without having an awful lot of him in you," says Holtz, who produced a national championship team in his third year at Notre Dame (1988) and has been a leading contender for that title ever since. As long as I'm coaching, as long as Earle Bruce is coaching, as long as Bill Mallory is coaching, Woody Hayes will always be coaching. Everything we do is probably influenced by Woody Hayes. I haven't drastically changed my approach, my philosophy, the things I believe, since I left Ohio State. Coach Hayes just had that manner. Not only was he successful, but he did it the right way, the proper way, with good discipline and good fundamentals. He was hard-nosed, and he was concerned about his football players. Whether it was handling the staff or recruiting or any-thing else, Woody Hayes just had that way of influencing you."

Woody's strength as a coach? Holtz has a surprising twist: "Coach Hayes' greatest strength was that he didn't care whether you, as a coach or as a player, liked him. He didn't care whether the news media liked him or not. He didn't care what they wrote. What he worried about was players and coaches being the best they could be—having a standard for them, the hard-work ethic, good solid fundamentals. There isn't a guy who played for him or coached for him that didn't love him. You didn't love him when you were there. He had a standard that you might think was unrealistic. But doggone, when you looked back after reaching that standard, you felt good about being around him. He pushed you farther than you thought you were capable of going. You didn't like it while you were doing it, but if he worried about you liking him, he couldn't have done that."

Other keys to Hayes' success, Holtz feels, were "his intelli-gence and his inordinate ability to work and study. I don't know anybody who worked as hard as he did or read as much as he did. He was a great influence on me."

Holtz relates "Woody stories" in his speeches—and he makes about as many as Woody did—but one he likes especially concerns a personal experience during his first summer on Hayes' staff: "I went over to the office on a Sunday night," he says, "and I took my little children along. Skip was then about eight and Luanne about six. I thought we were alone in the building. There was a long hallway in the Athletic Department, and the kids got one of the secretary's chairs. One would sit in the chair and the other would push it down to the end of the hall, both of them screaming and yelling. Then they'd switch places and scream and holler some more.

"Coach Hayes had a unique ability to concentrate, but he came out of his office—at the time, we didn't know he was there because his door was closed—and he said, 'Goddammit, whose kids are those?' I came out of my office and said they were mine. He said, 'Boy, they sure are healthy, aren't they?' and went back into his office. I thought that was funny, but the real point is that I went to the office on a Sunday night in the summertime, and Coach Hayes was there, working! That was typical of his work ethic. He was just a tremendous guy. A super individual!"

Bill Mallory, who may have matched Hayes for intensity and emotion, turned Indiana into a bowl team and a Big Ten contender. "We're all different people," he stipulates, "but the man had tremendous influence on me and others. I find that a lot of things he believed in, I believe in. I think that when you look back, you see that there were a lot of things you were learning from Woody that you didn't realize at the time—his dedication, hard work, academics. A lot of the things I do today are structured on the same philosophy he had academically: the tutoring program he set up, the overall emphasis on graduation."

Lou McCullough once said that anyone who worked for Woody learned about hard work. Mallory agrees: "I marvelled at how hard Woody worked, his tremendous dedication to the game, how much he put his heart and soul into it. He never stopped looking for a different way to do things. He built such a good, stable, quality program. He was long-lasting and so consistent in producing that he was able to work through the lean years. He had his lean years, but he was able to work through them. He had what I call "elephant skin"— critics' barbs simply bounced off Hayes."

Mallory empathized with Earle Bruce, whom Woody once "fired" as "movie coach." Bill got "fired" as "weather coach" during his time on Woody's staff. "I had the misfortune to be the 'weatherman' when I came on the staff," he relates, "and Woody was so caught up in the [practice] field being covered. I asked Ralph Guarasci [in charge of athletic facilities] to cover the field, but he was reluctant because he thought the grass needed the rain. He didn't want it to die. But Woody didn't give a damn, he didn't want the field muddy. So I was kind of a referee.

"One Sunday night it started to rain, and I wondered if Ralph had covered the field. I ran out to the facility, and unfortunately the field wasn't covered. I went to Woody and told him we had a problem because the field wasn't covered, and he said, 'You're damned right, we got a problem!' The defensive staff had already gone, but we got hold of McCullough, Earle Bruce, and Sark [Esco Sarkkinen]—the offensive coaches were still meeting. Larry Catuzzi always took pride in the way he dressed, and he was wearing a nice sweater; and Tiger [Ellison] had been to church and still had his suit on.

"We all went out to the field, and it was raining cats and dogs. We tried to unroll that big tarp, but the wind caught it and blew it way up like a Barnum and Bailey circus tent. Woody was stuck out in the middle of the field with the tarp waving all around him—and screaming for us to get the doggone thing back down! We fought that baby for two hours. We worked our butts off, and in the end, by the time we got the tarp on, it stopped raining. I wish you could have seen us. We were all sopping wet. Catuzzi's sweater looked like a mini-skirt, and Tiger's suit shrank.

"I'd just come on the staff that year, and I'll never forget Hugh Hindman's quip: 'How do you like the big time?' Lou Holtz was the new member of the staff in 1968, so Woody fired me and gave the weatherman job to Holtz. That was one of my happiest days at Ohio State."

George Chaump spent 11 years on Woody Hayes' staff, which was 10-3/4 more than he anticipated at one stage of their working relationship. "My first year [1968] we were getting ready for spring practice," he relates. "Woody was at the blackboard lecturing like a school teacher, and we were like pupils. He was lecturing on the belly play [numbers 26 and 27, a tight T-formation]. He went through all the coaching points and on and on."

George, whose coaching experience had been at Harrisburg (Pennsylvania) High School, listened and took notes, disagreeing to himself. When Woody came back for the afternoon session with more talk about the belly play, George raised his hand and asked: "Is this the offense we're going to run this year?" Woody said yes, "Unless you know something better."

Young and new to Woody's convictions, Chaump said he did and proceeded to expound on the I-formation. Woody asked him what play he'd run first, and Chaump replied, "I'd run the tailback off tackle from the I-formation." Woody then asked him why, and Chaump thought he gave him all the positives. But Woody said, "It'll never work. You got the [tail]back seven yards deep, and the fullback leads him where he's going. That's lighthouse football, that I-formation. You got the fullback showing where every play goes. If you think you're going to come in here and make my fullbacks into glorified blocking guards, you're in the wrong place. I'm a fullback coach and you better know that. The fullback play is a lot better for a number of reasons: He's closer to the ball, he hits better, he's more flexible, the ball can go inside or outside. You can run that thing right or left. It's the most deceptive play in football."

The rookie coach made his second mistake. "I put up an argument," Chaump admits. "With that he said, 'Anybody tells me an I-back off tackle is better than a fullback isn't going to work for Woody Hayes. You get the hell out of here.' I was shocked. I must have been chartreuse. I went back for my pen and out the door. Woody came out after me and said, 'George, get back here! I've never fired anybody in my life, and I'm not going to break my record on you.'"

One of the other coaches suggested that maybe young George's ideas merited consideration. Woody listened. He was a great listener and more amenable to change than his reputation suggested. He ordered films from several schools that successfully ran the I-formation, and Chaump points out, "We opened up the season that fall with the I and used the belly play on short yardage and inside the 20 [yard line]."

But, confesses the present Naval Academy head coach: "Twenty-two years later, you know what? Woody's famous 26-

27 is still a great play. When we played Army, the belly play went for 48 yards for a touchdown. Every time I run that damn play, I think of Woody—that old son-of-a-gun had so much wisdom!

"Everybody who ever coached for Woody is a better person and a hell of a coach because you learned all the practical things that make you win football games. You learned why you win: the simple things that everybody else takes for granted but that Woody emphasized: the simple, basic, fundamental things, the value of the people part of football—he was a master at motivating people and underscoring the importance of execution in the success of a play."

Woody considered play 26-27 "our trademark." Once asked why he ran it so much, he said, tongue in cheek, "We're going to keep running it until we get it just right." Chaump remembers, "When we added the outside option, Woody said we'd call it 38-39. Somebody asked why not 28-29 and he said, 'Hell with it, 38-39 is what I know, and that's what we're calling it.' Every time we'd take on a new play, which Woody liked to do, he'd say, 'What can we call it?' Somebody would say that it ties in with this and that, and he'd say, 'Naw. What numbers haven't we used yet? Pick a number.'"

"Woody stories" are something that all of Hayes' disciples share. But as Mallory puts it, "There are a lot of Woody stories, but they're all done with respect. He was unique."

Even his most blindly defensive backer would concede that Woody Hayes had a temper both quick and volcanic. Even he made that concession, sometimes ruefully, though rarely apologetically.

Athletic Director Jim Jones recalls a time when one of the Buckeye football players landed in jail for taking part in a student prank. "I had the unenviable task of telling Woody," he recalls. "He was in the projection room over at the Biggs Facility, and he dumped over every chair in that room. He hit some, kicked some, threw some. When he finally got done, he set up a chair, sat down and said, 'Now, what are we going to do about this?' He was a master at that. He'd get it all out and then he'd say, 'How are we going to solve this problem?' Then HE'D solve it!"

Which led Bill Myles to proclaim Woody "the problem solver." It also parallels the old coach's approach to personal disputes: He'd erupt, get it out, and let life go on.

"If you had an argument with Coach Hayes," says Lou McCullough, an OSU staff member for nine years, "the next day it was forgotten."

As many a player could attest, it usually didn't take overnight. Give him half an hour. Assuming, that is, that the object of his disaffection was on "our side," someone he liked. If not, forgetting might take a little longer.

23

WARTS AND ALL

The December chill gave Woody Hayes' face a bluish cast, appropriate to the mood within. His 1978 Ohio State football team had lost the regular-season final to bitter rival Michigan for the third straight year, missing at least a share of the Big Ten championship for the first time in six years and only the second time in the last ten.

This day he had reassembled the squad to begin preparation for a bowl game, but not one of the "Big Four." The Buckeyes had been in the Rose Bowl six times in the previous ten seasons and in the Orange Bowl and Sugar Bowl once each. This time it would be the Gator Bowl—and not even on New Year's Day, but December 29.

One hand anchored on his knee, fingers of the other hand groping through tousled gray hair, he roused himself from staring at the office floor and looked to a solitary visitor. "I can't coach anymore," he said simply. "It's tough to coach after you're 50, and I'm 65, a pretty damned tired old 65 right now. I should have retired when I wanted to last August."

His retirement had been a subject of lively press speculation for seasons, speculation he rather enjoyed. Friends and fans kept calling Mrs. Hayes after each rumor, telling her not to let him retire, or they delivered the same message to him in person. "Frankly, it's a great compliment," he confessed. "You can't help but appreciate it."

But through the years, he always demurred: "I don't know what I'm going to do. Before I leave coaching, I've got to find a job I like better." And everybody knew he'd never find anything better than coaching.

So in August of 1978, had he decided to make the move from the coaching line? "Yeah," he conceded. "But my coaches talked me out of it."

Why August? "If I'd retired in August [with fall football practice imminent], I could have slid _____ in there as head coach without all that other stuff, and my football would have gone right on." "That other stuff" meant the standard University process of appointing a screening committee, interviewing candidates, and weeks later finally hiring a replacement.

But why retire? "It probably was time." Though he didn't explain further, one reason seemed apparent to those closest to him: fatigue. He came in from practice some nights, plopped down on the leather cot that occupied half his office, and sat for a long time, maybe unlacing his cleated shoes, maybe just resting.

His schedule, suggested one of his doctors, would have "put an ordinary man six feet under." But this was no ordinary man. Although the engine had been racing at high speed for so long, it had begun to show wear—and then there was the diabetes, for which he had medication, though he rarely remembered to take it. "He didn't feel well the last two, three years he coached," attests Dr. Robert Murphy, OSU team physician from 1952 to the present and the Hayes family physician. "The diabetes took a real toll."

But there was always one more long-coveted prize, often at his fingertips, each time snatched away. Before calling it a career, he wanted another jewel in his coaching crown, another national championship. Since the Buckeyes' last title in 1968, the vision had agonizingly diminished.

His 1970 team, unbeaten, number one in the polls, and with six All-Americans in the lineup, had charged toward a national title, but was upset by underdog Stanford in the Rose Bowl. Though once beaten, the 1972 team might have been a national champion had it defeated the eventual poll winner, USC, in the Rose Bowl. But the Buckeyes lost big.

A 10-10 tie with Michigan in 1973 so damaged the Buckeyes in the pollsters' eyes that even a 42-21 show of power against USC in the Rose Bowl could lift them no higher than third (in UPI). A loss to Michigan State notwithstanding, Ohio still had a shot at the national championship in 1974. But a one-point loss to Southern Cal in the Rose Bowl banished Ohio to third (UPI) and fourth (AP).

The 1975 team, with second-time Heisman Trophy winner Archie Griffin and three other All-Americans, arrived at the Rose Bowl with an 11-0 record, and a solid number-one ranking. They were facing a UCLA team they had defeated by 21 points in the regular season. So bitterly disappointed was Hayes by UCLA's 23-10 Rose Bowl ambush that he closed the dressing room to all visitors after the game and escaped to the team bus without speaking to the press.

An early defeat and tie crippled hopes in 1976, and a jarring 22-0 beating by Michigan finished them off. The 1977 team dropped a 29-28 last-second heartbreaker to Oklahoma in one of the all-time great Ohio Stadium games, but any national recognition disappeared with later losses to Michigan and Alabama.

The Alabama game was a lavishly ballyhooed Sugar Bowl match-up of two football giants, Bear Bryant and Woody Hayes, the number-one and number-two career winners among active coaches. The Crimson Tide boosted the Bear's victory total by one and inflicted a galling mark in Woody's loss column. He gave the Louisiana Superdome crowd a hint of his feelings as he left the field at halftime, the Buckeyes trailing 13-0. He slammed his left fist into the goal post—fortunately well-padded—with knockout power.

Now came 1978, a season that began in controversy and ended in chaos. Woody beat Michigan in an off-field skirmish in February, seven months before the first on-field scrimmage of September.

Max Schlichter's family, on a farm near Bloomingburg, 40 miles south of Columbus, included an 18-year-old son whose athletic ability had drawn college recruiters from all over the nation. Lithe and handsome young Arthur Schlichter reigned as king of the year's high school quarterback crop. While leading his high school team to 29 wins and a tie in 30 games, the 6-foot-3, 190-pounder overheated statisticians' calculators with 4,397 yards passing (264 completions in 478 attempts), 1,660 yards rushing, and a grand total of 75 touchdowns accounted for. He kept busy in the off-season as a point guard for the school's basketball team, which twice reached the state tournament.

Hayes already had an outstanding quarterback, but signing Schlichter became an absolute must for the old master recruiter. His chief opposition in the spirited battle, which matched
the on-field "war" for intensity, was none other than Michigan's
Schembechler. Bo had entertained Art on the weekend of the
1977 Ohio State game in Ann Arbor, which Michigan won. The
following Thursday, Thanksgiving, Woody and Anne joined the
Schlichter family for that day's traditional turkey-and-all-the-
trimmings farm-style feast—with Hayes' subtle salesmanship as
a side dish.

Art revealed later that "I was brought up watching Ohio
State football," which helped stack the odds against Schembechler.
He also confessed that, though a Michigan guest at the game, "I
was cheering for Ohio State. I was considering Michigan pretty
heavily for a long time, but those people up there were anti-Ohio,
and that kinda turned me off."

Young Schlichter's decision created great jubilation among
Buckeye followers and an immediate quarterback controversy.
Or, if not exactly controversy, at least rife speculation: Would
Woody stay with two-year starter Rod Gerald, a brilliant option
operator, with Schlichter as backup? Would he install the freshman as the starter, with Gerald as back-up, or switch him to
another position? All through preseason practices in September,
the guessing game continued. Both worked at quarterback, with
Gerald also taking a turn at wide receiver. Woody coyly delayed
any public decision.

While Penn State kicked off and the Buckeyes took posses-
sion on their own 20 in the season's opening play, Gerald and
Schlichter stood together at Hayes' side. Then he sent both on the
field to an approving roar of the home crowd. Schlichter lined up
under center, Gerald as wide receiver.

A Penn State team that would eventually finish fourth in
the nation rudely initiated the rookie quarterback into big-time
college football. But though the experience jolted him, it didn't
intimidate him. Schlichter went on to establish Ohio State passing, total offense, and touchdown records that weren't approached
during the ensuing decade and could well survive for a century
(7,547 yards passing; 8,850 total offense; 85 TDs accounted for).

Schlichter's arrival may have been another reason Hayes
elected to stick with the job in 1978. And once he had made the
decision, he coached with no less intensity than in the previous

27 seasons. His will to win never wavered, though in August he had nearly put it on the shelf permanently.

Now, after a disappointing 7-3-1 record and fourth place in the Big Ten, the Gator Bowl represented one last chance to salvage something, to go out with a bowl victory—if Hayes actually would make this his last stand. The game would be nationally televised, opposing Clemson, ranked seventh in the polls, and the Buckeyes were definite underdogs—the kind of challenge Woody always relished. Hayes plunged into the effort like a man on a mission. In the mud of a high school field, he drove his squad hard, and in rain, wind, and cold that turned most Jacksonville, Florida, practices into ordeals.

A gag gift at a Gator Bowl luncheon the day before the game proved bitterly ironic in light of later events. In introducing Hayes, sportscaster Keith Jackson presented him with a pair of boxing gloves, the bowl committee's joking allusion to Woody's combative reputation. Hayes did not appear amused, nor was he thrown off-stride. He delivered his usual crowd-pleasing speech.

On game night, midway through the final quarter of the 1978 Gator Bowl, Ohio State trailed 17-9. But freshman Schlichter led his team 88 yards, scoring his second TD of the game to close the margin. He was stopped short on a two-point conversion try that would have created a 17-17 tie.

Minutes later, middle guard Tim Sawicki revitalized Buckeye hopes and snuffed out a Clemson threat with a fumble recovery on the Tigers' 44. Schlichter continued his brilliance in a drive to third down and five on the Clemson 24. He dropped back to pass, retreated under a rush, then threw. Clemson middle guard Charlie Bauman dropped out of the line—as Jim Stillwagon used to do with such success—and intercepted.

"I was throwing to [tailback] Ron Springs," a red-eyed Schlichter explained after the game. "He wasn't open for a minute, but when I rolled out, I saw him come open and I came back to him. I didn't see the linebacker." With only 1:59 remaining, Woody's hopes—and his team's—were shattered again. He had poured full effort into the quest for victory and, as All-American linebacker Tom Cousineau said, the Buckeyes had "laid everything on the line."

Bauman was tackled at the sideline, almost at the feet of OSU coaches and players. As he jumped up with the ball, Woody stunned him, his own team, and a nationwide television audience by lashing out, landing a half-clenched right fist to Bauman's neck, just below his face mask.

Defensive coordinator George Hill and Buckeye players, notably guard Ken Fritz, grabbed the frustrated head coach, and he eventually calmed down. After the officials marched off a 15-yard penalty against Ohio State, Hayes incurred another 15 for a vehement protest that too much time had disappeared from the game clock.

Bauman was hesitant to talk about the incident to sports writers in the dressing room after the game or later, but attested that he had been surprised but not hurt by the blow. But Woody WAS hurt by it, as much as a man could be hurt. He didn't speak to reporters either after the game or "on the record" for another month. Hill represented him at a postgame press conference outside the locker room.

Athletic Director Hugh Hindman, who had watched from the press box, entered the locker room grim-faced and exited a few minutes later, still grim-faced. The players and assistant coaches left by buses for their hotel. Most of the media had gone when Hill motioned for me and said, "He wants to see you."

Woody was sitting on a metal chair in a dingy cubicle off the main locker room. What happened in the following 30 minutes I didn't consider journalistic privilege. I discovered later that my tape recorder had been running inadvertently, but I listened to only a portion of it then and have never since played it.

I have called the session a "soliloquy of anger and frustration"; I might have added "career termination." The old coach, alternately angry and depressed, suggested he'd prefer a quick departure from Jacksonville rather than waiting for the planned next-day jet flight to Columbus. I offered a seat on the *Dispatch* plane waiting at the airport for immediate takeoff. He quickly reconsidered, deciding to stay with his team.

Senior student manager Mark George was stowing gear, but fortunately he was out of the line of fire when Woody punctuated his monologue by hurling a metal folding chair at a covey of lockers, with a resounding clatter. "I'm so damned sick and tired of losing I don't know what to do!" he snapped.

Eventually he draped his coat over his arm and we stepped outside the locker room. Only a half-dozen fans were still around, hardly noticing as the 65-year-old, gray-haired man walked slowly, head down, to a waiting automobile. It was one of the saddest moments of my life—and his. As I feared, I was watching not only the end of a great career, but the end of a glorious era in Ohio State football.

Anne and Steve Hayes had returned to the hotel with the Ohio State party, unaware of what had happened. "From where we were in the stands, we didn't see anything," Mrs. Hayes recalls. "We didn't know anything until Dr. Bob [Murphy] came back to the hotel and told us."

University President Harold Enarson was equally unaware. He and his party had left the stadium early to return to their guest quarters in a private home in Ponte Vedra.

Hindman hurried from the press box to the dressing room and closeted with Hayes. "In the opening game against Penn State that year, Woody was physical with one of our kids on the sideline," relates Hindman, brought to Ohio State by Hayes as an assistant coach and later promoted to athletic director. "The next day, I told him that if he ever did that again, there was no way I could support him. He went through the season in great shape; nothing even close to a confrontation for the rest of the year, until the end of this [Gator Bowl] game. I told him, 'Coach, we've got a problem. I'm in a position where I've got to go to the president. You need to expect the worst possible decision.'"

Hindman drove to Ponte Vedra and conferred with Enarson and several of his administrative associates. They decided one way or the other, Hayes had to go. They composed two news releases: "The first said that Woody was announcing his retirement," Hindman explained. "If he wouldn't retire, then he would be released from his coaching position."

A press conference was scheduled for 9:30 the next morning, and Hindman delivered his news to Hayes at about 7:30 a.m. He admits that reports describing their meeting as "stormy" were not exaggerated. "At one point, Woody asked if we were going to let him resign," Hindman recalls. "I told him he had that right. But he said, 'No, goddammit, you bastards are going to have to fire me.'"

Hindman left, and shortly before 8 a.m. Woody called for me at the *Dispatch* sports department. I had already left for home, having had no sleep since early morning December 29. The call was transferred, and at my salutation the voice from Jacksonville said: "This is Woody. I always promised that when I decided to retire, you would be the first to know. I'm retiring as of now."

I pressed for details, but he insisted, "That's all I'm going to say. I've retired. Let it go at that." I immediately called Tim May on the *Dispatch* sports desk and relayed the information. He wrote a quick story. Our first edition was about to go to press; it was delayed only a short while and then appeared with our largest, blackest type on the front-page headline: "WOODY HAYES RESIGNS." In later editions, after the story unfolded further, "RESIGNS" would give way to "FIRED."

Since all the *Dispatch* writers had flown home during the night, May immediately called for Hindman in Jacksonville. But he wasn't available, nor were any other Ohio State officials. By now, the *Dispatch* report of Hayes' resignation was on the Associated Press wires, but Hindman's official word on the firing went out immediately after 9:30 via AP, UPI, and other media.

Hayes, his coaches, and team had left their Jacksonville hotel 45 minutes before the press conference. Mark George recalls that a deputy sheriff had been sent to escort the team buses, "So we managed to get Woody down a back stairs and to the bus without the media seeing him."

The players obviously knew what had happened on the sideline during the Gator Bowl, and they may have suspected that some disciplinary action would be forthcoming. But they had no inkling of its finality. They were stunned when, as their charter jet approached Port Columbus, Woody announced over the intercom: "Gentlemen, I regret that I will not be your coach next year."

Mark George admits, "I was crying because my hero had fallen," and explains that the PA system and the noise of the plane made Woody's announcement difficult to hear. Some players didn't catch it, but the word got around quickly. A sober, somber, dazed group filed out of the plane. Reporters could coax only a few curt comments: "I'm shocked." "I can't believe it!" "After all Coach Hayes has done for the University!" "He deserves better."

Hayes was whisked from the plane to his Upper Arlington home by the State Highway Patrol. He expected to arrive in Columbus with newspapers and other media proclaiming his "retirement." But by then the headline had changed.

In mid-afternoon, while I assembled and rewrote Hayes material for the *Sunday Dispatch*, he called and asked if I would come to the Biggs Facility. He was in his office, clearing out books and other items he'd accumulated over the years. George and former "brain coach" Jeff Kaplan were packing the boxes and loading them into his truck.

As they continued to work, Woody and I adjourned to the nearby squad room, where he had held meetings with his players, conducted staff meetings, and watched millions of miles of film during his years at Ohio State. He sat on his customary wooden folding chair behind the big, flat-top desk, chalked football instructions still on the blackboard. He seemed surprisingly relaxed, but I suspected that the reality hadn't yet hit home: After 28 years, he was no longer head football coach at Ohio State.

He still maintained—and other witnesses agreed—that after the interception, the Clemson linebacker had "waggled" the ball at the Buckeyes, which Woody considered a taunt to his players. Beyond that, he declined to discuss the catastrophic punch. He confirmed that after "cooling down" from Hindman's visit, he soon thought better of it, "and that's when I called you. I had retired as of that moment." In his own mind, anyway.

I returned to the office to write my impressions of Woody's first day as ex-coach, a story carried nationwide by the AP. Being on the go for over 40 straight hours had some compensation: I had no time to brood about what had happened to a man I knew as a close personal friend, admired with the depth of that knowledge and understanding, and regarded as a towering figure on the right and good side of sports, education, and life.

Like many others, I didn't protest the penalty, only the manner in which it was imposed. After devoting his life to the job and the institution; after making "building character" and "education first" realities (rather than clichés) with several thousand young men who came under his influence as players; after being such a positive force in the community for so long; after touching the lives of so many people, I felt he had earned the right to retirement with dignity. The dust should have been allowed to settle after the Gator Bowl.

Hindman, Enarson, Mrs. Hayes, the assistant coaches' wives and families, and all others in the Ohio State party left Jacksonville by plane in the early afternoon of December 30. The press conference should have been scheduled after everybody returned to Columbus.

Hayes' retirement, as announced in the noon edition of the December 30 *Dispatch*, should then have been affirmed and accepted by the University. Even a "with deepest regret" would have been appropriate. Instead they rushed to send out the new line: "Look, don't be mad at us; we fired the bad old guy."

Hindman emphasizes that Hayes "was never fired from the University; he was relieved of his coaching duties." Of Hayes' declaring his "resignation" or "retirement" to me, Hindman firmly insisted, "He doesn't resign to you. He resigns to me or the president. Telling Paul Hornung he's resigning doesn't mean a thing. You weren't his superior. We gave him that opportunity and he refused."

The hasty press conference, which was attended by no representative of Columbus' major newspaper, went on, he insists, "because of the media furor that would have erupted during that lag time. It wouldn't have been fair to Woody. They would have dredged up every bad situation. He had previously been put on notice. I had to take action. Everybody in America saw the incident. The University would have been really criticized for delaying. People would have wondered why we were waiting so long. It would have created a horrible situation."

On one point everyone can agree: It was a tragedy that such a storied career had to end with such a story.

Only one physical knockdown, his first heart attack, on the morning of June 5, 1974, occurred during Woody's active coaching days. Obviously, it immediately raised doubt about whether the then 61-year-old Hayes could continue as OSU's coach, and at his customary level of commitment. He seemed less concerned than anybody, although he did submit to hospitalization without protest, on orders from team physician Bob Murphy and heart specialist Joe Ryan.

"This sounds funny," he conceded, "but I programmed that damn thing to have it on vacation time. I held off and kept going, and I only had two speeches left on my schedule. But then I broke down and had to go to the hospital.

"I had planned to take off the whole month of June. I was going down to Noble County and get myself back in shape. I walked nine miles a day the last time I was down there. This thing [the heart attack] beat me by two days."

The day after the chest and arm pains caught up with him, Woody dictated a letter to his squad. "I knew they'd be wondering," he explained. "I told them the chances were very good that I would be back coaching next fall. I'd say it's 99 percent likely. It's obvious I didn't have a bad heart attack."

It was 100 percent sure by September. Coach Woody Hayes was raring to go when his players assembled for fall workouts, and he was in his usual sideline position for the Buckeyes' opening game. He promised to tone down his intense prowling and gyrating, which had long caused fans to divide their attention between the field and the sideline. That good intention lasted less than one-half of the season opener. But the 1974 football team helped limit stress on the old coach by going 9-1 before losing in the Rose Bowl.

Ohio State-Michigan, each season's finale, never lacked pomp and ceremony, but 1974 presented a unique sidelight. Both teams were coached by recovering heart patients. Bo Schembechler had returned to full duty after being stricken with a coronary only hours before the 1972 Rose Bowl.

24

EARLY WARNINGS

I n homes around Ohio and the nation, a special group of men sat before their television sets in late evening, December 29, 1978, stunned and saddened. Woody Hayes' former players, those who knew him best and loved him most, saw the sideline swing on Clemson's Charlie Bauman and shared a sickening feeling that Hall of Famer Jim Parker expressed in his living room: "I told my wife he'd be gone by tomorrow!"

Some may have joined walk-on Tod Alles, who confessed, "I cried when it happened, because I knew what the outcome would be." Some undoubtedly agreed with All-American punter Tom Skladany, who felt, "he shouldn't have been there. Woody Hayes doesn't coach in Gator Bowls, he coaches in Rose Bowls."

Michigan's Bo Schembechler, in California, had his mind on his team's upcoming Rose Bowl, but his heart figuratively flew the 3,000 miles to Florida. He admittedly broke down emotionally when Woody's firing was confirmed. "I wasn't there," he said of Hayes' Gator Bowl outburst, "but I'm convinced this is what happened: He had had a long, trying season, we'd beaten him, he was in the throes of the final game, he was tired, he'd neglected his medicine, and his blood sugar was out of whack. He said to me later, 'All I was trying to do was wrestle the ball from [Bauman's] hands.' I asked him if he'd seen the film or the replay, and he said no. I told him, 'That's not what you were doing.' I think in his own mind, he thought that's what he was doing. People don't believe that, but I do."

After watching the film a number of times, Schembechler accepted Woody's claim that, following the fateful interception, Bauman, had "waggled" the ball at the Buckeye sideline. "He flaunted it at the [OSU] players," Bo decided.

Schembechler also was among those who urged Hayes to apologize. A couple of weeks after the Gator Bowl, in a dramatic coup, WBNS-TV arranged for Woody and Bo to meet for a filmed reminiscence of the "Ten-Year War." The opening scene showed limousines speeding headlong toward each other, one carrying Woody, the other Bo, each in coaching "uniform." The bumpers come within a yard of impact at—you guessed it—the Ohio-Michigan line.

Their TV meeting actually took place at the Bowling Green home of former OSU assistant and BeeGee head coach Doyt Perry. "When we met at Doyt's place," recalls Bo, "I was trying to tell Woody to apologize and he said, 'I'm not going to. Should I apologize for all the good things I've done?' I said, 'No, but people don't know you like we do. They look differently at something like that.'"

Parker visited Woody some months later, at least partly on a similar mission. They walked over to the Holiday Inn on Lane Avenue for breakfast, and this is Jim's account: "I asked Woody to do me a favor: 'That accident you had when you were into the game and made a mistake, I know you didn't do it intentionally. Why don't you go public and get it over with?' I thought he was wrong for hitting that boy but he gave me a thousand reasons why he shouldn't apologize. When we walked out of the breakfast room, I was teed off because Woody didn't break the guy's arm. He told me some of the things he had done for players, for the University; he geared me up."

The word "sorry" lodged in Woody's throat. But he would dance around it to an extent that one knew the feeling did exist inside. "Of course I regret it," he once said. "Who got hurt the most by it?" The answer was obvious. It was one rash moment in the Gator Bowl that had cost him the job that represented vocation, avocation, family, religion, and passion for nearly half of his 65 years.

He spent two weeks in self-imposed exile at his home in Upper Arlington following his dismissal as Ohio State's head football coach. The days were marked by a steady stream of visits from former players and coaches, some close friends, some local media—and by evidence that many others cared: a flood of mail inundated the living room sofa.

But Woody refused to apologize directly until a chamber of commerce luncheon three weeks later. "I'm sick of people running around apologizing for things they've done," he said. "I got what was coming to me, and I've taken my medicine."

This was not the first time Hayes had been involved in an incident that had brought unwanted—if unwarranted— attention, which some regarded as an unfavorable reflection on the University. During a game against Indiana in 1958, he charged onto the field in the fourth quarter to protest what he considered overly rough play by the visiting team. "The way things were going, somebody was going to get hurt, and the officials weren't doing anything about it," he explained later. The officials marched off a 15-yard penalty, but Woody didn't mind; the Buckeyes led 35-0 at the time. Moreover, he felt he had made his point: On the very next play, the Hoosiers were assessed 15 yards for unnecessary roughness. Big Ten Commissioner Tug Wilson and OSU Athletic Director Dick Larkins publicly chided Woody, and several rival coaches expressed annoyance, but he never backed down.

Some of the early attention-getting antics occasioned more amusement than censure. Ohio State trailed 8-0 at Iowa in 1952. Seeking to fire up the troops, Woody ripped off his sport coat and flung it by one sleeve in the direction of the bench. Instead, it sailed into the front rows of the stands, which were occupied by some Iowa fans. When a student manager attempted to retrieve it, the Iowa fans initially refused to give it back.

Michigan seemed to bring out the best (or worst) in Woody. Michigan Stadium still used heavy, octagonal wooden yard boxes in 1951, Woody's first trip to Ann Arbor. The Buckeyes were losing 7-0, and he prowled the sideline. As he backed away from the field at one point, he tripped over one of the wooden markers and nearly fell. Regaining his balance, he angrily kicked the box and hurt his foot. As he turned, striving mightily not to show pain, he shot a menacing glance at the bench, where the players hid their laughter in towels and parka hoods.

Hayes did win a later battle with a piece of Michigan Stadium equipment. End Rich Michael had apparently recovered a fumble in the 1959 game, giving Ohio State an opportunity to cut the Wolverines' lead. But the officials ruled the ball down before the fumble. Hayes kicked a nearby wooden folding chair, splintering it. Afterward, Michigan officials considered presenting Ohio State a bill, but rethought the wisdom of further provoking the Buckeye coach.

Another call for the home team aroused Woody's ire in the 1963 game at Michigan. Buckeye Paul Warfield apparently caught a touchdown pass, but officials declared him out of the end zone. Hayes charged toward the offending official, propelling his 220 pounds with sprinter form, if not speed. A Detroit news photographer caught a classic picture of the flight, showing Woody pumping his arms, both feet off the ground, pants legs above his short white socks and cleated shoes.

"Coach Hayes and I used to play a lot of handball—and man, was he a tough competitor!" relates former defensive coordinator Lou McCullough. "A week after that game when he chased the officials, he showed me his leg. The back of it was solid black. He had pulled a muscle all the way down his hamstring. From that time on, he played very little handball. He couldn't! But he was right in confronting the officials, because Warfield caught the pass and definitely made a touchdown just before the half, and we didn't get it."

That incident paled by comparison with Woody's 1971 outburst in Ann Arbor. To set the stage: Fourteen 1970 OSU starters, six of them All-Americans, had graduated. Then a staggering rash of injuries struck the squad, starting with the preseason loss of future All-American tackle John Hicks to a knee operation. Thirty-nine different players started during the season, and Hayes was constantly forced to patch up the first platoons.

But the Buckeye survivors had managed to win six of their nine games and trailed Michigan, which had already clinched the Big Ten title, by only 10-7 in the fourth quarter. With time slipping away, Ohio State began a drive that raised hopes of a tying field goal or a long-shot touchdown for the upset of the year. But on a pass play, Michigan safety Tom Darden leaped over Buckeye receiver Dick Wakefield to grab the ball. Schembechler considered it "a great interception." Hayes knew it was interference. The officials ruled in Michigan's favor, crushing Ohio State's valiant comeback bid.

Woody dashed onto the field, confronting the officials and pleading his case with characteristically demonstrative vigor.

Unconvinced, but surrendering to futility, he finally marched off the field. As he reached the sideline, he grabbed the yard markers and hurled them onto the field in a final gesture of protest. "It was definitely interference," he contended. "I knew they'd penalize me, but when they gave [Michigan] the ball and first down with some 50 seconds [to play], the game was over. That [an interference penalty] would have given us first down on their 32-yard line with almost a minute left. Whether we could have gotten a field goal or another first down, I don't know. But when you see officials decide a ball game, I'm bitter. So I went out there to let them know I was bitter. That's why I don't like officials."

Films and TV clips seem to substantiate Hayes' protest. As the ball approached, Wakefield's helmet appeared to be down over his eyes, the result of Darden's diving over him. But such vindication hardly soothed Woody's feelings. He said firmly, "After seeing the pictures, I would have been ashamed of myself if I hadn't gone out there to protest."

The Big Ten commissioner did not, as Woody expected—or hoped— "call him on the carpet" for this one. Nor did OSU Athletic Director Ed Weaver, who explained, "I defended what he did because I knew why he did it. We got a bad call. That didn't mean I sanctioned his doing what he did. But knowing Woody like I did, I understood it. We were moving and the lack of an interference call could well have cost us the game."

Hayes' last appearance in Michigan Stadium, 1977, DID land him in trouble with Commissioner Wayne Duke. Trailing 14-6 with four minutes remaining, the Buckeyes reached the Wolverine ten-yard line, where quarterback Rod Gerald was hit hard and fumbled. Michigan recovered on its 18. Dashed were Ohio State's hopes for so much as a tie.

Woody ripped off his headphones and slammed them to the turf in disgust. "We were going down the field with a chance to score in a great game for a great championship," he related afterward, "and we lost the ball and a chance to score a touchdown. I was sick about it and as I turned around, right there in my face was this damn television camera. I took a swing at it."

The usual conflicting accounts followed, but the roundhouse left apparently did not hit the camera or ABC cameraman Mike Freedman. When the incident was mentioned in the postgame press conference, Woody stalked out. True to form he also refused to apologize, although he did say at the postseason appreciation banquet, "I'm sorry for what I did, sure. Do I make mistakes? Sure, I make lots of them. We all do. Now as far as I'm concerned, that thing's over."

When Freedman was assigned to work the January 1, 1978, Sugar Bowl game between Ohio State and Alabama in the New Orleans Superdome, Woody talked with him and they had their picture taken together. Bygones were gone.

But not for Duke. He conceded that the game films showed that Freedman was in violation of the NCAA-approved TV restraining line and that he was within two to four yards of Hayes, not eight to ten as had been claimed. Nonetheless, Duke slapped Hayes with a one-year probation for the swing.

OSU President Harold Enarson issued a statement that would later assume a certain irony. In accepting the probation he said, "The cruel fact is that a coach is subjected to great provocation. However, this does not justify assault upon another person. Coach Hayes understands that.... In all fairness, there is something that cries out to be said. Over the years, the Ohio State University teams coached by Woody Hayes have been noted for clean play and good sportsmanship.... These [good] things do not just happen. They are due to our entire Athletic Department and Coach Hayes."

The Big Ten probation ended after the Buckeyes played the 1978 regular-season finale against Michigan, the loss that established the Clemson-Ohio State matchup in the Gator Bowl.

An earlier pair of Hayes "incidents" were, as he suggested, "blown out of proportion" because they took place on the West Coast. He had never been the darling of the California media, starting with his first Rose Bowl trip in 1954 and proceeding downhill from there.

He rarely allowed West Coast reporters into Buckeye workouts in Pasadena. He held jovial, informative, and often expansive press briefings at the Huntington Hotel press room daily, but maintained his usual policy—in force in Columbus as well—of shielding his players from probing journalists and TV cameras, except occasionally under controlled conditions.

Ohio State played Southern Cal in a night game at the Los Angeles Coliseum in 1959 with disastrous results. Not only did the Buckeyes lose 17-0, but they were so battered and bruised that the training room resembled the aftermath of a bus crash. Seventeen were injured.

Writers were never permitted in a postgame Hayes locker room, and certainly not before the squad prayer, Woody's talk with the players, and his check on the injured. But two West Coast writers barged in, and he ordered them out.

Their version of the story and his, which was backed by the players, conflicted. He insisted that he did not strike either scribe, but conceded that he did push one back out the door. Suddenly, the game was almost forgotten in the furor of another Woody Hayes-vs.-the media clash.

I was there, but I didn't take it very seriously. For one thing, I learned early in my career that the reading—or listening—public cares little about the hardships journalists encounter in doing their job. One of my predecessors as *Dispatch* sports editor wrote a scathing column about the poor treatment to which he had been subjected in covering a Cincinnati Reds baseball game. As one of our printers fit the type into the sports page that day, he glanced at the column and wondered what his problem was: Was the free beer in the press box warm?

Another overblown affair concerned a pesky Los Angeles cameraman prior to the 1973 Rose Bowl. Art Rogers of the *Los Angeles Times* charged that Hayes had grabbed the lens of his camera and pushed the camera back into his face as he was taking a picture. He went to first aid for a checkup, reportedly "because I had a pretty good abrasion on my nose. There was no blood, no cut." He returned to work the first half of the game, then left because "I began to get this problem with double vision."

The *Times* carried a small story on the sports pages in early editions, but by late editions it had mushroomed to a front-page spread, complete with a huge picture of Rogers re-enacting his part for a Pasadena policeman. Reports and discussions of the pregame "incident" all but overshadowed the game in the press box. When a *Times* writer brought up the subject in what had been a solemn but amiable postgame press conference—considering that the Buckeyes had lost 42-17—Hayes stalked out, knocking over a microphone in the process.

The next day, television camera crews and newspaper reporters invaded the Huntington looking for Woody or any other University official—but they found none. It was the story of the day on L.A.'s local TV and in the West Coast press.

Finally, in early evening, three Ohio sports writers were summoned to the room of Athletic Director Ed Weaver for

Woody's explanation. Also present were University President Harold Enarson, Associate AD Hugh Hindman, and Assistant AD Jim Jones. "I did not shove the camera in his [Rogers'] face, and I did not strike him in any way, as was alleged," Woody declared firmly in opening the conference. "We [Hayes and his assistants] get together before the game, after the team has gone back into the dressing room and just before three coaches take off for the press box. At home we meet under the goal posts. But because the band was under the goal posts in this instance, we had our meeting to one side, but definitely still IN the field, where photographers aren't supposed to be.

"We have two minutes to go over a lot of things. First, we talk about choice of goals and the way the wind is blowing, which was a very important item in this game. Second, I ask the coaches how our linemen warmed up, whether they were firing out. If not, I have to fire them up.

"I want to know what the coaches going to the press box want me to tell their [position] players; and last, we go over again what play we want to use to open the game. It's a sort of ritual. We think this is real important, and we have about two minutes to go over everything.

"There were about seven or eight photographers there, and I asked them to step back. They all honored our wishes except this one. He persisted. He even got between the coaches' legs to snap pictures. One of the coaches dropped his jacket to screen him off. It was extremely disconcerting.

"As we broke up the meeting, a photographer had his camera stuck in my face, not more than a foot away. I shoved it [the camera] and said, 'Get out of here.' I used a word I shouldn't have used. I shoved the camera sideways, not in his face. It did not go in his face. I made no effort to injure him, and he did not appear to be injured at all. I did not strike him in any way.

"Defensive coordinator George Hill said, "I saw the whole thing. Woody did not strike the guy, and he did not push the camera in his face. It's ridiculous." Other coaches agreed.

Dr. Enarson, only a month on the job as OSU president, declared "This incident has been blown all out of proportion. The entire incident is regrettable, but they [the *Times*] have done a systematic badgering of Woody all week." Hayes chimed in with the thought, "I'm wondering if that [camera incident] was not contemplated harassment."

The photographer confirmed that "the Ohio State coaches were gathered in a huddle on the sideline, and there were a half-dozen or maybe a dozen photographers shooting. I kneeled down and tried to photograph Woody between the other coaches' legs, and all of the sudden—boom—I got it."

The late Bill Foley, the *Dispatch's* ace photographer, had covered Ohio State games for years and was on the sidelines in Pasadena that day. He gave Rogers no support, explaining, "When we pick up our credentials, we understand we aren't supposed to be on the field. You never see me on the field."

At the time of the evening press briefing, Hayes already had in hand what he called a "notice to appear" in Pasadena court to answer charges filed by Rogers. He said he wouldn't be back, but would be represented by a lawyer. After several postponements, the legal action against Woody was finally dropped. But it was another morsel for Hayes' critics and detractors and another step closer to the "last straw," the Gator Bowl.

Woody even attracted media attention when he wasn't coaching football. He, Anne, Steve, and John Bozick attended a Cleveland Indians game in the summer of 1969 that began with a small debate at the box office. "Woody was at the ticket window and the guy didn't want him to pay," Bozick relates. "Woody finally put his money through the bar and said, 'We're paying for the tickets,' so the guy took the money."

John blames himself to a certain extent for what happened afterward. "On the way to Cleveland," he remembers, "I remarked that there was a 'hot dog' playing first base, because Vic Power was the kind of 'hot dog' that liked to show off with the glove." As a long-time follower of Indians Baseball (he rooted for all Ohio pro teams, for that matter), Hayes became less and less enchanted with Power's performance in the field and when a ground ball went past him, it was too much. Woody arose from his box seat on the first base side and shouted: "Power, you ARE a hot dog!" Bozick adds, "Power got shook after hearing Woody. It was a standard remark almost any fan would make. Woody wasn't nasty or malicious, and that was the extent of his statement, nothing more. He didn't entice the guy, he didn't ride him.

"Power had no idea who Woody was. But he came over and asked, 'Is that your wife?' and then made some nasty remarks about Anne." She recalls that "Woody's knuckles were white, he was gripping his fingers so tightly, trying to keep from going out on the field after him."

"Powers said he'd fight Woody after the ball game and Woody said he'd be there," Bozick added. "We were out there waiting for him, but he didn't show up. Woody was a gentleman all the way. When it happened, a few people behind us said they'd be glad to go to court with him if he wanted to press charges about the remarks [Power] made. The newspapers grossly exaggerated the incident and made a big to-do of it." Indians general manager Frank Lane criticized Woody as an ungracious "guest of the club," but when he learned Hayes had paid for the tickets, he sent the coach a letter of apology. Nevertheless, Woody was in the headlines again, even off-season.

For all their sound and fury, the vast majority of "incidents" involving Hayes were harmless exhibitions of pique. Iowa obviously wasn't a "traditional foe" of the Buckeyes, à la Michigan, but Hawkeye coach Forest Evashevski—a Michigan grad—enlivened the meeting with Ohio State. He seemed to relish bugging Woody.

One year, after arriving at Iowa several hours before game time, the players and coaches walked out on the field to test the turf, as was their custom. Woody began a slow burn. He judged the grass much too high, suspecting that Evvy had allowed it to grow to slow down the speedier Ohio State backs. He demanded that the stadium crew mow the grass immediately. He was refused, but not defused. Now he was upset, which may have been Evashevski's original intent.

On another cold afternoon in the Iowa stadium, during pregame warmups, Woody spotted a half-dozen large heaters trained on the Hawkeye bench, but no such comfort was provided the visiting Buckeyes. He had a student manager wheel several of the heaters from the Iowa side to the Ohio bench. Evvy watched, then sent his student managers to retrieve the heaters.

But Woody had his moment. After one Ohio State victory, the Iowa crowd booed him as he left he field. He stopped, pointed to the scoreboard and smiled his way to the dressing room.

All of these unscheduled happenings, and a few others like them, enlivened the "Woody Hayes Era," the most colorful as well as the most successful in Ohio State's first 100 years of football. Unfortunately, one of them ended it.

Woody Hayes campaigned for years, sincerely and vigorously, for instant replay. "We MUST come to it," he said after the January 1, 1974, Rose Bowl, about the umpteenth time he'd tried to sell the idea. "As it stands now, a coach has no recourse."

He recalled a play where "I saw their [USC] right tackle move ahead of the ball. I yelled at the man [official] standing on the sideline, but of course he ignored me. After the game, Herman Rohrig [Big Ten supervisor of officials] came to me and said he'd seen it from the press box. He said, 'Coach, you were absolutely right. We saw it on instant replay.'" It wasn't the plaint of a losing coach, either. Hayes' Buckeyes had smashed the Trojans 42-21.

Woody burned a little when the NFL experimented with instant replay and eventually implemented it as part of the pro game. He'd be bitter today that his sport, college football, still hasn't "come into the electronic age," as he once phrased it. His proposal for instant replay differed from the pros': he would have penalized a team 5 yards if the coach called for a review and was proven wrong. A second mistaken call for replay would have cost 15 yards.

25

BREAD ON
THE WATER

Funny thing about generous people: While they naturally inspire a generous response in others, they're often uncomfortable having the focus on themselves. Rex Kern tells two stories about Woody Hayes that show how the coach found it much easier to give than to receive.

Kern remains one of Ohio State's all-time favorite athletes and personalities—a multitalented quarterback; a youth, religious, and community leader; and an excellent student who eventually earned a Ph.D.—a prime example, in short, of Woody's "quality person."

But an injury in his freshman year cast doubt on his ever playing a varsity game. "Toward the end of spring practice I found out that I had a ruptured disc in my back," Kern recalls. "They decided to operate. As I was going into surgery, Woody told my mom and dad, 'Mr. and Mrs. Kern, whether Rex ever plays a down for Ohio State or not, be assured that he will get his college degree from Ohio State, and I'll see to that!' That really stuck in my mind, and in my parents' minds, too. Woody would take care of you, keep you on scholarship, and that sort of thing." Kern recovered, of course, to be Hayes' starting quarterback for three glorious years, 1968-69-70, during which the Buckeyes won 27 games and lost only two.

Kern also remembers a time when Woody was the reluctant patient. "He'd just had an operation, and I called him to see how he was getting along," says Rex. "Woody never liked to talk

about himself, and the first thing he said to me was that he'd
heard I was having trouble with my back again. He switched the
whole conversation around. I told him, yes, I was having trouble
with my back and he said, 'By God, Rex, we've got the best
doctors in the world here at Ohio State. We've got to get you back
here to see some of our doctors.'" Hayes had been giving and
giving for so long, he couldn't see when it was time to take–even
when the only thing to be taken was attention.

Among the many truths his players learned from Hayes
was his primary principle of preparation: work harder than the
other guy. Shortly after his dismissal, the players went to work
to prepare a tribute that even generous-to-a-fault Woody couldn't
deflect. Spearheaded by Moose Machinsky and All-American
end Dean Dugger, the 1979 reunion brought together members
of Hayes' 28 Ohio State squads. More than 460 former players
and assistant coaches came from all over the country, from his
first team to the last, from stars to "scrubs," at their own expense.

No "outsiders" were allowed to crash the party. This was
just Woody and his guys, the OSU football "family." Jack Tatum,
the superstar roverback of the great 1968-69-70 Buckeye teams,
once said, "The thing I liked about Woody was that he would see
me ten years after I finished playing for him, and he'd ask about
every member of my family and call them by name. He did that
with every guy he knew." Woody did a lot of that before, during,
and after his banquet.

"I saw player after player go up to him," relates Machinsky,
a former All-Big Ten tackle, "and he not only immediately knew
their names, but their wives' names, where they were living and
working, a lot about their children, and in most cases the names
of their parents."

"When you start living in the past," Woody liked to say,
"you're done for." But on that night, Woody allowed himself to
revel in the nostalgia he had so long disdained.

Michigan's Bo Schembechler delivered the main speech of
the evening, and many thought it was the speech of his life. It was
unquestionably a speech from the heart. Schembechler had
played for Woody at Miami, been his assistant coach at Ohio
State, and for ten epic years an intense, spirited, but deep-down
respectful coaching adversary.

Woody was unabashedly moved by the tribute and by
seeing all those familiar faces again, but his players, "working

harder than the other guy," had saved the big play for last: Hayes used his 23-acre plot of strip-mining land in Noble County, Ohio, as a retreat to hike the hills, think, write, and enjoy the therapeutic benefits of nature. He slept in the back of his El Camino truck until he could have a 100-year-old cabin roughly reconstructed.

As their gift of appreciation to their old coach, the players had the cabin refurbished and modernized. Bill Trautwein, a 1950 tackle and captain, drew the plans; and Bill Wentz served as overseer of the project. Later, about 40 players spent a weekend installing a driveway and walk. At Woody's insistence, the cabin was sparsely furnished with few amenities–specifically, no distracting telephone, TV, or radio.

This climactic tribute revealed, the banquet came to an end, but there was too much feeling in the air—too much love—to allow the festivities to end. The party adjourned to a large suite in the hotel, which became a sort of revolving door parade, with ex-Buckeyes elbowing in and out—and a capacity number staying. "The guys just couldn't seem to tear themselves away," reported Bill Cummings, a former tackle. "It was just so great being with Woody again and sitting around listening to him, having a lot of laughs about things that happened 'way back." Woody and the last group left about 6:30 the next morning.

Afterward, Woody savored the grand scale of the reunion. "No man could have had a finer tribute," he said. "That was the biggest single affair I've ever had. I'm not sure I deserved it, but it makes you feel like you may have done some things right. Those doggone kids were wonderful! To have those fellows come back when they didn't have to, it meant something.

"You know, in football you truly get to know them. It's not just 'hello' and that junk. You get to know them under enormously emotional conditions. When you see them again, you pick up right where you left off. They mean an awful lot to me. The great players I've had here at Ohio State, not just as football players, but as fine students and outstanding citizens—a fellow who wouldn't be proud of that, there'd have to be something wrong with him."

It was a night to be remembered and almost three decades of memories to be savored.

Not many things this side of whipping Michigan elated Woody Hayes more than Lou Fischer's gesture to his old school and his old coach. Lou lettered as a guard in Woody's first year (1951) and went on to make it big with a chain of hamburger joints along the East Coast. Woody became convinced in the late 1960s that Ohio Stadium should be outfitted with the newly developed synthetic turf, but the Athletic Department budget couldn't absorb the tab. So Fischer came forward, promising Woody $280,000 to cover the installation of Astroturf, ostensibly for the 1970 season. As a heartwarming touch, he made the donation in memory of a former teammate and close friend, Joe Campanella, who had died suddenly—and young—of a heart attack.

An overjoyed Hayes gave me the turf story, which the Dispatch splashed on page one. But it proved a year premature. One of Astroturf's rivals in the synthetic grass business tied up the University with legal action, and by the time that was untangled, football season fast approached. Thus Hayes' troops had to perform their maneuvers on the real mowing-type turf for another year. Besides Woody's slow burn, the delay spawned an indelicate but apt bumper sticker: "Even on grass, we'll beat their ass!" As a fitting farewell to nature's sod, the Buckeyes trampled Michigan 20-9 in the season-ender for their third straight Big Ten championship and their second Rose Bowl trip in three seasons.

Woody sprang a bit of philanthropy, with a tart aside, at the annual appreciation banquet. He announced that he'd invited half a dozen retired OSU coaches and the retired stadium groundskeeper and their wives to make the California trip with the football team. To the surprised Athletic Department brass, he jibed: "If you can't get the money, I'll raise it. Only this time, don't let it get into litigation."

Just before the bulldozers arrived to begin the turf project, the Athletic Department announced that fans could call at the stadium on Sunday morning for a free chunk of the hallowed old sod. "We were swamped," Athletic Director Ed Weaver remembers. Cars were finally aligned in a drive-in mode, with Woody himself tossing rolls of sod into trunks and accepting voluntary contributions for the athletic fund. One fan brought a check for $20.09, commemorating the 1970 Michigan game score. The stadium crew hurriedly cut more sod, and the last roll departed in mid-afternoon.

By football season 1971, the Astroturf was in place, and the Buckeyes initiated it with a 52-21 romp over Iowa. Woody liked it so much that he eventually moved practices there. Then he decided "the purchase was too great" and feared the flawless footing might increase injuries. He ordered the stadium crew to drench the field with hoses before each practice, figuring players would slide, rather than stopping too suddenly. Buckeye players renamed it "Lake Hayes."

In the inevitable cycle of progress, the field was reconverted to natural grass in 1990.

26

A NEW START

"A good football player finds out that he gets knocked down dozens of times," the old coach said. "But he gets up, and the first thing he knows he's knocking other people down. The great thing about football is that when you get knocked down, you get up and go again. You don't lie there and moan and groan and rail against the fates."

That was Woody Hayes' answer to those of us who worried about his ability to adjust to "life after football." He suddenly had no involvement in the axis around which his entire life had revolved for more than 38 years, we reasoned. His mission had evaporated. His lifeline had been severed. Traumatic!

"I don't take this thing as seriously as most people," he maintained with a familiar jaw set. "To hell with it! I'm not going to let anything get in my way. If they expect me to grovel, they're mistaken!"

We had underestimated the fibre of this incredible man. We did him the injustice of questioning his resiliency and strength of character. He simply changed directions and continued to contribute to the University, the community, the state, his country, and all mankind only from a different base. The old soldier did not fade away. He embarked on a new life.

"I don't live in the past," he declared. "I'm a student of the past, and I try to learn from the past, although a lot of people will say I haven't done a very good job of it. But for me to live in the past, hell no!"

By the time he emerged from 1711 Cardiff Road for his first public appearance at the January 18, 1979, Columbus Chamber of Commerce luncheon, the furor over Jacksonville had subsided. One of his former assistants, Earle Bruce, had been hired to replace him, with the usual fanfare. This was the first new coach at Ohio State in 28 years. Basketball season was in full swing. The world moved on.

The chamber speech proved a watershed. Some in the standing-room-only crowd of 1,200 jammed into the Neil House ballroom undoubtedly came with chips on their shoulders, daring Woody to win back their admiration and support. Many people in the radio audiences were still angry over his Gator Bowl transgression.

Woody arrived after the Neil House diners had finished the salad course. If the standing ovation that greeted him then was a matter of polite custom, the one that erupted after he finished his speech shouted acceptance, admiration, and affection unrestrained.

He was magnificent in that 45-minute soul-baring—contrite, uncharacteristically apologetic, philosophical, whimsical, amusing, emotional, and totally charming. He praised Bruce, admitted his warm regard for long-time rival Schembechler, and cited his familiar homilies on football and life. And he admitted he was bitter—not as some expected at the University, for being fired—but "toward me because . . . we got beaten down there when I thought we were going to win."

He'd struggled for hours the day before to outline the points he wanted to make, but he let his heart dictate the sure-fire clincher: a poignant declaration of his great love for Ohio State and a plea for "good thoughts for EVERYBODY at the University."

The *Dispatch* covered the event the following day, then published the entire text of the speech in its Sunday editions. Woody was back! The audience said so; those who heard on radio and TV said so; a fresh flood of mail said so; and renewed requests for speaking engagements and public appearances confirmed it.

Surprisingly, his return to the world did not include football. "Earle is the Ohio State football coach," he maintained. "I'm not going to horn in on him in any way. It's his show now."

During his self-imposed exile and without Bruce's knowledge, he did everything he could (within the rules) to keep high school players he had been recruiting before the Gator Bowl thinking OSU as their college choice. It might have been human nature to resent his successor, but Hayes wished only success for Bruce. They had been head coach and assistant, they had maintained a healthy friendship, and reasoned Woody: "As hard as I worked to keep this program up as long as I did, I don't want to see anything happen to it now. Sure, I'm going to give Earle all the help I can, if he wants it."

The help was welcomed. "I think of Coach Hayes for the great support he gave me when I was coach at Ohio State," Bruce said several years after his departure from Columbus. "When I had a problem, I went and talked to him about it. He would call me up and give me advice. He was very, very supportive of everything. Coach Hayes loved Ohio State University. He wanted to see that program go well. I think he would have done anything for that school."

Hayes had several opportunities to follow a typical pattern for old coaches, scouting college talent for a pro team or the NFL combines. He would have been good at it and might have come to enjoy it, as did his good friend Pappy Waldorf, formerly of Northwestern. But he said, "I decided when I got out of football, I'd really get out of it, and I've done that. Sure, I miss it! But like Satchel Paige, I'm not going to look back; they might be gaining on me. I find other things to do. I keep moving. There's no use sitting around."

Entitled to a University office as an emeritus professor, Hayes was assigned a large corner room on the second floor of the Military Science Building. Many thought that the location was a recognition of his well-known love for things military, but this happened to be the only office available in the immediate area of his former base.

Woody could sit at his desk and look through the big office window at Ohio Stadium, the scene of 124 of his 205 Buckeye victories. The location also afforded him an opportunity to talk with the Army, Navy, and Air Force ROTC instructors about two of his favorite subjects, history and the military.

Woody had booked some speeches before the Gator Bowl, but his calendar filled up quickly after the chamber of commerce comeback. "The responses of people have been unbelievably fair-minded," he said. In fact, his re-emergence as a "celebrity" worried him. "Everywhere I go, I seem to sign more autographs than I used to," he observed. "Kids crowd around me. I'm afraid it might be for the wrong reason—because of the [Gator Bowl] publicity I got."

In the years immediately following his "retirement" from football, Hayes logged a lot of air miles and almost ran the tires off his sophisticated truck. "A big company flew me to Miami yesterday in its private jet to give them a luncheon speech," he casually mentioned one morning when I stopped by his office. "That's the sixth or seventh time I've been to Florida. I've been to Dallas twice, Houston twice, Boston one day, and Philadelphia the next, and Chicago after that. I've been in Seattle, San Francisco, Los Angeles, San Diego, and Denver; and I've been in South Carolina three times for speeches. Those people in South Carolina [where Clemson is located], well shoot, they couldn't have treated me nicer.

"I make a variety of speeches. I have a high school speech today and another tomorrow. I could make three speeches a day if I wanted to. I'd like to get into the grade schools and junior highs, because young kids today are faced with all kinds of temptations and distractions. If something I say can help them just a little bit, my time's well spent."

Had his football grads been present, they would have recited in unison: "The most valuable gift you can give anyone is your time." Woody had said it to them again and again during their careers.

Between trips and speaking engagements, Hayes greeted visitors to his hard-to-find office—former players and coaches, friends, fans, students; he worked at catching up on his voluminous correspondence with help from his secretaries, first Betty Garrett, then Sandy Trelay; he talked on the phone scores of times a day; he read and underlined books.

He also began gathering material and writing, in longhand, the first chapters of a fifth book, examining the correlation between military and football.

He spent more time at the Faculty Club, mainly at lunchtime at the "long table." He preferred to walk across campus, and as he did students went out of their way to say hello or to chat briefly. And he still dropped in on classes and lectures of special interest to him.

Hollywood came calling too. During a visit to Los Angeles, Hayes signed a contract with two producers who planned to film his life story. Budd Schulberg wrote a script, but the project never reached the lights-camera-action stage. Woody was told that financing had become prohibitive, but the Rev. Daryl Sanders, who helped him with the negotiations, suspects that Schulberg's researcher "brought back such a good picture of Woody that they lost the edge of his passion, and it ended up not being a marketable thing."

ABC-TV proposed an interview to be conducted between halves of the 1979 Ohio State-Michigan game. Woody seemed agreeable—until the subject of the interview was mentioned: the Gator Bowl affair. End of negotiations! "I've taken my punishment and said nothing," he explained, with sizzle around the edges. "I'm going to keep it that way." He did submit to a number of TV and press interviews in the next five or six years, but always with an abrupt ending if the Gator Bowl came up.

Bruce invited his old coach to dinner with the football squad before the 1979 opener, and Woody enjoyed seeing all of the players he'd coached only the year before. He'd recruited all but two of the 22 starters. He attended no practices or games, although he did watch games that were telecast.

"There's nothing they need from me," he insisted, "and if I came around, it probably would be misunderstood. Earle's doing a great job." A great job indeed! The Buckeyes stormed through their 11 regular-season games unbeaten and lost in the Rose Bowl by a single point.

When Michigan game week arrived in 1980, Bruce asked Hayes to deliver the speech at the "Senior Tackle." This is an annual ceremony in which senior players hit a tackling dummy or more recently, a blocking sled to symbolize the impending completion of their college careers. The old Hayes eloquence and fire reignited as the football squad, coaches, marching band, and several thousand fans alternately listened and roared approval. Bruce, once a graduate assistant and full-time assistant under Woody, just beamed.

In May 1981, Woody experienced the first of a series of misfortunes that precipitated his physical decline. He underwent an operation for removal of a pestiferous gall bladder. Almost six weeks later, he developed an abscess. It was discovered, much to the University Hospital's embarrassment, that it was caused by a surgical sponge that had been left in the abdominal cavity. Woody feigned annoyance and deadpanned, "Isn't that something! In all the years I coached football, I never made a mistake." Then he laughed and suggested to the relieved surgeon, "Let's get it out."

The infection and the second operation hit him hard. He dropped from the rounded 220 pounds that Ohio Stadium fans remembered to 158, and friends began to worry. But within a couple of months, he had regained 30 pounds and resumed his nonstop schedule. "It wasn't that bad," he insisted. "Shoot, I've seen people who were a lot worse off than I was, and they came out of it. I do get a little tired if I drive 300 miles for a speech, but I'm coming back."

Among Woody's hundreds of get well cards was a thank you letter from OSU President Harold Enarson in appreciation for his response to the surgical mistake. That misplaced little sponge could have brought big bucks to the old coach, but he never considered legal action. Not against his beloved University!

That fall, for the first time, Woody quietly returned to Ohio Stadium. He watched all the home games from a radio booth above the press box and continued to do so for four of the next five seasons.

On Friday before the Buckeyes' 1981 trip to Michigan, he hyped the Buckeye Boosters luncheon audience at noon and the Senior Tackle crowd a few hours later. Afterward, Bruce insisted that he accompany the team to Ann Arbor for the Big Ten championship showdown.

Hayes was assigned a seat in the press box for the game, unfamiliar territory for him. Unaware of the first dictum of that professional setting—no cheering in the press box—he angered some of the writers, and Michigan officials even more, with obvious and vocal support for the Buckeyes.

Of his early predecessors at OSU, Woody had especially admired the gentlemanly Jack Wilce. The late Dr. Wilce had coached the Buckeyes to their first Big Ten championship in 1916, Ohio State's fourth year in the league and his fourth as head football coach. He gave up coaching in 1928 and became director of the University Student Health Service. "No one ever heard him say one word of criticism about an Ohio State coach," reported Woody, who occasionally joined Dr. Wilce for lunch at the Faculty Club. The same could later be said of Woody Hayes. Sitting with him in his assigned radio booth at Ohio Stadium games, I heard him comment on, but never second-guess, Earle Bruce's handling of the team or the game. He backed them with quiet enthusiasm. But fancy-dan ball-carriers bothered him just as much as a spectator as when he was a coach. "C'mon now, back," he'd mutter, "level off!" But that was the extent of his long-range advice.

More popular than ever with the public, Woody put that popularity to work for charity causes. He became interested in the Heinzerling Foundation, which ministered to severely impaired children and adults. He hosted an annual "Woody Hayes Birthday Party" in a shopping center as a Heinzerling fundraiser. He also became host of the "Woody Hayes Sports Spectacular," a golf pro-am featuring many of his former stars and other celebrities. The outing benefited Children's Hospital, an institution he visited often.

Dick Paugh, a Columbus fundraising consultant, recalls turning to Woody in 1985, after USO's funds had been cut. "He not only signed 1,000 letters to top businessmen in central Ohio," Paugh says, "but he allowed the responses to come to his office, giving more clout to the plea. The campaign was successful."

Woody helped the Operation Feed drive for food for the homeless; he backed the diabetes campaign; he did his bit for the Recreation Unlimited Fund, a pet project of TV sportscaster Jimmy Crum that provides summer camp time for handicapped children and adults; and he was one of the "Columbus Greats" honored at the Central Ohio Lung Association gala.

Two of Woody's good friends, Dr. John Peter Minton, an internationally known cancer surgeon, and Dr. Manuel Tzagournis, established the Woody Hayes Cancer Fund in the OSU College of Medicine, which would assist in research and treatment of the disease. Woody suggested voluntary contributions to the fund from fans who received autographed pictures, and many obliged.

He ventured into the political arena, too. Hayes never hid his loyalty to the Republican Party. He appeared with Richard Nixon and Jerry Ford when they came to Columbus on the campaign trail. He backed Jim Rhodes for governor. He was a friend of George Bush. He claimed, in fact, that he had once nearly given up his coaching chores at Ohio State for the party and had second-guessed himself for not doing it.

On a banquet dais with former President Ford, the coach gained his usual momentum as he spoke: "I like to feel President Jerry Ford is somewhat a product of football," Woody said, noting that Ford had played center at Michigan and was once a Yale assistant coach. But then he plunged to the heart of his message. "I'm often asked if I had it to do over, would I be a coach? Yeah, except for two weeks in 1976. I could have taken the doggone ball and thrown it to my assistants and said, 'Here, you fellows play the ball game, I'm going on to a bigger game.' We [the Republican party] just lagged by 7,500 votes in Ohio. I could have gotten those 7,500 votes for this man [Ford], and he'd be in the White House where he belongs!"

In 1981, however, the Republicans felt they might gain the pivotal seat on the Columbus City Council until a series of TV commercials began appearing, in which Woody stumped for Democrat Ben Espy. Espy won the Council seat. "It shocked a lot of people," admits Anne Hayes. But anyone who remembered that Espy had been a halfback on Hayes' 1962-63 Buckeye teams realized where his first loyalties lie. Nothing mattered but that Ben was one of Woody's guys.

Earlier, Woody had campaigned for former tight end and co-captain Greg Lashutka in a successful bid for Columbus city attorney. Lashutka was a Republican. Coincidentally it was Lashutka vs. Espy in the 1991 battle for mayor of Columbus. Woody undoubtedly would have stayed neutral, but button-bursting proud of both.

When President Ford came to Columbus to speak at the OSU winter commencement in 1974, the *Dispatch* dramatized Woody's status. He met the president at the airport and escorted him to St. John Arena. That evening's *Dispatch* carried a front-page picture of the two of them together with a caption reading, "Woody Hayes and Friend."

In the years following Hayes' coaching exit, the University, with leadership from President Ed Jennings, also recognized the man who had given it so much of his life for 28 years and who continued to be its most loyal booster. In April 1982 the street fronting Ohio Stadium was officially renamed "Woody Hayes

Drive" during a formal ceremony attended by much of the OSU brass. In June he received the Distinguished Service Award at the Commencement exercises in Ohio Stadium, prompting a standing ovation by the 1,100 graduates.

The clock began to toll in May of 1985. Woody suffered a stroke on an airplane en route to a speaking engagement in Vancouver, Canada. He was returned to Columbus on John Galbreath's private jet and checked into University Hospital, where he underwent several weeks of treatment and therapy.

During his early recuperation at home, he became a familiar figure along Cardiff Road, walking slowly with the support of his pale red cane, which was given to him by one of his great fullbacks, Champ Henson. He eventually managed to get back to the office on a limited basis, first on a walker, then on the cane.

His pride prompted him to resent both walking aids, but the choice was not his. Nor did he question that his office had been moved to a windowless first-floor location. He continued to lunch some days at the Faculty Club, pulling himself up by the railing to negotiate the front steps and grudgingly using the elevator to the second-floor dining room.

He attempted to drive his truck again as part of his after-stroke therapy, but the combination of physical unsteadiness and failing eyesight proved too much. He was forced to depend on others for transportation.

Already weakened, Woody was hit by a second heart attack, a lighter one, and he was back in University Hospital. After returning home for recuperation, he developed phlebitis, forcing another week in the hospital and producing ugly, nagging leg ulcers.

All that kept him from 1985 football games. But against all odds, he made it for the Senior Tackle. Rev. Sanders—who, with Archie Griffin, had been the first to visit the Hayes home after Jacksonville—picked him up at the hospital, drove him to Ohio Stadium, and loaded him into a wheel chair. Huddled in a topcoat, a wool shirt and a blanket, his voice weaker than normal, he still found the right words for a stirring challenge to the seniors, and the whole squad and coaches as well. They all lined up to shake his hand. A lot of eyes watered, but not from the chill of the late November afternoon.

Amazingly, Hayes refused to drop out. His indomitable will and mental clarity and toughness overcame the physical frailties. By December, he was struggling into his office four hours a day and even making more ambitious outings.

In January 1986, thin and with drawn face, Hayes flew to New Orleans in a private plane arranged by President Jennings to accept the Amos Alonzo Stagg Award and a standing ovation at the American College Football Coaches' Association convention. He was well attended. Two of his physicians, OSU College of Medicine Dean Dr. Tzagournis and Professor of Medicine Dr. Joe Ryan, accompanied him. Bo Schembechler met him at the plane and hosted him during the stay.

At the Columbus Touchdown Club in the same month, the 1,000 diners accorded Hayes two wild standing ovations as he presented Schembechler with the "Coach of the Year" trophy. Later in the summer, he went to Washington to receive a Vince Lombardi Memorial Award. The Masons of Ohio honored him; his hometown, Newcomerstown, saluted him, as did numerous other organizations.

Dr. Ryan, among others, didn't approve of all the activity. Aside from his other afflictions, Hayes' diabetes was "a real problem," Ryan said. Still, he decided that denying Woody would have been more detrimental than allowing him to keep going. "I was frankly amazed at his ability to keep functioning," confessed Dr. Bob Murphy, OSU team physician and Hayes family doctor, who later recalled that Woody suffered a lot of congestive heart failure. "Woody was in the hospital more than anyone knew," said Mrs. Hayes. One of those unpublicized visits was for a pacemaker.

President Jennings helped ease Woody's struggle in August 1985 by assigning to him an energetic student intern named Chris Boadt. Solicitous almost to a fault, Boadt reveled in being a companion, driver, aide, and arm-to-lean-on for the famous man, whom he genuinely liked and admired.

Even in the last week of his life, Woody remained active and in the public eye. Although Hayes had been the subject of a 1982 Columbus Roast, the organization—including a number of his former players—planned a repeat in 1987. Woody refused unless Earle Bruce would be included as co-roastee. That agreed upon, he called Schembechler, Lou Holtz, Bill Mallory, and Lou McCullough and "ordered" them to appear. They dutifully complied, despite previous commitments. None realized it would be the last time.

The dais outdid itself on the March 5 "Night with Woody and Earle." I stopped by Woody's office the next morning, checking on his health. "Good party, wasn't it?" he said. "I got a little tired, but I feel fine now. I couldn't coach today, though. Not after all the nice things that were said about me. I'd be too fatheaded."

He then related some highlights for a visiting threesome from Tulsa, Oklahoma, headed by Mayor Dick Crawford, formerly of Columbus and still a staunch Ohio State and Woody Hayes booster. After the visitors had gone, I mentioned that Holtz had flown in from Arizona for the roast and flown right back to Arizona for a Notre Dame alumni meeting. Woody became emotional, as he tended to do in his last years.

Schembechler had postponed an appearance in Dayton to make the roast, on the condition that Woody would then introduce him at the delayed Dayton banquet, which he did on March 10, 1987. Two days later, Woody Hayes died.

The menu for a February 1978 Miami Roast included a "Woody Hayes Potato." As served, it was roasted brown, almost burnt. So was the old coach by the time a celebrity panel zinged him. Woody absorbed all the barbs tossed his way at the $150-a-plate fundraiser for the University of Miami athletic scholarship fund, then served up an oratorical filet mignon that prompted a standing ovation by the 1,000 mostly-paying customers.

Former President Gerald Ford said, "In all modesty, I vote for Woody as one of the great coaches of all time. Of course, I voted for Barry Goldwater, Tom Dewey, and Alf Landon too."

MC Pat Henry introduced a speaker's table that included among others, entertainers Ann-Margret, Shirley MacLaine, Cloris Leachman, and Paul Anka, as well as sports figures Bud Wilkinson, Don Shula, Archie Griffin, Paul Hornung, Yogi Berra, and Bob Griese, claiming "Woody Hayes is the only unknown here tonight."

"I'm truly honored to be here to participate in this tribute to Woody Hayes," said MacLaine. "I don't know who the heck he is, but after listening to the speeches, I know WHAT he is."

Shula declared, "Woody is the most generous man I know. I've never seen a man give away so many bowl games." But the Miami Dolphins coach turned serious to add, "Woody is one of the most respected coaches in football."

Former Oklahoma coaching great Wilkinson told Hayes, "If they ever have a Heisman Trophy for coaches, you're my number-one choice."

Griffin thanked Hayes for helping him to two Heismans, suggesting, "Woody is a God-fearing man. It's nice to know he's afraid of somebody."

27

IN MEMORIUM

Two public memorial services marked Woody Hayes' death, each impressive in its own right. But perhaps most touching were simple, individual acts by persons unidentified, except as fans or admirers.

On March 12, 1987, and on the days immediately following, many came to Ohio Stadium to place bouquets on the huge scarlet and gray O that spanned the 50-yard line. Single red roses dotted the artificial turf, each set carefully to indicate a separate donor. A family left a picture of a baby wearing an Ohio State sweatshirt, with a football at his feet. Simple tributes, but eloquent in their message.

Eloquence also distinguished both the service at First Community Church on March 17 and the public ceremonies in the stadium on March 18. Each did signal honor to its subject.

More than 1,400 crowded into First Community for the televised service, with one section reserved for Hayes' former players and coaches. Across from the Hayes family, down front, were a former U.S. president, the former governor, the current Ohio governor, and Columbus' mayor.

On a table at the altar, beside a single flickering candle rested a black baseball cap with a scarlet O, a U.S. Navy flag folded three-corner, and a single red rose in a plain vase; simple but powerful symbols of the Ohio State partisan, the Navy man, and the Rose Bowl coach.

OSU President Ed Jennings said he would remember Woody most as a teacher because "he taught us that you must work as long and as hard as it takes to achieve your dream."

After a scripture reading and comments by Pastor Emeritus Arthur Sanders, former President Richard Nixon delivered the eulogy, without notes and with obvious sincerity:

> I vividly recall the time I first met Woody Hayes 30 years ago. It was right after the Ohio State-Iowa football game in 1957. It was a great game. Iowa led 13-10 in the middle of the fourth quarter. Ohio State had the ball on their own 35-yard line. A big sophomore fullback, Bob White, carried the ball 11 straight times through the same hole inside left tackle. It was three yards in a cloud of Hawkeyes. He finally scored. Ohio State won 17-13. It was Woody Hayes' second national championship.
>
> Afterwards, at a victory reception, John Bricker introduced me to Woody. I wanted to talk about football. Woody wanted to talk about foreign policy. You know Woody—we talked about foreign policy.
>
> For 30 years thereafter, I was privileged to know the real Woody Hayes—the man behind the media myth. Instead of a know-nothing Neanderthal, I found a Renaissance man with a consuming interest in history and a profound understanding of the forces that move the world. Instead of a cold, ruthless tyrant on the football field, I found a warm-hearted softie— very appropriately born on Valentine's Day—who often spoke of his affection for "his boys," as he called them, and for his family.
>
> I am sure that Woody wouldn't mind if I shared with you a letter he wrote to me shortly after Mrs. Nixon suffered a stroke ten years ago: "You and I are about the two luckiest men in the world from the standpoint of our marriages with your Pat and my Anne. I know that you will agree that neither of us could have done better and neither of us deserves to do so well."
>
> I saw another Ohio State game on New Year's Day in 1969. The Buckeyes were playing USC, Mrs. Nixon's alma mater, in the Rose Bowl. O.J. Simpson electrified the crowd in the first quarter when he made one of his patented cutbacks after going over left tackle and then sprinted 80 yards for a touchdown. But the Buckeyes came roaring back in the second half and crushed the Trojans 27-16. It was Woody's third national championship.

He could have quit then, with three national championships and seven Big Ten championships. He had to know that
it was a risk to stay on. It is a rule of life that if you take no risks,
you will suffer no defeats. But if you take no risks, you will win
no victories. Woody did not believe in playing it safe. He
played to win.

In the next nine years, he won some great victories,
including a record six straight Big Ten championships from
1972 to 1977. He also suffered some shattering defeats. The
incident at the Gator Bowl in 1978 would have destroyed an
ordinary man. But Woody was not an ordinary man. Winston
Churchill once said, "Success is never final. Failure is never
fatal." Woody lived by that maxim. He was never satisfied
with success; he was never discouraged by failure.

The last nine years of his life were probably his best. He
made scores of inspirational speeches all over the country. He
gave all of the honorariums from those speeches to the Woody
Hayes Cancer Fund at Ohio State University. He raised tens of
thousands of dollars for crippled children in his annual birthday and Valentine's Day phonathons. He gave pregame pep
talks to his beloved Ohio State team, now coached by one of his
boys, Earle Bruce. He basked in the warm glow of tributes that
were showered upon him by those who played under him and
others who had come to know him, love him, and respect him.

Last year, the National Association of College and High
School Coaches capped his career by honoring him with the
Amos Alonzo Stagg Award. They honored him as an outstanding coach, but even more importantly, they honored him as a
great humanitarian.

Two thousand years ago, the poet Sophocles wrote,
"One must wait until the evening to see how splendid the day
has been." We can all be thankful today that in the evening of
his life, Woody Hayes could look back and see that the day had
indeed been splendid.

First Community's Senior Minister Barry Johnson, in the
unenviable position of following Nixon, adeptly painted a word
picture of the Woody Hayes known to his family, players, close
friends, and ministers. The service ended with the singing of
"Carmen Ohio," the Ohio State University alma mater, one line
of which speaks of "hearts rebounding thrill with joy which
death alone can still."

More than 10,000 came to Ohio Stadium for the public
service, though it was held during weekday working hours with

students off-campus for spring vacation. President Jennings mentioned Woody's "rare gift for inspiring others to believe in themselves and to believe in what they could achieve."

Michigan's Bo Schembechler, who had enjoyed almost a son-father relationship with Hayes, despite the on-field rivalry, brought a few laughs when he suggested, "You may wonder why I'm here." He continued:

> But I did have the distinction of playing for Woody, of coaching with him, of competing against him over a ten-year period. While at Miami, we had a great team in 1950, and it was one of Woody's favorite ballclubs. We felt, and I think he did too, that we were instrumental in his getting the only job he ever really wanted, here at Ohio State.
>
> I came here with him in 1951 as a graduate assistant. I returned in 1958 as one of his assistants, and stayed until I became the head coach at Miami, a job he got for me in 1963.
>
> When I went to Michigan, I wondered how the old man would take it. As it turned out, the so-called "ten-year war" was fierce competition between two great schools. I'd always felt that that competition, as intense as it was, actually brought us closer together.
>
> I have many friends at Ohio State. I know many of the football players who played for Woody. Some of them I coached and some of them I just competed against, but it seemed like I knew them well. There's something about competition like that. You know you're competing against the best.
>
> When you know you're dealing with honesty and integrity, no matter how fierce the competition gets, it just brings you closer together. In the last eight years I've seen Woody Hayes many times, I've talked to him quite a bit. A great friend of mine, a very, very close friend of mine!
>
> I think I can speak for the 4,000 or so young men who got a chance to play for him, the numerous coaches who had a chance to work for him, and for the many coaches in the Big Ten Conference who competed against him, because during the 28 years that he coached, there is no question in my mind that he was the dominant force in the league.
>
> He's the greatest football coach the conference ever had. He set the tone. That's why you see little of the cheating and violations that occur throughout the country happening in our conference—because for 28 years, ladies and gentlemen, if you violated the rules, sooner or later you had to face the old man.

We all knew this was going to happen sooner or later, but you're never really prepared for it. So for all of you who played for him, because he was a players' coach, here was the coach of coaches. I hear so many people say he was more than a coach. No, he wasn't more than a coach, he just set a different standard for coaches, recognized that there are other obligations you have to commit to. He set a standard that was higher than most any of us could reach. And so now he is gone, but for those of us who were closely associated, there is forever the lasting impression Woody Hayes had on our lives. It will never leave us.

I'd also like to say in closing that I have tremendous respect for Anne Hayes. What a magnificent woman, who was as much a part of Woody's success, in the background, as Woody himself!

So he leaves us now. Let's all be joyful in the one thing we can all say: Somewhere along the line, this great man touched our lives, and he's made us better people because we knew Woody Hayes.

Earle Bruce, who coached under Woody Hayes and became his Ohio State successor, directed his emotional remarks mostly to the old coach:

Coach Hayes cared for me. He cared for you. He cared for Ohio State University and the football program. His heart was as big or bigger than his chest.

When I reflect on what's happened, it's kind of difficult to say thank you to the people who have done so much for you. I'd like to say thanks to Coach Hayes for caring for his players, caring whether they got an education or not, whether they graduated or not.

I came here at a time when [it was common practice at some institutions] if you got injured you lost your scholarship. And if you were low down on the team structure you were probably gone. But he cared for people at the top and the bottom of the roster. [A running back, Bruce suffered a severe knee injury the year before Hayes came to Ohio State. He returned home, but Hayes brought him back and hired him as a student-coach. He went on to graduate from Ohio State.]

Thanks for the great dedication you gave to all of the assistant coaches, and the hard-work ethic you demanded out of every one of us as we approached the game of football. You demanded the best effort and nothing less.

Thanks for the integrity you gave us in every endeavor. Thank goodness I worked for him, because he set a high standard for the game of football he loved so much. He felt cheaters never won in the end, and he held the game of football in high esteem.

He truly was one of a kind in his integrity and ability to help people. Nothing was ever too big or too small. Whatever time of the day it might have been, he'd give you the helping hand you needed to get you through.

Thanks for showing me that loyalty and love prevail over bitterness and hate. Thanks for the pay-ahead principle. You can never pay Coach Hayes back for all he's done for you. It would take forever. He is the best football coach in America.

I guess we're all faced with things today, to face up to what's happened. I love you, Woody Hayes; football loves you, Ohio loves you, the University loves you. You'll be missed at the Friday Senior Tackle. You'll be missed when things are tough. We'll miss your helping hand, encouragement, the idea to run "robust" and get the job done.

The following season, Bruce was dismissed by Ohio State, a development some felt might have been forestalled if Hayes had still been on the scene.

Steve Hayes closed the memorial, including accounts of family scenes—his father wearing a Darth Vader helmet, shooting a toy laser, playing with Steve's son, or holding one of Steve's daughter's dolls. "I cherish those memories of him," Steve said. With a glance to the sky, he added: "I submit that, come fall, he will have the best seat in the house."

After the ceremony, Schembechler stopped at Woody's office in the Military Science Building and quietly looked around, studying the huge, cluttered blackboard on which Woody had chalked the outline of a book he was writing; reading inscriptions on plaques and trophies; scanning the impressive display of books; musing over pictures on the wall, including an obviously ancient portrait of Ralph Waldo Emerson, which Woody had received shortly before his death and which he treasured.

"I just wanted to see all the things," the Michigan coach said simply, as he bade a private and personal farewell to "the old man."

On Woody Hayes' unpretentious headstone is a verse the coach quoted many times:

> *And in the night of death*
> *Hope sees a star,*
> *and listening love can hear*
> *The rustle of a wing.*

> —*Robert Green Ingersoll*

Appendix A

LETTERS TO WOODY

A veritable flood of mail followed termination of the football phase of Woody Hayes' career, December 30, 1978, as did his "coming out" speech to the Columbus Chamber of Commerce, January 19, 1979.

After his death, Mrs. Hayes donated all of Woody's memorabilia, including the letters, to The Ohio State University. She felt "that's what Woody would have wanted. He loved the University."

His office in the Military Science Building yielded more than 50 huge cardboard packing boxes full of trophies, plaques, commendations, sculptures, paintings, scarlet and gray rugs, pictures, notebooks, his coaching jackets, and sundry other items brought, or sent to him by fans.

In excess of 5,000 books were part of the Hayes donation, intended for use by present and future students through the University's libraries.

Before relinquishing a score of jammed manila folders containing letters received by Woody, Mrs. Hayes permitted me to excerpt a representative number. They are included here in the belief they are a part of the Woody Hayes story.

After the 1978 Gator Bowl

I know things have gone badly for you, but, as the old saying goes, one swallow doesn't make the Spring and one mistake doesn't wipe out decades of good leadership and good coaching. For that longer performance, I and your friends here at Notre Dame send you congratulations, not recriminations.

Father Theodore M. Hesburgh, S.C.S., President, University of Notre Dame

When you win you hear from everyone. When you lose you hear from your friends. You can be sure Pat and I will always be in the latter category. I ran across a quote from Churchill which I thought you might like to see. "Success is never final; failure is never fatal." Dolores Hope told me shortly after I resigned, "One who loves you is worth ten who hate you." Always remember there are many of us who love you." (handwritten note)

Former President Richard Nixon
San Clemente, California, January 1, 1979

Words are sometimes difficult to come by, but I want you to know I am your friend come "Hell or high water." I know how much good you have done for so many, including myself, so count me in if I can be of help in any way." (handwritten note)

Former President Gerald R. Ford

I have thought of you almost constantly during the past week. Recent events and actions were sad developments and seem so unfair when put into perspective. You have been a great coach, an outstanding citizen and a man who has had a positive influence on thousands of young men and millions of citizens of our nation. Thoughtful people will never forget it. You have been knocked down but you will never be out. You still have much to contribute to this country—and you will. (signed, Westy)

William C. Westmoreland, General
United States Army, Ret.

First: I do not blame you for what happened. I blame those people who pushed and pushed you beyond your limit to achieve their ends. You have given too much of yourself. I know of no man, including myself, who after many years of great responsibility and tremendous pressure, has not lost temporary control of himself; second, you have not lost any of my respect, my admiration, my confidence and above all of my deep feeling of friendship; third, there has never been a greater football coach/benefactor of young men than Woody Hayes and you must know there are tens of thousands of people all over the country who totally agree with me. (handwritten note)

Lewis W. Walt, General
U.S. Marine Corps

Because I had the privilege of playing for a great man who likewise respected you immensely, all of us have followed your career with much interest and admiration. Those of us who are now following the steps of those like you fully appreciate the sacrifices, discipline and perspective you stressed to your athletes through the years. That same perspective forces any detractors to focus on your enormous achievements over the years, rather than a single incident.

Bart Starr
Green Pay Packers great
(head coach at the time)

Those who would accentuate the negative and eclipse the contributions of Woody Hayes within the realm of collegiate athletics are nothing short of aloof to reality. As one who refused to follow the trodden path, but opted instead to go forward and leave a trail for those to follow, you are to be commended. To paraphrase the poet: Among life's dying embers/These are my regrets,/When I am right, no one remembers; / When I am wrong, no one forgets.

Gil Brandt, Vice-President
Dallas Cowboys

This man will miss you for being Woody Hayes, not Coach Hayes. You are remembered not for your record, but for the things you did for me that made me a better man. (handwritten note)

Lee Corso,
TV commentator
former head coach at Indiana

I just want you to know that I hold you in high regard as a gentleman and sportsman because of the many wonderful things that you have done for the coaching profession and for the boys that have played under you in your years of coaching. You have been a real inspiration to all of us who have competed against you and I want you to know sincerely that the teams at the University of Illinois have always held in high regard the teams at Ohio State that you coached. They have always been great sportsmen, and that reflects only the great techniques of their coach.

Ray Eliot
former head coach
University of Illinois

Please consider us friends and ones that will always remember Woody Hayes as a great coach, great American, and above all, a great and considerate man.

Anna and Woody Stillwagon
parents of former OSU player Jim Stillwagon

I write to express my appreciation for the many ways in which your career has been a credit to your profession, Ohio State and to you as a human being. . . You have been outspoken, courageous and successful.

You, as is true of all of us, have made mistakes, but the net of your career is a strongly positive one.

John Corbally
former Ohio State University administrator

Nobody can take your place in the hearts of the young men you have coached or the old men you have coached with or the loyal fans you have coached for. Your departure leaves an empty spot that will never be filled, but will always be remembered and the memory of it will be forever a tender thing, because, Woody, you were one hell of a coach, and you are still one hell of a man.

Tiger Ellison
former OSU freshmen coach

Please be assured that I appreciate the tremendous influence that you have been on literally thousands of students throughout your career. Your philosophy of life is one of the finest I have observed and your dedication to The Ohio State University and the State of Ohio and the United States of America is heartwarming indeed.

Roy M. Kottman, Dean
OSU College of Agriculture and Home Economics

I want you to know that I think the world and all of you as a person, as a coach and as a humanist.

Dr. John Peter Minton
Professor of Surgery, OSU
internationally known in cancer treatment and research

Your contribution to football and college life rank you with the great coaches of our times. . . . I am especially appreciative of your many contributions to minority youth both on and off the field. Through your interest and efforts many of them are now pursuing successful careers.

William Jimmerson Holloway
professor of education

Several times at the conclusion of one of your speeches, you would end with a poem about building a bridge over a chasm to make it less hazardous for those who follow. . . . Now, you can continue to build those bridges in some other fashion. Whatever method you choose, I do know one thing, the job will be done with enthusiasm and fervor and lives will be affected for that has been Woody's impact upon people.

Frank Ellwood
former OSU quarterback and assistant coach

I came to OSU to have fun and play football. It took a few years, but your insistence on education finally sunk in. By this time I had also obtained some amount of discipline and became aware of the advantages of sacrifice in obtaining a goal. . . . I gave up a lot of other things to become a lawyer. . . .Despite the fact that we were never on what I would call close terms, I feel that you have had a tremendous effect on my life. As the old cliché goes, "If I had a son, I'd like him to play for Woody Hayes."

Stan White, attorney
former OSU linebacker

The personal interest you showed in each one of us made me feel I was a part of a large family. As a member of that family, I thank you for the hard work and the successes, because you showed us they go hand in hand. You were never too busy to listen to players' problems, you never deserted us even if it would have been convenient to do so.

Alan Jack
former OSU guard

The rather traumatic events in that last game don't wipe out a lifetime of success and all the very good and positive things you have accomplished. . . . I believe I was one of the first fellows you recruited and you were my coach, my friend and my inspiration for 28 years, and nothing has occurred to change that.

John Borton
former OSU quarterback

I cannot begin to tell you the great, positive influence you have had on my life. . . . I have reflected upon many of the good things that have happened to me and my family, much of which is a direct result of your very positive influence on me during my years at OSU and the many things I learned from you. . . . I am a better person for having known you, and having the privilege of playing under you.

Bill Cummings, Jr.
former OSU tackle

I know what your frustration must have been to cause such a reaction, but love you for being so totally committed to excellence. You trained many of us well. No one man or action will ever detract from that. . . . There are many people who owe so much to you and stand behind you at this time.

Mike Current
former OSU tackle

Aside from my own mother and father I know of no one who has had a greater impact upon me than you have had. I know I am only one of thousands whose life was touched by your leadership, strength, unselfishness, your deep commitment to excellence and the deep commitment to your players and your coaching staff. You have given so unselfishly of yourself to so many people for so many years.

Chuck Clausen
former OSU assistant coach

There is no doubt in my mind that had I attended another university, I probably would have lost my scholarship when my heart murmur was discovered. Yet, you not only let me keep my scholarship, but forced me to keep close contact with you and the football team in a very rewarding capacity as assistant coach. I will have to credit you with the decision I made to go to medical school. . . . Your honesty, integrity and personal drive have been a great inspiration to me and something I hope I will be able to emulate. . . . My respect, admiration and devotion to you will never waver.

Dr. John Derbyshire
former freshman player
forced to quit football for health reasons

You developed me from a dumb country boy into a responsible, competitive and fairly intelligent citizen. . . .You taught me a value system that I still hold onto after all these years. You taught me that a man defeated has usually defeated himself. I've told hundreds of youngsters your story about the great sculptor who starts with a hunk of stone and just chips off what he doesn't want. You taught me respect for rules, teamwork, punctuality, fair play and patriotism. You made sure I received my education and you gathered blood donors for my dad when he was in University Hospital. Only we, who knew you as your players, will know your true value to society. I love you for all the things you did for me.

John Martin
principal, Avon Park, Florida middle school
former OSU player

When Tom was being recruited, I honestly was not very enthusiastic about Tom attending Ohio State. We stress academics in our family (somehow the sports take care of themselves) and we felt a degree would not be the number one priority at Ohio State. How wrong we were! Our minds were quickly changed when you visited our home. Your genuine interest and concern for your players' future was very evident. When Tom decided to attend Ohio State, I felt good that he would be playing for you.

Mrs. Lyle Levenick
mother of 1978 freshman player

The training table employees feel fortunate that we have had the opportunity to get to know you on a personal level. It has been a great pleasure to serve a man who has done so very much for this University and its athletic program. Our acquaintance with you will always come to mind as part of The Ohio State University.

Letter signed by 28 Ohio Union workers involved in serving dinner to OSU football players and coaches each weekday night during the season

You have made me proud to be a graduate of Ohio State University. While I was there I never attended a game, never supported athletics and frequently called you a fanatic. No more. Never again. Had I realized then the rightness of your values, your ability to teach, educate and elevate people to greatness. . . . it still wouldn't have mattered. I took you for granted. No more. You're a winner and we need winners. You care about people and we need that care. You're a hard taskmaster and we need that, too. Coach, so few people have all that you have to give. We need you to teach us to be proud and to win!

Gregg Schuler
OSU alumnus

After Chamber of Commerce Speech

I have just returned from the annual luncheon meeting of the Chamber of Commerce. . . . Outside of the very emotional impact your remarks make on everybody, I must say you grew a whole foot taller before that tremendous group. Their response to your presence was a magnificent tribute to Woody, "the man." Your remarks could be a historical document applicable to any young man or woman anywhere from fourteen to sixty. My feelings about integrity in sports and business coincide exactly with yours. . . . History will record the tremendous record you have made and all those fortunate enough to have heard you speak today went away from the meeting happy and emotionally better people than when they arrived. . . . I respect you, admire you and hope that you will always be a warm friend of mine.

John W. Galbreath
international financier and sportsman

I have been an admirer and supporter of yours since the first day you took over the head coaching job at Ohio State. . . . When I have had the privilege of introducing you, I have tried to say that beyond your won/lost record, you were a leader of men who has made almost unprecedented contributions to our University and to the coaching world—and I believed and felt that very sincerely. . . . My dad and others have told me that you proved that greatness the way you handled the Chamber of Commerce luncheon. . . . I wanted you to know. . . . Because of a previous business commitment in Canada. . . . I was unable to be with you that day.

Dan Galbreath,
John Galbreath's son and successor
former OSU trustee

Just learned that you have been honored by being selected for the College Football Hall of Fame. Congratulations on this richly deserved recognition. Over many years you achieved tremendous success as one of the finest football coaches of all time, but more importantly you were always a great leader for our youth and an inspiration to them. I treasure and cherish our wonderful friendship.

Former President Gerald R. Ford

I have just finished listening to your speech at the Chamber of Commerce. You brought much honor to yourself and our university. Your comments about the importance of sound family life for our youth of today in this type of world need to be repeated constantly... While I shall always remember your remarkable coaching record, I will always hold in greater esteem your concern for the total personal development of your and my students.

Kent P. Schirian
professor and chairman
OSU Department of Sociology

I was very lucky to hear your speech at the Chamber of Commerce and want to commend you. . . . Needless to say, you have inspired my life with your desire to win and to work for perfection.... I still admire your love for Ohio State and your feeling that an education is more important than winning or losing a football game. . . . It is sad to see you go but please remember one thing—Bill Mrukowski appreciates his education, football experience, coaching experience and finally, the opportunity to have been associated with such a fine gentleman.

Bill Mrukowski
former OSU quarterback

I saw the incident that cost us a great football coach and American. . . . I was awake until 5:30 a.m. recalling all the great things I have learned from you that have made me a better man. . . . I walked on your 1974 team when I was 26 years old and had been in service and started a family. I already knew about responsibility and hard work, but I didn't know about teamwork, love, respect, loyalty and the three Ds Arch made famous (desire, determination and dedication). . . . Before coming to Ohio State as a player and grad assistant, I had a chip on my shoulder. I felt I was shorted on breaks. Then I took my tough guy attitude onto your field just to see if I could be tough enough to make it. That was the greatest day of my life and the beginning of the greatest years of my life. I learned from you that breaks don't just happen, you make your own breaks, no one owes you a damn thing; that, as in one of your sayings, nothing in this world that comes easy is worth a damn. I am by far not the only one in 28 years you have reached, but I want you to know how much this man appreciates the righteousness you stand for. . . . You have been such an inspiration to me that my son is named for you: Justin Woodrow Alles.

Tod Alles
former OSU player

The populace writes, too

Famous radio news commentator Lowell Thomas penned a note to John Galbreath with an attached clipping which carried news of the Ohio Senate resolution commending Woody Hayes. Thomas' note, sent to Woody by Mr. Galbreath, said: "I was pleased to see this piece in the *New York Times*. Also perhaps at a later date I hope they name the stadium for him. In his own way he has been one of the giants of our time."

Your (Chamber of Commerce) speech, which I read in the *Dispatch*, was truly the mark of a great man . . . . I have received degrees from The Ohio State University and the University of Michigan. I must be honest and tell you that I have been and remain a loyal Michigan booster in sports. . . . Before reading your speech I am not sure I would have said this: Without meaning to convey disrespect or disloyalty to the great coaches that we have had in Ann Arbor, it would be nice if you had been one of them. Yes, I would have been proud of you as a coach of the Wolverines!

K.H. Moltrecht
professor, OSU Industrial Engineering

You have had a long and brilliant career and I hope you don't consider it over.... The press in this part of the country has been very complimentary and you have many, many boosters.... I suppose the years have taken great toll of the U.S.S. Rinehart crew members but those of us still around remember a hectic night off Wake Island when you saved the ship (and me) with some remarkable seamanship.... I can remember as though it were yesterday delivering to you the radio message that your son had been born.

Eugene J. Durgin
Vice-chairman, Howard Johnson's Board of Directors
served with Woody in the Navy

Patricia Dixon, a teacher at Sharon Elementary School in Columbus, asked her fifth and sixth grade classes to write a paper on one of several subjects, one of which was Woody Hayes. Steve H. submitted the following:

Woody Hayes was an Ohio State University football coach. He was fired about a week ago. My feelings are mixed. In some ways I think he should have been fired, in some not!

The incident that led him to his firing was when Clemson University intercepted a pass and the player got knocked to the sidelines. Woody gently walked up to him and punched him in the neck.

My good feelings about him are that he was such a nice man most of the time. Once in a drugstore, he sat down beside me and asked me if I wanted ice cream and when I said yes, he bought me some. He then signed his autograph and soon left.

I think he was responsible for perking up Ohio State. He is a good man and I don't think any coach outshone him! The new coach for OSU will never do as good as ol' Woody Hayes.

Bobby M. wrote directly to Woody:

I saw what you did. I thought it was kind of funny, but when I heard what they did to you, I was mad! Some people deserve it, you don't.

You are a champ to me. You are better than Elvis. He used to be my favorite star. Some people don't like you and a friend of mine called you an _____, so I hit him and broke his nose. I felt sad about it, but nobody is going to call my champ that!

From Lori:

Today is my birthday. I got a hamster. His name is Woody. I named him after you.

Fortunately, these and hundreds of other letters arrived before Woody's eyesight made reading difficult or impossible.

Appendix B

WOODY'S LETTER WINNERS 1951-1978

A

Adams, Douglas O., 1968-69-70
Adderly, Nelson W., 1965
Adkins, David, 1974-75-76-77
Adulewicz, Casimir T., 1959
Allegro, Joe, 1975-76-77
Amlin, George P., 1966
Anders, Billy J., 1965-66-67
Anderson, Kim, 1964-65-66
Anderson, Richard L., 1964-65
Anderson, Richard, 1952
Anderson, Thomas L., 1964
Anderson William T., 1968-69-70
Andrews, Lawrence F., 1951
Andria, Ernest, 1975-77-78-79
Andrick, Theodore K., 1964-65
Applegate, Richard, 1974-75
Arledge, Richard, 1951
Armstrong, Billy J., 1060-61-62
Armstrong, Ralph A., 1949-50-51
Arnold, Birtho, 1957-58-59
Aston, Daniel B., 1969
Atha, Robert, 1978-79-80-81
Auer, John J., 1953
Augenstein, Jack G., 1953
Ayers, Ronald, 1974-75-76

B

Baas, James W., 1965-66
Bach, Terry, 1977-78
Backhus, Tom A., 1967-68-69
Bailey, Ralph, 1958
Baldacci, Thomas G., 1955-56-57
Ballmer, Paul E., 1958
Bargerstock, Douglas, 1974
Barnett, Orlando T., 1963-64-65
Barrington, Thomas G., 1963-64-65
Bartley, Thomas A., 1967-68
Bartoszek, Mike,1972-73-74
Barwig, Ronald, 1977-78-79-80
Baschnagel, Brian, 1972-73-74-75
Battista, Thomas, 1971
Baxa, Thomas, L., 1972
Beam, William D., 1959
Beamon, Eddie, 1974-75-76-77
Bechtel, Earl R., 1952
Beecroft, Charles, 1971-72
Beekley, Marts E., 1951-52
Beerman, Raymond O., 1957
Belgrave, Earl, 1972
Bell, Farley, 1975-76
Bell, Todd, 1977-78-79-80
Belmer, Cliff, 1978-79
Bender, Edward A., 1968
Benis, Michael K., 1960
Betz, Wayne O., 1961-62
Bledsoe, John, 1971-72
Blinco, Thomas, 1976-77-79
Bobo, Herbert L., 1954
Bodenbender, David G., 1964
Bombach, Jaren D., 1967
Bond, Robert J., 1952-53-54-55
Bonica, Charles, 1970-71-72
Booth, William A., 1953-54-55

Borton, John R., 1951-52-53-54

Bowermaster, Russell L., 1956-57-58

Bowers, Brian, 1973-74

Bowsher, Gerald J., 1959

Bradshaw, Morris, 1971-72-73

Breehl, Edward L., 1957

Brockington, John S., 1968-69-70

Brown, Aaron, 1974-75-76-77

Brown, Jeff, 1972

Brown, Leo M., 1955-56-57

Brown, Timothy, 1978-79

Brubaker, Carl R., 1953-54

Brudzinski, Robert, 1973-74-75-76

Bruney, Fred K., 1950-51-52

Bruney, Robert O., 1962-63

Brungard, David A., 1967-68

Bryant, Charles S., 1959-60-61

Bugel, Thomas E., 1963-64-65

Buonamici, Nicholas, 1973-74-75-76

Burgin, Asbury L., 1965-66

Burke, Timothy, 1978-79

Burris, Scott, 1978-79-80

Burrows, Norman, 1978-79-80

Burrows, Roger W., 1970

Burton, Arthur F., 1967-68-69

Butts, Robert W., 1960-62

C

Cairns, Gary L., 1966-67

Campana, Thomas, 1969-70-71

Campbell, Paul, 1976-77-78-79

Cannavino, Joseph P., 1955-56-57

Cappell, Richard A., 1969-70-71

Cassady, Craig, 1973-74-75

Cassady, Howard (Hop), 1952-53-54-55

Castignola, Gregory, 1977-78-79

Cato, Byron 1975-76-77-78

Cheney, David A., 1968-69-70

Chonko, Arnie, 1962-63-64

Cisco, Galen, 1955-56-57

Clark, Donald, 1956-57-58

Clotz, Dennis R., 1961

Coburn, James A., 1970

Cochran, Terrence A., 1965

Cole, Robert, 1956

Collmar, William J., 1954-55

Colzie, Cornelius, 1972-73-74

Conley, William N., 1970-71

Connor, Daniel D., 1961

Conroy, James, 1969

Conway, Blair, 1972-73

Cook, Ronald L., 1955-57

Cope, James, 1972-73-74

Cousineau, Tom, 1975-76-77-78

Cox, Garth, 1974-76-77

Cowman, Randy, 1972

Crapser, Steven R., 1969

Crawford, Albert K., 1956-57-58

Crawford, Thomas E., 1957

Cummings, John, 1972

Cummings, William G., 1956

Cunningham, Charles, 1971

Curcillo, Anthony, 1950-51-52

Current, Michael, 1965-66

Curto, Patrick, 1973-74-75

Cusick, Martin, 1977

Cusick, Peter, 1972-73-74

Cutillo, Dan, 1971-72-73

D

Dale, Michael D., 1970

Dannelley, Scott, 1972-73-74-75

Dansler, Kelton, 1975-76-77-78

Datish, Michael, 1975

Davidson, James, 1963-64

Davis, Jeff, 1971-72-73

Davis, Jerome, 1973-74

Dawdy, Donald A., 1953

Debevc, Mark C., 1968-69-70

DeCree, Van, 1972-73-74

DeLeone, Thomas, 1969-70-71

Denker, Irv., 1952
Detrick, Roger, 1959-60
Dillman, Thomas M., 1954-55-56
Dillon, Daniel D., 1966
Disher, Larry L., 1957
Dixon, Joe, 1975-76-77
Dixon, Ken 1970-71
Doll, John, 1972
Donley, Douglas, 1977-78-79-80
Donovan, Brian P., 1968-69-70
Doyle, Richard A., 1950-52
Dreffer, Stephan D., 1962-63-64
Drenik, Douglas J., 1962-63-64
Dugger, Dean, 1952-53-54
Dulin, Gary, 1976-77-78-79
Dwyer, Donald W., 1965-66-67

E

Eachus, William N., 1965-66
Ebinger, Elbert C., 1955
Ehrsam, Gerald R., 1966-67-68
Elia, Bruce, 1972-73-74
Elliott, Samuel, 1965-66-67
Ellis, Ray, 1977-78-79-80
Ellwood, Franklin D., 1955-56
Endres, Robert L., 1951
Epitropoulos, John, 1978-79-80
Ervin, Terry L., 1966-67
Espy, Bennie E., 1962-63
Ezzo, Billy, 1972-73-74

F

Facchine, Richard, 1955
Fair, Robert F., 1963
Farrell, John R., 1960
Federle, Tom, 1963-64
Fender, Paul E., 1967
Ferguson, Keith, 1978-79-80
Ferguson, Robert E., 1959-60-61
Ferko, Richard, 1970-71
Ferrelli, Jeffrey, 1975-76

Fertig, Dwight L., 1967
Fields, Jerry E., 1958-59
Fiers, Alan, 1959-60
Fill, John M., 1964-65-66
Fischer, Louis C., 1950-51
Fitz, Thomas, 1964
Fletcher, Kevin, 1970-71-72
Foley, David, 1966-67-68
Fontes, Arnold P., 1965-66
Fontes, Leonard J., 1958-59
Fortney, Harrison, 1963
Foster, Rodney, 1961-62
Fox, Tim, 1972-73-74-75
France, Doug, 1972-73-74
Francis, David L., 1960-62
Fritz, Kenneth, 1976-77-78-79
Fronk, Daniel A., 1957-58
Funk, Robert, 1964-65

G

Gaffney, Mike, 1972
Gage, Ralph G., 1958
Galbos, Richard, 1971-72
Gales, Richard, 1971-72
Gandee, Sherwin K., 1948-50-51
Gentile, Jim M., 1968-69-70
Gerald, Rod, 1975-76-77-78
German, William, 1959-60
Gibbs, Jack G., 1954
Gillian, Lonnie R., 1967-68-69
Givens, Dan O., 1971
Goodsell, Douglas R., 1951-52
Gordon, Les, 1975
Gradishar, Randy, 1971-72-73
Graf, Lawrence, 1973
Greene, Cornelius, 1973-74-75
Greene, Horatius A., 1969
Griffin, Archie, 1972-73-74-75
Griffin, Duncan, 1975-76-77-78
Griffin, Ray, 1974-75-76-77
Grimes, Robert L., 1950-51-52
Guess, Michael, 1976-77-78-79
Guthrie, George P., 1951-52

Guy, Richard S., 1954-55-56
Guzik, Frank A., 1953

H

Hackett, William J., 1967-69
Haer, Archie H., 1967
Hague, Thomas R., 1952-53
Hamilton, Ray L., 1949-50-51
Hamlin, Stanley A., 1965
Hansley, Terrence, 1959
Hardman, von Allen, 1961
Hare, Gregory, 1971-72-73
Harkins, Donald L., 1962-63-64
Harkrader, Jerry, 1953-54-55
Harman, Timothy A., 1970
Harrell, James, 1975-76-77
Harris, Jimmie L., 1969-70-71
Harris, Tyrone, 1974-75-77
Hart, Randall J., 1967-68-69
Hartman, Gabriel C., 1958-59-60
Hasenohrl, George, 1970-71-72
Hauer, Oscar A., 1958-59-60
Haupt, Richard A., 1961
Hayden, Leophus, 1968-69-70
Hazel, David, 1972-73-74
Heid, Robert C., 1949-50-51
Henson, Harold, 1972-73-74
Henson, Luther, 1977-78-79-80
Herbstreit, James H., 1958-59-60
Herrmann, Harvey J., 1959
Hess, William W., 1960-61-62
Hicks, John, 1970-72-73
Hicks, Tyrone, 1978-79
Hietikko, James L., 1950-51
Hilinski, Richard, 1953-54
Himes, Richard D., 1965-66-67
Hlay, John, 1950-51
Holloway, Ralph B., 1968-69-70
Holycross, Tim, 1972-73-74
Hornik, Joe, 1975-76-77-78
Houk, Ronald, 1959-60
Houston, James, Sr., 1957-58-59

Houston, James, Jr., 1978
Howard, Harry, 1969-70-71
Howell, Carroll, 1952-53-54
Hubbard, Rudy, 1965-66-67
Hudson, Paul, 1964-65-66
Huff, Paul, 1967-68
Hughes, John, 1970-72-73
Hunter, Charles, 1977-78-79
Hutchings, John, 1978-79-80
Hutchision, Charles, 1967-68-69
Hyatt, Bob, 1974-76

I

Ingram, Robert M., 1959-60-61
Ireland, Kenneth D., 1962

J

Jack, Alan R., 1967-67-69
Jackson, Matthew, 1976
Jaco, William, 1976-77-79
Jacoby, George R., 1951-52-53
James, Daniel A., 1956-57-58
Janakievski, Vlade, 1977-78-79-80
Jankowski, Bruce D., 1968-69-70
Janowicz, Victor F., 1949-50-51
Jenkins, Joseph, 1967
Jenkins, Thomas G., 1961-62-63
Jentes, Charles A., 1960
Jesty, James B., 1970
Jobko, William K., 1954-55-56
Johnson, Kenneth E., 1960-61
Johnson, Ricky, 1977-78-80
Johnson, Pete, 1973-74-75-76
Johnson, Robert T., 1965-66
Jones, Ben, 1960
Jones, Arnold A., 1972-73-74
Jones, Herbert M., 1956-57
Jones, Herman, 1975-76-77
Joslin, Robert V., 1951-52-53

K

Kain, Lawrence, 1973-74-75
Kasunic, Gerald S., 1963-64
Katterhenrich, David, L., 1960-61-62
Kaylor, Ronald L., 1964
Keeton, Mike, 1973
Keith, Randal, T., 1971-72
Kelley, Dwight A., 1963-64-65
Kelley, John L., 1966-67
Kelly, Robert, 1971
Kern, Carl, 1972-73
Kern, Rex W., 1968-69-70
Kiehfuss, Thomas C., 1962-63 64
Kilgore, David S., 1958-59
King, Gerald L., 1970
Kinsey, Marvin C., 1971
Kirk, Roy E., 1963
Klaban, Tom, 1974-75
Klein, Robert J., 1960-61-62
Klevay, Walter S., 1949-50-51
Koegel, Vic, 1971-72-73
Koepnick, Robert E., 1950-51-52
Kohut, William W., 1964
Kregel, James, 1971-72-73
Kremblas, Francis T., 1956-57-58
Krisher, Gerald Glenn, 1951-52-53-54
Kriss, Frederick C., 1954-55-56
Krstolic, Raymond C., 1961-62
Kuhn, Richard, 1968-69-70
Kuhn, Kenneth W., 1972-73-74-75
Kumler, Karl W., 1962
Kurz, Theodore R., 1968-69

L

Lago, Gary M., 1970-71-72
Lambert, Howard L., 1961
Lamka, Donald, 1969-70-71
Lang, Mark, 1974-75-76-77

Lashutka, Gregory S., 1963-64-65
Laskoski, Richard D., 1961
Laughlin, James, 1977-78-79
LeBeau, Charles R., 1956-57-58
Lee, Ben, 1978-79-80-81
Leggett, William D., 1952-53-54
Lewis, Donald B., 1955
Lindner, James E., 1959-60
Lindsey, William L., 1964
Lippert, Elmer H., 1971-72-73
Lister, Robert C., 1961
Livingston, Brian, 1965
Logan, Jeff, 1974-75-76-77
Logan, Richard I., 1950-51
Long, David W., 1971
Long, William E., 1966-67-68
Longer, Robert M., 1964
Lord, John C., 1958
Luckay, Raymond J., 1951
Ludwig, Paul L., 1952-53-54
Luke, Steven N., 1972-73-74
Lukens, William, 1974-75-76
Luttner, Ken, 1969-70-71
Lykes, Robert L., 1965
Lyons, James D., 1963

M

Machinsky, Francis C., 1953-54-55
Maciejowski, Ronald J., 1968-69-70
Mack, Richard W., 1972-73-74
Mackie, Douglas, 1976-77
Mamula, Charles, 1962-63
Mangiamelle, Richard C., 1962
Manyak, John N., 1952
Marendt, Thomas L., 1971-72
Marsh, James R., 1970
Marshall, James, 1957-58
Martin, Harold P., 1952
Martin, John C., 1955-56-57

Portsmouth, Thomas, 1965-66-67

Powell, Theodore, 1972-73

Provenza, Russell D., 1957

Provost, Ted R., 1967-68-69

Pryor, Ray Von, 1964-65-66

Purdy, David B., 1972-73-74

R

Radtke, Michael, 1967-68-69

Rath, Thomas, L., 1950-51

Reese, Wayne G., 1961

Reichenbach, James, 1951-52-53-54

Rein, Robert E., 1964-65-66

Rich, Rocco J., 1971-72-73

Richards, David P., 1955

Richley, Richard C., 1965

Ricketts, Ormonde B., 1961-62-63

Ridder, William E., 1963-64-65

Riticher, Raymond J., 1952

Roach, Woodrow, 1973-74-75

Roberts, Jack C., 1961

Roberts, Robert L., 1952-53

Robinson, Philip, 1956-57

Robinson, Joseph, 1975-76-77-78

Roche, Tom, 1974-76-77

Roman, James, T., 1966-67-68

Roman, Nicholas G., 1966-67-69

Ronemus, Thor, 1950-51

Roseboro, James A., 1954-55-56

Ross, Paul, 1976-77-78

Ross, Richard L., 1960

Rosso, George A., 1951-52-53

Roush, Gary S., 1968

Rowland, James H., 1959

Ruehl, James, 1952

Ruhl, Bruce, 1973-74-75-76

Rusnak, Kevin G., 1967-68-69

Rutherford, William A., 1966

Ruzich, Stephen, 1950-51

S

Sander, Willard F., 1963-64-65

Sanders, Daryl T., 1960-61-62

Saunders, Keith, 1977

Savoca, James, 1974-75-76-78

Sawicki, Tim, 1976-79

Scannell, Michael P., 1971-72

Schafrath, Richard P., 1956-57-58

Schiller, Richard T., 1952

Schlichter, Arthur, 1978-79-80-81

Schmidlin, Paul R., 1967-68-69

Schneider, Michael, 1977

Schram, Fred, 1971

Schumacher, James W., 1952-53

Schumacher, Kurt, 1972-73-74

Schwartz, Brian, 1976-77-78-79

Schwartz, Gerald, 1952

Scott, Dan, 1971-73

Scott, Robert, M., 1962

Seifert, Rick E., 1970-72

Seilkop, Kenneth, 1959

Sensibaugh, Mike, 1968-69-70

Shedd, Jan W., 1955

Simon, Richard E., 1969-70-71

Simon, Charles, 1974

Skillings, Vincent, 1977-78-79-80

Skladany, Thomas, 1973-74-75-76

Skvarka, Bernie G., 1950-51

Smith, A.G., 1950-51

Smith, Bruce R., 1970

Smith, Carroll J., 1950-51

Smith, Huston R., 1966-67

Smith, Larry W., 1965

Smith, Robert G., 1967-68-69

Smith, Robert P., 1968

Smith, Ted, 1973-74-75

Smurda, John R., 1972-73

Snell, Matthew, 1961-62-63

Sobolewski, John J., 1966-68

Sommer, Karl, W., 1956

Spahr, William H., 1962-63-64
Sparma, Joseph B., 1961-62
Spears, Thomas R., 1953-54-55
Springs, Ron, 1976-77-78
Spychalski, Ernest T., 1956-57-58
Stanley, Bernie D., 1963
Stephens, Larry P., 1959-60-61
Stier, Mark H., 1966-67-68
Stillwagon, James R., 1968-69-70
Stock, Robert H., 1964
Stoeckel, Donald C., 1953-54-55
Storer, Greg, 1975-76-77
Stottlemyer, Victor R., 1966-67-68
Stowe, John H., 1968
Strahine, Michael, 1977
Straka, Mark, 1973
Strickland, Phillip S., 1968-69-70
Strong, Terry, 1970
Sullivan, Mark, 1975-76-77-78
Sutherin, Donald P., 1955-56-57
Swartz, Donald C., 1952-53-54

T

Takacs, Michael, J., 1951-52-53
Tatum, Jack D., 1968-69-70
Taylor, Alvin, 1978
Teague, Willie M., 1970-71-72
Ternent, William A., 1952
Theis, Franklyn B., 1955
Thomas, Aurelius, 1955-56-57
Thomas, Richard J., 1951-52
Thomas, Will C., 1965-66
Thompson, Ed, 1974-75-76
Thompson, Kenneth, 1955
Thornton, Robert F., 1952-53-54
Tidmore, Samuel E., 1960-61
Tingley, David R., 1959-61
Tolford, George K., 1959-60-61
Trapuzzano, Robert, 1969
Trivisonno, Joseph J., 1955-57
Troha, Richard J., 1969
Tyrer, James E., 1958-59-60

U

Ulmer, Edward, 1960-61
Unverferth, Donald, V., 1963-64-65
Urbanik, William J., 1967-68-69

V

Van Horn, Douglas C., 1963-64-65
Van Raaphorst, Richard W., 1961-62-63
Vanscoy, Norman J., 1960
Vargo, Kenneth W., 1953-54-55
Vargo, Thomas W., 1965
Varner, Thomas A., 1960
Vavroch, William B., 1952
Vecanski, Milan, 1970-71
Vicic, Donald J., 1954-55-56
Vogel, Robert L., 1960-61-62
Vogelgesang, Donald A., 1960
Vogler, Terry, 1977-78
Vogler, Tim, 1975-76-77-78
Volley, Ricardo, 1977-78-79

W

Wagner, Jack W., 1950-51
Wakefield, Richard, 1969-70-71
Walden, Robert L., 1964-65-66
Walker, Jack E., 1960
Walker, Stephen E., 1971
Walther, Richard E., 1950-51
Ward, Chris, 1974-75-76-77
Warfield, Paul D., 1961-62-63
Warner, Duane A., 1960
Washington, Alvin, 1977-78-79-80
Wassmund, James A., 1956
Wasson, Richard, 1963
Watkins, Jene, 1959
Watkins, Robert A., 1952-53-54

Watson, Otha, 1978
Waugh, Charles A., 1970
Waugh, Thomas, 1976-77-78-79
Weaver, David A., 1953-54-55
Weaver, J. Edward, 1970
Weed, Thurlow, 1952-53-54
Wentz, William A., 1959-60
Wersel, Timothy, 1972
Whetstone, Robert E., 1953-55
White, Jan, 1968-69-70
White, Loren R., 1957-58-59
White, Stanley R., 1969-70-71
Whitfield, David A., 1967-68-69
Wiggins, Larry, 1972
Wilkins, Dwight, 1972
Wilks, William C., 1951
Willard, Robert, 1973
Williams, David M., 1953-54
Williams, Lee E., 1955-58
Williams, Robert D., 1968
Williams, Shad, 1970-71-72
Willott, Louis, 1974-75
Willis, Leonard, 1974-75

Wittman, Julius W., 1949-50-51
Wittmer, Charles G., 1959-60-61
Wolery, Scott, 1974
Worden, Dirk J., 1966-67-68
Wortman, Robert C., 1964
Wright, David W., 1970
Wright, Ernest H., 1958

Y

Yonclas, Nicholas, 1963-64
Young, Donald G., 1958-59-60
Young, Richard A., 1953-54

Z

Zawacki, Charles E., 1955
Zelina, Lawrence P., 1968-69-70
Ziegler, Randall K., 1963
Zima, Albert J., 1962

WOODY'S ASSISTANT COACHES 1951-1978

Adolph, David, 1977-78
Arnsparger, Jr., William, 1951-53
Bruce, Earle, 1966-72
Bugel, Joe, 1974
Catuzzi, Larry, 1965-67
Chaump, George, 1968-78
Clark, Lyal, 1954-65
Clausen, Charles, 1971-75
Ellison, Glenn, 1963-68
Ellwood, Frank, 1958, 1962-64
Fekete, Gene, 1949-58
Ferkany, Edward, 1972-73
Fiers, Alan, 1961
Gibbs, Alex, 1975-78
Godfrey, Ernie, 1929-61
Gunlock, William, 1961-62
Herbstreit, James, 1961-62
Hess, William, 1951-57
Hietikko, Jim, 1954
Hill, George, 1971-78

Hindman, Hugh, 1963-69
Holtz, Lou, 1968
Hubbard, Rudy, 1968-73
Jackson, Mickey, 1974-78
Larson, Gordon, 1959-60
Mallory, William, 1966-68
Mason, Glen, 1978-85
McClain, David, 1969-70
McCullough, Lou, 1963-70
Mummey, John, 1969-76
Myles, Bill, 1977-84
O'Hara, William, 1952-53
Perry, Doyt, 1951-54
Rush, Clive, 1955-57, 59
Sarkkinen, Esco, 1946-77
Schembechler, Glenn, 1958-62
Slaughter, Gene, 1960
Staub, Ralph, 1970-76
Strobel, Harry, 1949-67
Tranquill, Gary, 1977-78
Urick, Max, 1963-65
Walker, Richard, 1969-76

Appendix C

W.W. "WOODY" HAYES' RECORD 1951-1978
Won 205, Lost 61, Tied 10

1951
Captain: Robert C. Heid

OSU		
7	Southern Methodist	0
20	Michigan State	24
6	Wisconsin	6
10	Indiana	32
47	Iowa	21
3	Northwestern	0
16	Pittsburgh	14
0	Illinois	0
0	Michigan	7
109		104

Won 4, Lost 3, Tied 2
Big Ten Finish: 5th

1952
Captain: Bernie G. Skvarka

OSU		
33	Indiana	13
14	Purdue	21
23	Wisconsin	14
35	Washington State	7
0	Iowa	8
24	Northwestern	21
14	Pittsburgh	21
27	Illinois	7
27	Michigan	7
197		119

Won 6, Lost 3
Big Ten Finish: 3rd

1953
Captains: Robert V. Joslin,
George Jacoby

OSU		
36	Indiana	12
33	California	19
20	Illinois	41
12	Pennsylvania	6
20	Wisconsin	19
27	Northwestern	13
13	Michigan State	28
21	Purdue	6
0	Michigan	20
182		164

Won 6, Lost 3
Big Ten Finish: 4th

1954
Captains: C. Richard Brubaker,
John R. Borton

OSU		
28	Indiana	0
21	California	13
40	Illinois	7
20	Iowa	14
31	Wisconsin	14
14	Northwestern	7
26	Pittsburgh	0
28	Purdue	6
21	Michigan	7
20	*Southern California	7
249		75

Won 10, Lost 0
Big Ten Champions
National Champions
*Rose Bowl

1955
Captains: Frank C. Machinsky,
Kenneth W. Vargo

OSU		
28	Nebraska	20
0	Stanford	6
27	Illinois	12
14	Duke	20
26	Wisconsin	16
49	Northwestern	0
20	Indiana	13
20	Iowa	10
17	Michigan	0
201		97

Won 7, Lost 2
Big Ten Champions

1956
Captains: Franklin D. R. Ellwood, P.
William Michael

OSU		
34	Nebraska	7
32	Stanford	20
26	Illinois	6
6	Penn State	7
21	Wisconsin	0
6	Northwestern	2
35	Indiana	14
0	Iowa	6
0	Michigan	19
160		19

Won 6, Lost 3
Big Ten Finish: 4th (tie)

1957
Captains: Galen B. Cisco,
Leo M. Brown

OSU		
14	Texas Christian	18
35	Washington	7
21	Illinois	7
56	Indiana	0
16	Wisconsin	13
47	Northwestern	6
20	Purdue	7
17	Iowa	13
31	Michigan	14
10	*Oregon	7
267		92

Won 9, Lost 1
Big Ten Champions
National Champions
*Rose Bowl

1958
Captains: Francis T. Kremblas,
Richard P. Schafrath

OSU		
23	Southern Methodist	20
12	Washington	7
19	Illinois	13
49	Indiana	8
7	Wisconsin	7
0	Northwestern	21
14	Purdue	14
38	Iowa	28
20	Michigan	14
182		132

Won 6, Lost 1, Tied 2
Big Ten Finish: 3rd

1959

Captain: James E. Houston

OSU		
14	Duke	13
0	Southern California	17
0	Illinois	9
15	Purdue	0
3	Wisconsin	12
30	Michigan State	24
0	Indiana	0
7	Iowa	16
14	Michigan	23
83		23

Won 3, Lost 5, Tied 1
Big Ten Finish: 8th (tie)

1960

Captains: James Tyrer,
James Herbstreit

OSU		
24	Southern Methodist	0
20	Southern California	0
34	Illinois	7
21	Purdue	24
34	Wisconsin	7
21	Michigan State	10
36	Indiana	7
12	Iowa	35
7	Michigan	0
209		90

Won 7, Lost 2
Big Ten Finish: 3rd

1961

Captains: Thomas Perdue,
Michael Ingram

OSU		
7	Texas Christian	7
13	UCLA	3
44	Illinois	0
10	Northwestern	0
30	Wisconsin	21
29	Iowa	13
16	Indiana	7
22	Oregon	12
50	Michigan	20
221		83

Won 8, Lost 0, Tied 1
Big Ten Champions
National Champions
(Football Writers)

1962

Captains: Gary Moeller,
Robert Vogel

OSU		
41	North Carolina	7
7	UCLA	9
51	Illinois	15
14	Northwestern	18
14	Wisconsin	7
14	Iowa	28
10	Indiana	7
26	Oregon	7
28	Michigan	0
205		98

Won 6, Lost 3
Big Ten Finish: 3rd (tie)

1963
Captains: Ormonde Ricketts, Matthew Snell

OSU		
17	Texas A&M	0
21	Indiana	0
20	Illinois	20
3	Southern California	32
13	Wisconsin	10
7	Iowa	3
7	Penn State	10
8	Northwestern	17
14	Michigan	10
110		102

Won 5, Lost 3, Tied 1
Big Ten Finish: 2nd(tie)

1964
Captains: James Davidson, Wiliam Spahr, Thomas Kiehfuss

OSU		
27	Southern Methodist	8
17	Indiana	9
26	Illinois	0
17	Southern California	0
28	Wisconsin	3
21	Iowa	19
0	Penn State	27
10	Northwestern	0
0	Michigan	10
146		76

Won 7, Lost 2
Big Ten Finish: 2nd

1965
Captains: Dwight Kelley, Gregory Lashutka

OSU		
3	North Carolina	14
23	Washington	21
28	Illinois	14
7	Michigan State	32
20	Wisconsin	10
11	Minnesota	10
17	Indiana	10
38	Iowa	0
9	Michigan	7
156		118

Won 7, Lost 2
Big Ten Finish: 2nd

1966
Captains: John Fill, Mike Current, Ray Pryor

OSU		
14	Texas Christian	7
22	Washington	38
9	Illinois	10
8	Michigan State	11
24	Wisconsin	13
7	Minnesota	17
7	Indiana	0
14	Iowa	10
3	Michigan	17
108		123

Won 4, Lost 5
Big Ten Finish: 6th

1967
Captains: Billy Ray Anders, Samuel Elliott

OSU

7	Arizona	14
30	Oregon	0
6	Purdue	41
6	Northwestern	2
13	Illinois	17
21	Michigan State	7
17	Wisconsin	15
21	Iowa	10
24	Michigan	14
145		120

Won 6, Lost 3
Big Ten Finish: 4th

1968
Captains: David Foley, Dirk Worden

OSU

35	Southern Methodist	14
21	Oregon	6
13	Purdue	0
45	Northwestern	21
31	Illinois	24
25	Michigan State	20
43	Wisconsin	8
33	Iowa	27
50	Michigan	14
27	*Southern California	16
323		150

Won 10, Lost 0
Big Ten Champions

1969
Captains: David Whitfield, Alan Jack

OSU

62	Texas Christian	0
41	Washington	14
54	Michigan State	21
34	Minnesota	7
41	Illinois	0
35	Northwestern	6
62	Wisconsin	7
42	Purdue	14
12	Michigan	24
383		93

Won 8, Lost 1
Big Ten Co-Champions

1970
Captains: Rex Kern, Jan White, James Stillwagon, Douglas Adams

OSU

56	Texas A&M	13
34	Duke	10
29	Michigan State	0
28	Minnesota	8
48	Illinois	29
24	Northwestern	10
24	Wisconsin	7
10	Purdue	7
20	Michigan	9
17	*Stanford	27
290		120

Won 9, Lost 1
Big Ten Champions
*Rose Bowl
National Champions (NFF)

1971

Captains: Harry Howard,
Tom DeLeone

OSU		
52	Iowa	21
14	Colorado	20
35	California	3
24	Illinois	10
27	Indiana	7
31	Wisconsin	6
14	Minnesota	12
10	Michigan State	17
10	Northwestern	14
7	Michigan	10
224		120

Won 6, Lost 4
Big Ten Finish: 3rd (tie)

1972

Captains: Richard Galbos,
George Hasenohrl

OSU		
21	Iowa	0
29	North Carolina	14
35	California	18
26	Illinois	7
44	Indiana	7
28	Wisconsin	20
27	Minnesota	19
12	Michigan State	19
27	Northwestern	14
14	Michigan	11
17	*Southern California	42
280		171

Won 9, Lost 2
Big Ten Co-Champions
*Rose Bowl

1973

Captains: Greg Hare,
Richard Middleton

OSU		
56	Minnesota	7
37	Texas Christian	3
27	Washington State	3
24	Wisconsin	0
37	Indiana	7
60	Northwestern	0
30	Illinois	0
35	Michigan State	0
55	Iowa	13
10	Michigan	10
42	*Southern California	21
413		64

Won 10, Lost 0, Tied 1
Big Ten Co-Champions
*Rose Bowl

1974

Captains: Steve Myers,
Archie Griffin, Arnold Jones,
Neal Colzie, Pete Cusick

OSU		
34	Minnesota	19
51	Oregon State	10
28	Southern Methodist	9
42	Washington State	7
52	Wisconsin	7
49	Indiana	9
55	Northwestern	7
49	Illinois	7
13	Michigan State	16
35	Iowa	10
12	Michigan	10
17	*Southern California	18
437		129

Won 10, Lost 2
Big Ten Co-Champions
*Rose Bowl

1975

Captains: Archie Griffin, Brian
Baschnagel, Tim Fox, Ken Kuhn

OSU		
21	Michigan State	0
17	Penn State	9
32	North Carolina	7
41	UCLA	20
49	Iowa	0
56	Wisconsin	0
35	Purdue	6
24	Indiana	14
40	Illinois	3
38	Minnesota	6
21	Michigan	14
10	*UCLA	23
384		102

Won 11, Lost 1
Big Ten Champions
***Rose Bowl**

1976

Captains: Bill Lukens,
Ed Thompson, Tom Skladany

OSU		
49	Michigan State	21
12	Penn State	7
21	Missouri	22
10	UCLA	10
34	Iowa	14
30	Wisconsin	20
24	Purdue	3
47	Indiana	7
42	Illinois	10
9	Minnesota	3
0	Michigan	22
27	*Colorado	10
305		10

Won 9, Lost 2, Tied 1
Big Ten Co-Champions
***Orange Bowl**

1977

Captains: Chris Ward, Jeff Logan,
Aaron Brown, Ray Griffin

OSU		
10	Miami (FL)	0
38	Minnesota	7
28	Oklahoma	29
35	Southern Methodist	7
46	Purdue	0
27	Iowa	6
35	Northwestern	15
42	Wisconsin	0
35	Illinois	0
35	Indiana	7
6	Michigan	14
6	*Alabama	35
343	120	

Won 9, Lost 3
Big Ten Co-Champions
***Sugar Bowl**

1978

Captains: Ron Springs, Tim Vogler,
Tom Cousineau, Byron Cato

OSU		
0	Penn State	19
27	Minnesota	10
34	Baylor	28
35	Southern Methodist	35
16	Purdue	27
31	Iowa	7
63	Northwestern	20
49	Wisconsin	14
45	Illinois	7
21	Indiana	18
3	Michigan	14
15	*Clemson	17
339		216

Won 7, Lost 4, Tied 1
Big Ten Finish: 4th
***Gator Bowl**

Appendix D

EXCERPTS FROM WOODY HAYES' COMMENCEMENT ADDRESS

delivered before the faculty, graduates and guests of The Ohio State University, March 14, 1986

Graduates, Mr. President, faculty members, friends, and families of the graduates who have done so much to make this possible.

Today is the greatest day of my life.

And, Mr. President, you have certainly helped to make it that way. I appreciate so much being able to come here and talk to a graduating class at The Ohio State University, a great, great University.

I would like to start with something I have used in almost every speech, and that is, "paying forward." And that is the thing that you folks can do with your great education for the rest of your life.

Try to take that attitude toward life, that you're going to pay forward. So seldom can we pay back because those who helped most—your parents and other people—will be gone, but you'll find that you do want to pay. [Ralph Waldo] Emerson had something to say about that: "You can pay back only seldom." But he said, "You can always pay forward, and you must pay line for line, deed for deed, and cent for cent." He said, "Beware of too much good accumulating in your palm or it will fast corrupt." That was Emerson's attitude, and no one put it better than he did.

I'd like to give you a little advice today. I'll try not to give too much, just a little bit. One thing you cannot afford to do—

that's to feel sorry for yourself. That's what leads to drugs, to alcohol, to those things that tear you apart. In football we always said that the other team couldn't beat us. We had to be sure that we didn't beat ourselves. And that's what people have to do, too—make sure they don't beat themselves.

———

So many times you have found here at the University people who were smarter than you. I found them all the way through college and, in football: bigger, faster, harder. They were smarter people than I. But you know what they couldn't do? They couldn't outwork me. I ran into opposing coaches who had much better backgrounds than I did and knew a lot more football than I did. But they couldn't work as long as I could. They couldn't stick in there as long as I could. You can outwork anybody. Try it and you'll find out you can do it.

And I had a great, great association with my coaches. No one ever had better people than I did. Or better football players, and we outworked our opponents. The only way we got beaten was if we got a little fatheaded, if we didn't train well, if we had dissension on the squad, if we didn't recognize our purpose in life. Those are the people you win with.

———

Mr. Barthalow was my history and English teacher in junior high school. He was the best teacher I ever had, and I am so honored to have him here today. And to have my sister and my wife and friends, just as you're happy to have your parents here today, who have meant so much to you. A family life is unbelievable.

With good people, and this goes all the way back to my grandmother and all the way down the line, she didn't tell my dad, "Now you go to the study table." No, no. She said, "I'll meet you at the study table." And that's where your good parents and your good teachers are.

But when you deal with youngsters, when you get into jobs of any kind, don't *send* people to the job. Meet them there and help them do it. And you'll be amazed how it works.

In football we learn some wonderful, wonderful things. And one of them is this: When you get knocked down, which is plenty often, get right up in a hurry, just as quickly as you can. Do you know what to do then? You probably need more strength. Do you know where you get it? You get it in the huddle. You get it by going back and getting a new play and running that same play together with your teammates. That "together" is the thing that gives you the buildup to get ready to go again.

In your lifetimes, you'll find that how well you can work with people will depend on how quickly you get back to them and get together.

In football, you'll find out that nothing that comes easy is worth a dime. As a matter of fact, I never saw a football player make a tackle with a smile on his face. Never.

There's one more thing I want to get into, and then I will let you get graduated. I know you want to do that. That's what you came to college for. That's what your parents sent you to college for. We've had a great, great heritage. And so many times we've been so lucky that you can't believe it. The odds against us were unbelievable. In the battle of Salamis, 500 years before the birth of Christ, the Persians were attempting to conquer Greece and burned Athens down. The old men and women and the children were over on the beachhead at Salamis when the Persians came in to whip them.

But the Greeks had been getting ready for ten years. They had discovered silver on Mt. Laurium. And they had taken that silver to help them make good, small ships that could move. And they coaxed, they mousetrapped those Persians into the Bay of Salamis. And then they attacked them with the metal prows on their ships. They busted into them. The Persians couldn't get out of the way: their big troop-carrying ships were too awkward. So in one day, the Greeks sank the Persian fleet and drove them out of the Greek waters and all the way back to Persia.

Then the Greeks got busy. And you know what they did? They went over and rebuilt their city and decided they needed a new type of government. They even had a name for it: "de-mo-cra-tos." Have you ever heard of de-mo-cra-tos? People rule. That was the beginning of democracy. Right there on the Bay of Salamis is where we got this great system we have today.

To give you an appreciation of de-mo-cra-tos, a few years ago the mayor of Stuttgart, Germany, was here, and I interviewed him on television. He was the son of the great World War II general, Rommel. I asked him, "Did your father agree with Hitler's order to stop on May 24, 1940, when they were within 40 miles of the English Channel?" And he said, "Wait a minute, Coach. There's something you're not thinking about. My father did not have choices at all. He lived in a dictatorship." He went on to say, "I live in a democracy now, and you live in the greatest in the world, a great democracy. You and everyone else in your country have choices and decisions to make almost every day. My father didn't."

That night when I got home, I started wondering why he had become so upset. And then I recalled the last decision his father had made on this earth: the decision to take poison so that this boy and his mother could live. You can appreciate democracy when you look at it that way.

▬▬▬ ▄▄▄

My next story is much more recent. Another underdog victory. The fellows who did it were your age. They were four-to-one underdogs against Hitler's hordes at the Battle of Britain. At that time even the American ambassador to England was reporting that he didn't think the British could win. A matter of fact, every night the radio announcer would say with a mournful dirge in his voice, "This is London."

The British didn't look at it that way. They all fought— men, women, and the boys who flew those planes. And they did something greater than that. Their mathematicians and their scientists had done something that the German arrogance didn't think could happen. They had broken the German code—the Enigma Code. So that those British with their coding machines, the best in the world, broke that German code.

So the British knew where the German forces were coming from. They knew what time they'd arrive. They knew the point of attack, the formation, everything about them. Then British fighter planes—manned mainly by British but some Americans, some Polish, some Canadians—would strike them just as they were ready to lower their bombs.

Air Marshal Dowding didn't send the planes out over the Channel. He didn't have that many. He was outnumbered more than two-to-one. He didn't want to waste time or fuel or strength. These young fellows—just your age, mind you—wanted to get up there and fight and then get back for a couple hours to sleep under a shade tree and then go up and fight again. That's the way they fought and won.

And then after the British had won, General Dowding was criticized and fired. Well, there have been a lot of great men fired—MacArthur, Richard Nixon, a lot of them. But rather than knighting him for what he had done—and he had fought an unbelievably great war—they sent him out recruiting. He could very easily have straightened them out by telling them of the coding secret, but he wouldn't do that. He knew it was going to be needed for the rest of the war. And it wasn't told for 35 years after that. This man went to his death keeping it sealed. And that was Air Marshal Dowding, all honor to his great name. All honor.

They won. They won for us because if Hitler had whipped England and got the English Navy (that was a year-and-a-half before we ever got into the war), we'd have never joined the battle. And Hitler would have been over here after us, you can believe that.

So that's how fortunate we were to have those great British people. And you know what the greatest man in the war said about those fliers? He said, "Never has so much been owed by so many to so few." He was referring to those British fliers who won the Battle of Britain.

———

I'd like to tell one more story. And it's referred to still as a miracle, the miracle of Midway. Underdogs! You can't believe it. The Japanese had eight battleships in the area. We had eight too, but they were in the mud back at Pearl Harbor. This was six months after Pearl Harbor. The Japanese had 14 cruisers; we had 5 heavy cruisers. They had 45 destroyers; we had 15. They had a whole flotilla of submarines and eight admirals in the area. We had two, and one of them was a substitute. But that substitute made some of the greatest decisions ever made in combat.

Intelligence—yes, it was there. We had broken the Japanese code, and we knew where they were coming in. At least, Admiral Nimitz at Pearl knew. In Washington they didn't know. They'd have gotten mousetrapped like they did at Pearl Harbor six months before, but Admiral Nimitz knew. He had a great man, a Commander Rocquefort, as his intelligence officer. He had spent three years in Japan before the war studying their language, and now he broke their code. He broke it so we knew they were coming to Midway.

So Admiral Prugh and the substitute sent the planes off early because they knew the Japs were going for another strike on Midway. They hit their carriers when they had gasoline hoses and land bombs and everything else all up on the decks.

At 10:30 the Japanese were winning the war; at 10:36 they had lost it. Three carriers—the Kaga, the Akagi and the Soryu—were sunk in six minutes. They didn't go down until the next day, but they were mortally wounded. Ensign George Gaye was in the water for 30 hours and was the only one of his torpedo squadron who survived. He told me he had to hold his eye open to see the battle. His left eye was burned shut. But he said, "I held it open with my two hands, and I watched the battle. We'd hit it." Do you know why we'd hit it? Teamwork. Because George Gaye and Torpedo Squadrons Seven, Eight, and Nine went in there and were practically totally decimated.

But you know what the Japanese did? They brought in the air umbrella, the Japanese Zeros, to hit them. When they came down, our high-level bombers overflew them, and in six minutes it was over.

It took us three more years in the Pacific. To win the war, Harry Truman had to use the atom bomb to save a million of our servicemen and a million Japanese lives. You may have heard other opinions about that decision, but the truth is that he sat down with great men and he concluded that he had to use it to save our lives. I never voted for Harry Truman, but I fought for that.

Wars always bring bigger problems than they settle. We can't have that. It's up to us to have such a good democracy that other people want it too. That's a job that will be in your future.

Hard work, tough decisions, teamwork, family values, and paying ahead will help to change this world and make it a better place. And I have no idea but that you have the attitude and the capacity and the ability here to go on and help to make this a greater world.

Godspeed in the meantime to all of you. Thank you very much.